I Want My Body Back

COLLEEN A. SUNDERMEYER, Ph.D.

I Want My Body Back

NUTRITION

AND WEIGHT LOSS

FOR MOTHERS

A PERIGEE BOOK

A Perigee Book
Published by The Berkley Publishing Group
A member of Penguin Putnam Inc.
200 Madison Avenue
New York, NY 10016

First edition: March 1998

Published simultaneously in Canada.

The Penguin Putnam Inc. World Wide Web site address
is http://www.penguinputnam.com

Library of Congress Cataloging-in-Publication Data
Sundermeyer, Colleen A.
    I want my body back : nutrition and weight loss for mothers /
Colleen A. Sundermeyer.
        p.   cm.
    "A Perigee book."
    Includes bibliographical references and index.
    ISBN 0-399-52384-7
    1. Postnatal care.   2. Puerperium—Nutritional aspects.
3. Weight loss.   I. Title.
RG801.S86   1998
618.6—dc21   97-22337
                                                        CIP

Printed in the United States of America

10   9   8   7   6   5   4   3   2   1

to Toni List,
whose loving
and caring nature
has enriched the lives
of so many children . . .

Contents

5. "Will I Ever Stop Feeling Depressed and Anxious?"

Fighting Depression and Anxiety with Nutrients   63

6. "What Vitamins and Minerals Do I Need?"
Vitamins and Minerals for Breast-feeding and Weight Loss 77

Acknowledgments

I would like to express my appreciation to my editors,
Suzanne Bober and Erin Stryker, for helping me
refine my ideas and create a finely polished book.

Introduction

*I*t's easy to find books on birth, baby care, child-rearing, and the importance of good nutrition during pregnancy. But the topic of nutrition and weight loss for mothers has been sadly neglected. No books or tapes focus on this topic. Even the medical profession has failed to recognize the benefits of optimum nutrition for mothers. One thing is certain: Hospitals and physicians offer no help when it comes to teaching mothers about nutrition and weight loss after pregnancy. Nevertheless, adopting a healthy nutrition program remains a practical, effective, and safe way mothers can care for their mental and physical well-being.

During pregnancy women receive an enormous amount of information on how much weight they should gain and what nutrients they need to ensure the health of their unborn child. They are bombarded by a vast array of opinions and books on how to care for their baby's nutritional needs, but not their own. New mothers are left to determine their own nutritional needs when they have neither the time nor the energy. It's easy to see why many mothers find it frustrating and difficult to lose weight.

The truth is, women need just as much nutritional guidance after pregnancy as they had during pregnancy. Without nutritional guidance most mothers simply relinquish control. They accept being told that "their bodies are going through a period of adjustment" and that "they will naturally return to their normal weight within two months of delivery," only to find themselves years later feeling like failures because their abdomens are still flabby and prepregnancy clothes have yet to fit. In most cases weight gained during pregnancy doesn't just melt away despite all the excess calories needed to produce milk. Breast-feeding alone doesn't automatically mean you'll lose weight. In fact, mothers who are breast-feeding often gain weight because they are hungrier. If you're nursing, your body chemistry differs dramatically from that of a mother who is not nursing. You feel—and look—physically different, and your hormonal state is affected by levels of prolactin.

Typically, a woman gains thirty to forty pounds during pregnancy, at least fifteen of them by increasing her fat-cell number. After she has the eight-pound baby and loses a lot of water she's left with fifteen pounds of fat. Without proper nutritional guidance she'll carry this fat with her for the rest of her life.

It's surprising how many mothers unknowingly fall into their deeply ingrained roles as caretakers. They exhaust themselves giving to others without ever truly understanding how essential it is that the nurturer be nurtured. After all, our ability to trust later in life begins as babies, when we achieve satisfaction from being nurtured. Then as toddlers we gain major satisfaction from taking control over our bodies and feeling powerful. Now, after giving birth, we must once again gain a sense of mastery over our bodies so we can experience more satisfaction—and less anxiety. Gaining this sense of mastery over our bodies can prevent us from using food as a temporary escape or quick fix.

In order to be genuinely loving and committed to our children we must experience our own sense of well-being and satisfaction. Taking the time to care for ourselves physically and emotionally is the greatest contribution we can make to our families.

For me, becoming a mother was a real eye-opening experience. After fifteen years as an eating-disorder counselor and after writing two books on this topic, it wasn't until I became a mother that I realized weight loss for mothers requires specialized nutrition. It was obvious that the nutritional rhetoric of the weight-loss industry ignored the specific nutrients mothers need.

Once a woman has a baby she changes significantly. Her body's chemistry undergoes specific biochemical and biological changes. These changes create the need for specific nutrients, which ultimately determine how much and how soon she'll lose weight. Nutrients also determine how soon she'll recover from the physical stress of healing, postpartum depression, sleep deprivation, and hormone and brain chemical changes. It's also important to understand that calories are just one factor in our diets and that vitamins, minerals, and water are another. Without a proper balance of vitamins and minerals we cannot transform food into the energy our bodies need to lose weight.

The central purpose of this book is to serve as a "mother's helper." This is not some funky, silly, "in" diet. It is about helping you take care of yourself by making smart and satisfying choices about what you eat. You'll receive the nutritional guidance you need to feel good about yourself after your first baby, or even your third or fourth. No matter how long it's been since you've had children, the information in this book will help you lose weight. Therefore, some of you may choose to read this book from beginning to end. Others, however, may have a particular concern and go straight to the chapter that can help.

The book begins by defining two terms used frequently in nutritional science: *metabolism* and *nutrients*. I have found during my fifteen years of counseling that most women are confused by these terms. I then go on to explain how to identify and adjust to your metabolic type, so you stop comparing yourself to other mothers, relax, and lose weight.

If you've heard that pregnancy raises your basal metabolic rate, you've heard right. But what pregnancy doesn't change, unfortunately, is your ability to make new fat cells. However, some of your weight gained in pregnancy is a different kind of weight, one that comes from the temporary filling of fat cells.

Next I define the six general classes of nutrients considered necessary for life and how they're utilized in your body. Once you understand a little about the biochemistry that controls your weight and recovery, you can accomplish a lot in a short time. In chapters 4 and 5 you'll find out about the brain chemicals called neurotransmitters, which control hunger and satiety and can help overcome depression and anxiety. It is estimated that 500,000 women each year in the United States experience postpartum depression, partially due to changes in reproductive hormones. Hormones have a great effect on such neurotransmitters as serotonin, norephinephrine, ephinephrine, dopamine, and acetylcholine, which are responsible for ensuring that nerve impulses complete the jump from one neuron to another.

You'll learn how the production of these neurotransmitters depends upon the availability of specific nutrients. For example, you need both vitamin C (ascorbic acid) and B_6 (pyridoxine) to convert amino acid precursors, such as phenylalanine and tyrosine, to norepinephrine and dopamine. And when the supplies of these neurotransmitters become depleted, depression, increased hunger, and memory loss often can result.

Another example is zinc's astounding biological influence on hunger and satiety control. The depressed acuity of taste and smell show up quite readily in early stages of zinc deficiency and can adversely affect the regulation of hunger. After pregnancy meeting the Recommended Dietary Allowance (RDA) of 12 milligrams for zinc is not easy to do, even if you're consuming 3,000 calories a day.

In chapter 6 you'll learn more about which vitamins and minerals are essential to losing weight and breast-feeding. You might not know, for instance, that fat has a rich blood supply—it contains miles of capillaries for every pound—and when fat is lost, so are valuable minerals like iron and potassium. Or did you know that your baby takes about 2.3 milligrams of vitamin E (tocopherol) from your breast milk each day? To meet your need for vitamin E and the needs of your nursing baby, the RDA is set at 12 milligrams. It is now confirmed that this fat soluble nutrient plays an important role in the functioning of the nervous system.

If you're having trouble sleeping, chapter 7 will explain why sleep is vital to your recovery and weight loss. You'll discover that certain hormones, nutrients, and eating patterns will help you sleep without interrupting natural sleep patterns or causing respiratory failure, like some prescription drugs do. Most sleep medications activate what are called benzodiazepine receptors to promote sleep. Nutritional studies have revealed that vitamin B_5 (pantothenic acid) is required for this activation to take place. B_5 is just one of several nutrients found in the food you eat that activates the proper neurotransmitters for sleep, and also helps metabolize fat.

Chapter 8 examines the ever-popular subject of fat, and discusses how much fat you need to lose weight and regulate your hormones. Did you know you need fat to burn fat? Nearly 60 percent of the energy supplied during rest is provided by the metabolism of fat. To release this energy you need a balance of essential fats from both the omega-3s and -6s, which are two groups of polyunsaturated fatty acids that regulate fat metabolism. Chapter 9 discusses the importance of protein in losing weight and breast-feeding. For example, L-Isoleucine, an amino acid, is vital for muscle protein synthesis, which determines your ability to burn fat.

Next, in chapter 10, you'll be surprised to learn that vaginal yeast infections commonly experienced by mothers can produce symptoms such as depression, difficulty in concentrating, irritability, and often fatigue. To prevent the yeast from converting to harmful fungal forms, vitamin and essential fatty acid supplements can be used. For example, a supplement containing biotin, a B vitamin, can effectively reduce pathogenic invaders such as *Candida albicans* to their inactive forms.

Read chapter 11 if you're suffering from the physical and psychological discomforts of edema. Swelling and discomfort can make you feel fat and discouraged, or cause you to overeat or lose your appetite completely. Don't worry, there's help. This chapter shows you how to combat edema. It lists food additives you must avoid, and includes information on how to regulate your sodium intake. For example, in 1976 manufacturers voluntarily removed monosodium glutamate (MSG) from baby food because of claims it harmed the developing brains of children. But what about "adult" food? Even in adults, MSG is harmful and can interfere with weight loss.

If you're having problems with constipation and hemorrhoids, then read chapter 12. The easiest way to prevent or eliminate these problems is to avoid refined sugars and processed foods. Another way is to learn what type of fiber, digestive enzymes, and beneficial bacteria (such as *lactobacillus bifidus* and *lactobacillus acidophilus*) work best. In fact, over 96 percent of all the flora that a breastfed infant possesses is in the *lactobacillus bifidus* strain.

At the end of this book you'll find Forty Helpful Review Tips, which will get you off to a good start, along with an Everyday Herb Chart and Food-Substitute Chart, which can be used as handy references when making other recipes or creating your own. There are four week-long menu plans that show you how to whip up wholesome and flavorful meals, and still have time to relax. The food is different each day, so you can freeze leftovers and repeat a menu that you like. You'll find over fifty recipes, including snack suggestions, that look, smell, and taste terrific. The recipes are quick and easy to prepare, and are rich sources of the specific nutrients you need. After each recipe you'll find a list of the key nutrients contained in the dish. Since you don't have the time to run around, all recipes use common ingredients found in most local supermarkets.

You'll be delighted to know that fat, sugar, salt, and eggs have not been eliminated. Instead, all ingredients have been carefully incorporated so that each recipe reaches its desired flavor point, which is when food tastes its best and is still healthful. Keep in mind that once the flavor point has been reached, any addition of sugar or fat will only add to caloric value, not flavor.

Do you want your body back? To accomplish this you need not become an extremist or health nut, nor do you have to give up everything you love to eat. You can have your cake and eat it, too, as long as it's not too much cake too often. Whether or not you are aware of it, nutrition can help you enormously. Incredible though it may seem, every vitamin, mineral, and protein found in the food you eat has a distinct and specific effect on both your mind and body. Therefore, it doesn't matter how long it's been since you've given birth; the information in this book can help you acquire the energy and vigorous good health you need to keep up with your kids.

I Want My Body Back

"Why Has My Metabolism Changed?"
Understanding How Your Body Chemistry Alters After Pregnancy

What do you think the word *metabolism* means? Do you have a slow metabolism? Or do you have a fast metabolism? Maybe you think you have *no* metabolism. No matter what type of metabolism you think you have, it's important that you understand its true scientific meaning. Otherwise, it's easy to fall prey to marketing tactics that use this term inappropriately to sell you phony weight-loss drinks or chocolate "energy" bars that claim to increase your metabolic rate and melt away fat.

The scientific truth is that even a candy bar will increase your metabolic rate. And one egg is nutritionally better balanced than any weight-loss drink. Believe me, there are no magic properties in any weight-loss product. So you can stop spending your money on these useless products and instead get to know your body.

Knowledge Is Power

Once you read this chapter you'll be able to distinguish between the persuasive advertising of the weight-loss industry and the factual data of nutritional science. You'll learn how the digestion, absorption, transport, and metabolism of all foods will increase your overall metabolic rate.

The more you know about your own body, the more patient you'll be—and the more you'll increase your chances of losing weight without a struggle. It is absolutely essential that you give your body all the time it needs to make the necessary metabolic changes. Changes in your body's hormone levels from a pregnant to a nonpregnant state will alter your metabolism. It's a mistake to try to force your body to lose weight by restricting food or overexercising. It will only slow down weight loss by causing more metabolic confusion. Losing weight after pregnancy takes time, and the more you work with your body the less time it will take.

It's like trying to force your child to walk before he or she is ready. It just doesn't work. Don't get me wrong. You can encourage your child to walk, just like you can encourage your body to lose weight. But a healthy body is going to be stubborn and will make the necessary metabolic adjustments when it's good and ready!

Looking Past the Mirror Image

Now that you've had a baby you are a changed person. You need to get to know and understand the new you both physically and psychologically. To do this you must nurture your body by making gentle and subtle changes in your eating and exercising. You must also nurture your self-esteem by giving yourself credit for any progress you make. Being a mother is a difficult job. Avoid making any extreme changes and continue to pay attention to what is going on inside your body. Listen to your body's hunger and satiety signals like you did when you were pregnant.

Try to look past the mirror image and take a look at what is happening inside your body after pregnancy. This is not an easy task, but as you read on and understand what is happening inside your body, the mirror image will begin to fade. You'll become less interested in the surface changes, and more interested in the internal changes and your health. It doesn't matter how long it's been since you've given birth because you'll need all the energy and vigorous good health possible to keep up with your kids! So let's get going, and learn about how your body works.

Metabolism Is Life

Right now, as you read this sentence, you're using energy. Your body is constantly using energy, even at rest. You don't have to be exercising to use energy. The transformation of food into energy, the formation of compounds such as hormones and enzymes, the growth of bones and muscle tissue, the destruction of body tissue, and many other physiological processes are part of the metabolic process that uses energy. Metabolism represents the sum total of all the physical and chemical changes that take place within your body.

Metabolism involves two fundamental processes, anabolism and catabolism. When a compound is being synthesized (built) in the body, the process of metabolism is referred to specifically as *anabolism*. Whereas the breaking down of compounds through chemical reactions is called *catabolism*. *Metabolism* is the overall term indicating either or both of these processes.

Your body is constantly using energy to build up and to break down components within your cells. In the first six months after childbirth countless metabolic changes occur. Your uterus shrinks back to the size of a pear, blood volume is decreased by a third, four pounds of fluid disappear, and your hormones shift gears. Your body had to repair any damaged wounds in the womb where the placenta was attached; repair tears or stitches, strained muscles, and stretched tissues; normalize your urinary and intestinal tracts; and much more. The good news is that all these physical and chemical changes require energy, and will therefore increase your metabolic rate and keep it elevated for as long as it takes for your body to heal.

Even the release of energy from food itself requires energy to facilitate digestion, absorption, and the transport and metabolism of food. When you eat, your digestive process breaks down carbohydrate, protein, and fat into simple compounds that are absorbed into your body and are then transported to various cells for metabolism. Within the cells, the nutrients are chemically transformed through several metabolic processes. In the following pages we'll take a closer look at how carbohydrates, protein, and fats are metabolized.

Metabolism of Carbohydrates: Energy for Your Body

I'm sure the last time you ate a bowl of pasta you weren't thinking about metabolizing the carbohydrates. Instead, you probably were thinking about having a second serving since pasta is a fat-free food. Unfortunately, it's not that simple. You'd be better off eating a blend of carbohydrate, fat, and protein than you would be by loading up on carbohydrates alone. Here's why.

When carbohydrates are metabolized in your body the process involves many chemical reactions. Glucose (blood sugar) is the form of carbohydrate used to provide your body with energy. The major function of carbohydrate metabolism is to supply energy. When glucose enters a cell, it is broken down through the process of catabolism and is used in your body in three different ways :

1. Glucose: Released into the Blood

Glucose can be released into your blood to be carried to all your tissues and cells. Although glucose levels rise substantially above minimum values after eating, glucose levels in the bloodstream are regulated in healthy people at 80 to 100 milligrams of glucose per 100 milliliters of blood, or a little higher.

2. Glucose: Converted to Glycogen

Glucose can be converted into a carbohydrate called glycogen in the liver and stored there in this form until reserve carbohydrates are needed by your body. Although your liver and muscles are the storage reservoirs for glycogen, your liver contains the greatest concentration of glycogen. However, since its size is limited, the liver normally contains only about 75 grams of glycogen, or 300 calories.

An average person with about 30 kilograms (66 pounds) of his or her body weight consisting of muscle tissue could expect to have a total muscle glycogen content of about 300 grams or 1,200 calories. The greatest amount of carbohydrate stored in your body is in the form of muscle glycogen. This is because your muscle comprises such a large proportion of your body mass as compared to your liver. Total muscle glycogen content differs according to body size, and every gram of glycogen is stored with about 3 grams of water. When you restrict your food intake, your body uses the carbohydrate that is stored as muscle and liver glycogen to meet its energy needs. Most of the weight lost during the first few days of a diet is primarily due to a decrease in glycogen and water stores—not fat stores.

3. Glucose: Converted to Fatty Acids

Glucose can also be converted to fatty acids and stored primarily in the adipose (fat) tissue. So now you see why loading up on carbohydrates isn't a good idea. If you eat an excess of carbohydrates, they are converted to fat. What does this all mean? It means don't be so quick to start a diet or buy a product just because it's low fat. It may be too high in carbohydrates (sugar). The point is, if the energy from the foods you eat is not used through physical activity, or metabolic activity, it must be stored as fat. This is not just a myth or fallacy, it is the factual data of nutritional science.

Finally, as I've said before, a well-balanced diet requires that you eat a blend of carbohydrate, protein, and fat as well as appropriate quantities of vitamins and minerals. A well-balanced diet also requires that you evaluate your serving sizes. Servings and serving sizes are discussed in the next chapter. Let's move on and learn how protein is metabolized in your body.

Metabolism of Protein: The Building Material for Your Body

The diets emphasizing protein over carbohydrates that were so popular in the 1960s have made a big comeback in the 1990s. There's no question, however, that high-protein diets are dangerous, and can cause dehydration and the loss of valuable nutrients. Restricting carbohydrates and loading up on meat isn't safe, especially after pregnancy. Like excess carbohydrates, excess protein is converted to fat and stored. A high-protein diet also can can strain your kidneys and liver. It can destroy lean muscle and actually *lower* your metabolism.

This destruction of muscle is caused by the loss of water from your muscle. Your body gets rid of the nitrogen-containing waste product of protein metabolism, called urea, through urination. This water loss is your body's method of filtering out the urea from your bloodstream. If you consume too much protein, this process can cause severe dehydration, electrolyte imbalance, and loss of lean muscle mass. What you see on the scale is water loss, not fat loss.

Excess protein cannot be stored in your body, but is converted to either carbohydrates or fat. Protein breaks down into amino acids in your body, and certain amino acids, like alanine, may be converted to glucose in the liver. As we discussed previously, glucose can be converted to fatty acids for storage in adipose, or fat, tissue.

When protein is metabolized there's a dynamic situation between *synthesis* (anabolism) and *degradation* (catabolism) in your body. Numerous proteins are needed to be synthesized in cells and tissues throughout your body. So the amino acids necessary for the synthesis are removed from the amino acid pool in your liver and transported to sites where they're used in protein synthesis.

Did you know that protein is replaced constantly? Within a six-month period, all your protein molecules break down (catabolism) and are rebuilt (anabolism) from new or recycled amino acids. Thirty-five percent of your muscles are made up of the amino acids leucine, isoleucine, and valine. They are known as *branched-chain amino acids* because of their molecular structure. These three amino acids must be present for muscular growth and development to take place. A deficiency in any one of them will cause muscle loss, which decreases your ability to burn fat and slows down your metabolism.

All of the amino acids needed for protein synthesis must be supplied to your cells, and the lack of any necessary essential amino acid blocks synthesis of the protein being formed. The nonessential amino acid required for the synthesis may be provided directly from the blood. However, if specific nonessential amino acids needed for synthesis are not immediately available from your blood supply, they can be formed in the cells. This amazing process of protein metabolism is called anabolism (protein synthesis). This is truly a remarkable chemical reaction, and a perfect example of how capable your body is at taking care of you.

There are other metabolic processes that occur in the catabolism (degradation) of protein. This is when some amino acids are converted to similar compounds called amines by the removal of the acid group. An example of this would be the conversion of histidine, a nonessential amino acid to histamine which dilates your blood capillaries. Sooner or later, all amino acids in your body undergo a sequence of *catabolic* (degradation) reactions that result in the excretion of their components and the release of energy.

Metabolic Abnormalities: Phenylketonuria and Gluten Intolerance

Unfortunately there are some people who have impaired amino acid metabolism. The most widely publicized of these genetic defects of metabolism is *phenylketonuria,* often referred to as PKU. The primary defect is the inability to convert excess phenylalanine from food to tyrosine, resulting in an accumulation of phenylalanine in the cerebra spinal fluid and blood. The clinical manifestation of phenylketonuria is mental retardation. All hospitals in the United States are required by law to test newborns.

Treatment for PKU consists of a very carefully controlled diet in which only enough phenylalanine is provided to supply the body's need for this essential amino acid. This treatment halts the excessive accumulation of phenylalanine, which is the result of a missing enzyme, and therefore prevents mental retardation.

Another metabolic abnormality is *gluten intolerance*, which is defined as an intolerance to gluten, a complex protein found in wheat, rye, oats, and barley. It is caused by a sensitivity to a portion of the gluten protein called gliadin. Gluten is a component of modified food starch, which is used in most processed food. Gluten is used to make monosodium glutamate (MSG) and other flavor enhancers. If you have a gluten intolerance, consuming any foods containing gluten can damage the lining of the small intestine, decrease the absorption of nutrients, and result in poor digestion and diarrhea. People who are in good health normally use gluten from their diet efficiently. As you can see, learning about how your body works can help you appreciate being healthy.

Obtaining adequate protein in your diet is absolutely necessary for maintaining normal growth during pregnancy and after pregnancy. In chapter 9 you'll learn how much protein you need after pregnancy. Right now, however, it's important to remember that if you eat an excess of protein, it can be converted to either carbohydrates or stored as fat. The same holds true if you eat an excess of carbohydrate: It can be converted to fat and stored.

As I've suggested all along, a high-carbohydrate diet isn't any better than a high-protein diet. There is no single nutrient or diet pill that will change the way your body metabolizes carbohydrate, protein, and fat. However, maintaining a healthful balance of carbohydrate, protein, and fat can help you lose weight. Next, we'll examine how fat is metabolized.

Metabolism of Fat: Energy for Your Body

Although fat is one of the most criticized nutrients, it plays a significant role in nutrition and human physiological functioning. Dietary fats supply you with energy as well as essential fatty acids, and also function as a carrier for the fat-soluble vitamins A, D, E, and K.

During and after pregnancy your body is extremely efficient at storing energy as fat. During pregnancy your body produces a higher level of an enzyme called *lipoprotein lipase*, which is involved in the storage of fat. After pregnancy it takes time for your body to revert lipoprotein lipase to lower levels. Crash-dieting or skipping meals will simply interfere with your body's ability to make this adjustment.

The fat stored in your adipose tissue is an essential source of energy for your body, and contains approximately 100,000 fat calories. All fats in your body are metabolically active, and are constantly being exchanged with food fats. White fat found in fat cells that lie under your skin and brown fat that surrounds and protects your organs are in a dynamic equilibrium with the fats in your blood. The white fat is your energy or calorie-storage fat. This is where your body puts the extra calories from what you eat that you do not use. During pregnancy most women put on extra fat in their breasts, waist, hips, and thighs. This stored fat is then converted to energy for labor and for the demands of breast-feeding. When your body converts fat to energy it comes from a pool of fats throughout your body, not just from your hips and thighs.

Your body is sort of a big processing unit that stores energy (calories) and then uses it. Ninety-nine percent of your body fat is stored as *triglycerides,* the most common form of both dietary and body fat. A high level of triglycerides may increase the risk of blood vessel or heart disease.

During digestion, fats are emulsified with the aid of bile and broken down into fatty acids, glycerol, monoglycerides, and a few diglycerides by the action of pancreatic and intestinal lipases in your small intestine. Some absorbed products are then transported in your blood, but most are re-combined into trigylcerides and then combined with protein in prepara-tion for transportation to your blood as *chylomicrons* via the lymph system. Ultimately, fat is either stored in your body as fat or used for anabolic or catabolic reactions. These two scientific terms should be sounding very familiar to you by now.

The metabolism of fat by no means can be rushed. It is part of a very complex process called the *Krebs Cycle*, which uses fat to make several important substances, such as the sex hormones. And though you may be tempted to rush this process by skipping meals, eating a diet of grapefruit, or guzzling quarts of cider vinegar, it won't disturb one fat cell—just your stomach. Very few mothers return to normal quickly—for most it takes a year or longer.

What Is Your Metabolic Rate?

Your total metabolic rate consists of three components:

1. Basal metabolic rate (BMR): energy for basic life functions
2. Resting metabolic rate (RMR): energy needed for normal daily sedentary activities above BMR

3. Exercise metabolic rate (EMR): energy needed for active muscular exercise above BMR

Your BMR, RMR, and EMR will vary throughout the day. Your basal metabolic rate (BMR) is the amount of energy you use at rest. It's the rate at which your body needs energy for maintaining functions necessary for survival like maintenance of breathing, heartbeat, blood circulation, body temperature—everything excluding digestion and activity. Your BMR will also increase in cold climates because of muscular shivering and in hot climates because of increased cardiovascular demand and sweating.

Women usually have a BMR lower than that of men because men have more muscle tissue and less fat. The difference in BMR between the sexes is about 10 to 15 percent. As women age, their BMR deceleration is slowed 2 percent per decade after age thirty. This means your calorie (energy) intake must *decrease* with age and the food you eat must be more nutrient dense. *Nutrient density* is an important concept relative to the proportion of essential nutrients such as carbohydrates, fats, proteins, vitamins, and minerals, which are found in foods. A food with high nutrient density possesses a significant amount of a specific nutrient or nutrients per serving or for a certain amount of calories.

Foods that contain more nutrients will provide you with a greater feeling of satisfaction than foods that contain more flavor and fewer nutrients. Let's use vitamin C as an example. Two medium-size chocolate chip cookies contain 100 calories and have no vitamin C. On the other hand, a 100-calorie cantaloupe contains over 65 milligrams of vitamin C, which is more than the Recommended Daily Allowance (RDA). The cantaloupe has a higher nutrient density of vitamin C and will give you a greater feeling of satisfaction.

You must get a proper balance of nutrients from fewer food calories. The greater the nutrient density of a food, the greater your feeling of satisfaction. Remember this the next time you can't stop eating that bag of potato chips. By comparing the vitamin and mineral content of a bag of potato chips to the caloric content, you can easily determine why it is you don't feel satisfied after eating an entire bag. A bag of potato chips is a poor source of protein, vitamins, and minerals, and it consists mostly of fat calories.

Some calorie-dense foods include candy, cakes, cookies, soda, ice cream, fried food, and alcohol. The amount of nutrients and calories you need will change especially after pregnancy. Throughout your day try to make food choices based on the idea that you want to eat fewer calorie-dense foods and more nutrient-dense foods.

Determining Your Basal Metabolic Rate (BMR)

Determining basal metabolic rate (BMR) can be done in a laboratory or a hospital. You must fast for twelve hours, and then your oxygen consumption and carbon dioxide production are measured. Here's a simpler method you can use to estimate your BMR:

Add a zero to your weight in pounds.
Add your body weight to this value.
Example: 120-lb. woman
1,200 + 120 = 1,320 calories a day

This estimated BMR doesn't represent the amount of calories you need each day in order to maintain your body weight. It would if you remained in basal state all day, but you don't. You sit, stand, talk, walk, breast-feed, stay up at night with your children, and engage in other activities that increase your metabolic rate above BMR levels. When you sleep, you lower calorie expenditure below your BMR.

I'm sure you know that food provides energy for your body, but it doesn't stop there. The release of energy from food itself requires energy to facilitate the digestion, absorption, transport, and metabolism of the nutrient components in the food you eat. This energy required to utilize food is called specific dynamic action (SDA). This means that when you eat, you increase your BMR by 10 to 35 percent for the next two to three hours and burn more calories. But when you skip meals or restrict food your BMR decreases and you burn fewer calories. Also, skipping meals means you're taking in fewer of the vitamins and minerals that are necessary to losing weight.

Keep in mind that you do have some control over your BMR—it's not all in your genes. It's simple: Eating, not skipping, meals elevates your body's metabolic rate and burns more calories.

Metabolic Aftereffects of Exercise, Eating, and Pregnancy

Your exercise metabolic rate (EMR) is also under your control. Increasing your EMR is the most effective way to influence your overall metabolic rate. During exercise, almost all your body systems increase their activity in order to accommodate the increased energy demands of your muscle cells. Exercise not only increases the metabolic rate, but keeps the metabolic rate elevated during the recovery period. Research has shown that your RMR after exercise can increase by 7.5 to 28 percent above BMR and that this increase lasts four to six hours. Body temperature will increase, circulating hormones will continue to influence cellular activity, and other metabolic processes like circulation and respiration will remain elevated for a limited time. These are called the *metabolic aftereffects* of exercise.

Exercise can also diminish hunger because sustained slow exercise creates metabolic and hormonal changes that cause you to want to eat less. The first metabolic change is a *ketosis*, which occurs if fat reserves are used without sufficient carbohydrate intake. The second metabolic change that suppresses your appetite is *acidosis*, which is caused from the rapid breakdown of muscle glycogen into lactic acid.

Hormonal changes during and after pregnancy also affect your metabolic rate. The adrenal and thyroid glands secrete hormones that have important influences on your BMR. For instance, just a few weeks before your baby's arrival, your BMR increases. This phase is sometimes referred to as the "nesting instinct," since energy is often spent in making final preparation for your baby. It is due partly to the adrenal gland, which secretes adrenaline during periods of high emotion, causing an acceleration in BMR for as long as three hours. This is one reason it's so difficult to get to sleep during those last six weeks before delivery.

Perhaps the most common metabolic change after pregnancy takes place in the thyroid. The thyroid, which regulates your metabolism, reduces hormone production after pregnancy. The slowing of activity in the thyroid gland leads to a low level of thyroxine. Too little thyroxine slows your basal metabolism, which means your body needs fewer calories to function. I believe the slowing down of thyroid activity is one way your body tries to balance its energy (calories) supply in order to heal itself.

Most of the physical and chemical changes that occur after pregnancy require energy (calories) and will affect your metabolic rate and keep it elevated throughout your recovery period. In other words, there's a metabolic aftereffect that keeps you burning calories after you exercise, after you eat, and after you have a baby. As you have seen, your body is truly working in your best interests. Now, you need to work in your body's best interest by being patient and learning more about how it functions. Next we'll talk about how to identify and adjust to your own metabolic type so you stop comparing yourself to other mothers.

2

"Why Am I Not Losing Weight As Fast As Other Mothers?"

Identifying and Adjusting to Your Own Metabolic Type

"How come my friend Cindy is losing weight, but I'm not?" asks Susan. "It's not fair; I only eat one small meal a day." There's nothing more frustrating than comparing yourself to someone else, especially when you're comparing something as unique as your biological makeup. Susan might as well compare the size of her nose to Cindy's nose, and then ask why it's different. You have your own unique biochemistry and your metabolism is part of it.

It's best to stay focused on what's going on inside your body rather than waste time on comparisons. I've always felt that the quickest way to destroy a perfectly good friendship is to diet together. What another mother eats or how fast she loses weight should not mean anything to you. The only eating and exercise that affects your body is your own. Therefore, if you eat a cookie that contains 60 calories, that same cookie will not have the same caloric effect when eaten by another mother. Why? Because your metabolisms are different.

You need to find out what type of metabolism *you* have, and then stop comparing yourself to other mothers. Pay attention to your own body's hunger and satiety signals. Keep in mind that your body has undergone a transformation, part of which you can and can't see. Understanding and paying attention to what you can't see is extremely important. For instance, do you recall feeling warm when you were pregnant when everyone else was cool? This warm feeling was the result of an increase in your body's BMR of about 20 percent. Your body was responding and making the necessary adjustments to support the new life you were carrying. Try to remember that your body is always working in your best interest— even after pregnancy.

Once you have a baby your body changes significantly, and again it must make adjustments, both internally and externally. Your body is still using a lot of energy (calories) because it is working hard to make all the necessary biological and biochemical changes. Even once you drop back to your prepregnancy weight you'll be a changed person psychologically and biochemically. You'll be adjusting to a new baby, a new life-style, a new metabolism, and a new appetite.

As a result of all this adjusting your BMR will increase and remain elevated for as long as it takes for your body to recover and make the necessary changes in your energy level. If you're breast-feeding, your body requires 300 to 500 extra calories of energy per day to produce milk. Remember that what you eat influences your breast milk and therefore affects your baby.

Get on the Right Track: Your First Seven Steps

Getting off to a good start after pregnancy when your BMR is elevated is important to losing weight. Weight loss is usually rapid during the first several weeks after childbirth, and then it gradually slows down. Here are seven steps that will get you on the right track so you can start to feel better and lose weight.

This is what you need to do: First, identify your own metabolic type and then adjust your eating and exercise habits. Second, evaluate how much food you should eat (number of servings and serving sizes) to get all the nutrients you need without excessive calories. After all, for nine months you were eating for a growing fetus that was forming new bones, organs, and tissues, and now your body must adjust to a new appetite, and your mind must adjust to a new style of eating that is healthy and comfortable. Third, stop calorie counting and focus instead on foods that are nutrient dense. Fourth, identify and break old habits, and then replace them with new eating behaviors that will help you adjust to your new appetite and new style of eating so you can lose weight. Fifth, start eating smaller more frequent meals and controlled snacks, which will increase your BMR.

Your sixth step is to get rid of the bathroom scale. The scale doesn't offer you any predictability: Every day it can change dramatically even when the body is in excellent condition; it is not an accurate indicator. Finally, your seventh step is to begin a regular exercise routine and then continue to exercise faithfully. Don't start exercising right after your baby is born. Wait until the second week and then start to walk. Your activity level will depend on the age of your baby. Chasing around an active two-year-old will definitely increase your energy expenditure. Let's examine these seven steps more closely.

Step One: Identify Your Own Metabolic Type

Fast Metabolism

- I can eat and always have been able to eat what I want and not gain weight.
- I lose weight almost immediately when I cut back on eating.
- I'm a highly active person and always have been. I engage in vigorous activities (jogging, cycling, swimming, etc., for at least thirty to sixty minutes or more).
- It didn't take me long to lose my prepregnancy weight.
- I love to exercise.

Moderate Metabolism

- I sometimes have to cut back on my eating and be careful about what kind of food I eat.
- I lose weight slowly when I diet and will gain it back easily if I'm not careful about what I eat.
- I spend much of my time engaging in moderate activities (gardening, walking, housework).

- My prepregnancy weight has been coming off very slowly.
- I enjoy exercise.

Slow Metabolism
- I can't eat any of the foods I like, and if I do, I'll gain weight.
- I don't lose weight even when I'm on a low-calorie diet.
- I spend most of my time in sedentary activities (watching TV, reading, etc.).
- My prepregnancy weight has never come off.
- I don't enjoy exercise.

If you have identified yourself as having either a moderate or slow metabolism, you can move on to your second step. If you're one of those few women who have a fast metabolism, you can simply skip this chapter and go on to the next. Of course, that is, after you have a bite to eat.

Step Two: Evaluate How Much Food You Eat

If you're eating a variety of healthy foods like you did during pregnancy but are still not losing weight, try not to panic and make extreme changes. Instead, stick with the foods you've been eating, but make a small change in how much you've been eating.

What you need to do is to check your own serving sizes against labels and food guidelines. Understanding how much you should eat can be confusing. After all, what is a "serving size"? Are your "serving sizes" determined by the U.S. Department of Agriculture's (USDA) Food Guide Pyramid, the amount other mothers eat, the amount you usually eat, or the amount listed on food labels? All of the above are important. Yet, it's the amount *you* usually eat that is the most important.

The USDA created the Food Guide Pyramid in 1992, and each of its five basic food groups plays an important role in your daily food plan. However, the amount listed as "a serving" on the Food Guide Pyramid is just a guide. It helps you figure out how much of each kind of food you should eat to get all the nutrients you need. The Food Guide Pyramid recommends you eat six to eleven "servings" of bread, cereal, rice, or pasta. This may seem like a lot, but the serving is very small, just three to four plain crackers equal one serving. This is why the serving size on the label is important and why it's there to help you measure that specific product.

For instance, try pouring your usual bowl of cereal and then dump it into a large measuring cup. Keep in mind that one cup equals two servings, and two cups equal four servings. The Food Guide Pyramid also shows you that one cup of milk is equal in nutritional value to 8 ounces of yogurt, and that either is equal to 1 ounce of cheese, and recommends two to three daily servings. Two to three servings each day of meat, poultry, fish, dried beans, eggs, or nuts are recommended. The serving sizes are very small—only 3 ounces equal one serving.

Your body needs over fifty nutrients a day. In order to get these nutrients you need some food from meat, dairy, fruit, vegetable, and grain sources. And if you're not getting food from each of these five groups every day, you're not getting a balance.

Below you'll find the U.S. Department of Agriculture's food guide for the recommended number of daily servings and serving sizes. You can check your own servings against it and make a few small reductions in what you're eating. That's all. Even the smallest reduction in your serving sizes will help you lose weight. Don't avoid eating your favorite foods. The key is not to eat too much of any one food.

U.S. Department of Agriculture's Recommendation for the Number of Daily Servings and Serving Sizes

Grain group (bread, cereal, rice, pasta): 6 to 11 servings
Bread: 1 slice equals 1 serving
Rice or pasta, cooked: ½ cup equals 1 serving
Breakfast cereal: 1 ounce equals 1 serving
Plain crackers: 3 or 4 equal 1 serving
Cookies: 2 medium-size cookies equal 1 serving
Hamburger roll, bagel, or English muffin: 1 of these equals 2 servings

Protein foods (meat, poultry, fish, dry beans, eggs, nuts): 2 to 3 servings
Lean ground beef, cooked: 3 ounces equal 1 serving
Fish, cooked: 3 ounces equal 1 serving
1 egg equals 1 serving
Dried beans or peas, cooked: ½ cup equals 1 serving

Milk, yogurt, cheese group (preferably nonfat or lowfat): 2 to 3 servings
Milk: 1 cup equals 1 serving
Yogurt: 8 ounces equal 1 serving
Cheddar cheese: 1½ ounces equal 1 serving
Cottage cheese (4 percent fat): ½ cup equals ¼ serving

Vegetable Group: 3 to 5 servings
Any cooked vegetable: ½ cup equals 1 serving
Raw leafy greens: 1 cup equals 1 serving

Fruit Group: 2 to 4 servings
Whole fruit: 1 of these equals 1 serving
Canned fruit: ½ cup equals 1 serving
Unsweetened fruit juice: ¾ cup equals 1 serving

Fats, oils, and sweets
(butter, mayonnaise, oil-based dressing, cream, cooking oil, shortening, sugar, candy, etc.): Eat sparingly

If you're breast-feeding you don't need to stuff yourself with food to ensure that you are able to produce enough milk. The research on how many calories a breast-feeding mother needs to successfully nurse and still lose weight is not conclusive. Besides, not all calories are created equal—a fact that is discussed in the following step.

Step Three: Stop Calorie Counting

Food should not be viewed in terms of calories. The word *calorie* shouldn't send a fearful chill through your body. Calorie counting and weighing food before you eat causes you to think of food as "destructive calories" instead of a good food that contains valuable nutrients. Getting hung up on counting calories will only make you feel more anxious and frustrated, especially when you're working so hard to lose weight. So stop counting calories, and try to start thinking of food in terms of nutrients.

Foods that contain more nutrients will provide you with a greater feeling of satisfaction than will foods that contain more flavor and fewer nutrients. Nutrient density is an important concept relative to the proportion of essential nutrients, such as carbohydrates, fats, protein, vitamins, and minerals, that are found in foods. A food with high nutrient density contains a significant amount of a particular nutrient or nutrients per serving or for a certain amount of calories. For example, one jelly-filled doughnut contains approximately 225 calories and only a trace of potassium. Whereas one bran muffin is only 125 calories and contains approximately 100 milligrams of potassium. The bran muffin has a higher nutrient density of potassium and contains fewer calories.

You must get a proper balance of nutrients from fewer food calories. The greater nutrient density a food has, the more satisfied you'll feel after eating. Keep this in mind the next time you can't stop eating that bag of cookies. Read the nutrition label on a bag of cookies and compare the vitamin and mineral content to the caloric content, and you'll see why it is that you don't feel satisfied after eating an entire bag. Cookies are an inferior source of protein, vitamins, and minerals, and consist mostly of fat calories.

Ounce for ounce carbohydrates and protein supply the same number of calories (4 per gram), whereas fats supply more than twice as many (9 calories per gram). Also, the metabolism of protein in the body is more complex than that of carbohydrates and uses more energy. Protein, therefore, has a greater effect on your metabolic rate and increases the expenditure of calories, whereas water, vitamins, and minerals contain no calories.

Eating 1,000 calories of whole grains, fish, chicken, or fruit and vegetables isn't the same as eating 1,000 calories of cookies, ice cream, cake, and candy. It is not only the number but the kinds of calories you eat that matters. You may eat a piece of cake (simple/refined carbohydrate) that contains 135 calories or two pieces of whole-wheat bread (complex carbohydrates) that also contain 135 calories. The whole-wheat bread is a complex carbohydrate with more nutrient density (iron, B vitamins, calcium, and fiber) and is absorbed slowly, allowing your body more time to burn the food before storing it as fat for later use. The cake is absorbed quickly because refined sugar has little nutrient density and is more likely to be stored as fat in the body if not needed for immediate energy.

Simple or refined carbohydrates are simply or rapidly absorbed by the intestinal tract and sent to the liver in amounts too large for the liver to store. Some simple and/or refined carbohydrates include sugar, some fruits, cakes, cookies, white bread, white rice, and soda, all of which contain few vitamins and minerals. On the other hand, complex carbohydrates (such as starches and fiber) are absorbed more slowly and won't overload the liver. The liver then releases these nutrients into the blood, transporting them directly to the heart, which pumps them all over the body. As they go through the pancreas, insulin, which removes sugar from the blood, is secreted.

Sugars such as fructose (fruit sugar) and sucrose (table sugar) occur in simpler forms than the sugars found in vegetables and grains. Complex carbohydrates—like whole grains, vegetables, and some whole fruits—are composed of sugars linked together in such a way that the breakdown process takes longer. Because complex carbohydrates are absorbed slowly into the bloodstream, they do not stimulate a large rise in insulin levels. Simple carbohydrates, however, break down rapidly and absorption takes just a few minutes, creating a quick rise in blood sugar. It is also difficult to make an exact tally of calories consumed, since the caloric content of foods varies. For example, a large apple may contain twice the calories of a small one. Remember, calories express the amount of energy supplied by food, and your energy needs are met by carbohydrates, proteins, fats, and alcohol.

Step Four: Identify and Break Old Habits

Even though most mothers say they feel motivated to take care of themselves and their babies by eating healthful foods, they still have trouble controlling how much they eat, even when every calorie is counted. If you have this problem, you need to break some old habits, and rethink the way you've been eating. After all, eating for two has become a habit. For nine months you were eating for a growing fetus that was forming new bones, organs, and tissues, and now your body must adjust to a new appetite, and your mind must adjust to a new style of eating that is healthy and comfortable.

Old habits are tough to break and it is not uncommon for mothers to still have enormous appetites, especially when they're breast-feeding. If you're having trouble controlling how much you eat, you're going to have to break old eating habits by first identifying them and then replacing them with new eating behaviors.

A habit is something you do almost spontaneously, with little awareness of your actions. Do you nibble on the food you are preparing, or eat the leftovers as you clean up? Do you stand up and eat rather than sit down at the table, and then wonder why you are having trouble losing weight? These are unhealthy habits that you need to recognize and replace with healthy behaviors. Once a habit becomes a behavior you can better control it because now you are aware of it.

Your new behavior requires you to listen to your body's hunger and satiety signals. Eat just enough so that you feel comfortable, not stuffed. Don't leave the table hungry or skip meals. You must eat enough to keep your energy up, so you can keep up with your kids. But try to eat only foods that are nutrient dense, like 100 percent whole-grain bread, not white bread. Eat fresh whole fruit and vegetables, not canned.

After having a baby, staying at home more often and eating alone may be a new experience for you—one that is somewhat difficult to get used to. If you're unaccustomed to eating alone, you might find yourself eating too fast, too much, or even feeling rather lonely and uninterested in preparing meals. Remember, taking care of yourself is the greatest contribution you can make to your family. Putting together a fresh wholesome meal for yourself is not a waste of time but a way you can nurture yourself. Try to avoid eating packaged processed food, which is filled with unsafe additives. Often processed foods are packaged in large quantities, and this can lead to overeating if you don't divide and freeze leftovers when cooking for yourself. Whether or not you're breast-feeding, a well-balanced diet means you must eat a variety of wholesome fresh foods. Changing your eating habits gradually is the only effective way to lose weight.

Step Five: Eat Smaller, More Frequent Meals and Snacks

Skipping meals—especially breakfast—or eating only once a day will not speed up weight loss. It will create metabolic instability and slow down weight loss. Skipping breakfast is comparable to a small fast: It actually means you are not eating for twelve to fourteen hours. After eight to twelve hours without food, your body needs refueling.

If you avoid eating breakfast to save calories, you're going to make up for those lost calories by overeating at lunch or dinner. Research has shown that starting the day with a satisfying meal promotes a feeling of well-being and helps to control hunger later in the day. A balanced breakfast with an average amount of protein will help prevent the onset of mid-morning hunger that often leads to a doughnut. It is the protein that helps maintain normal blood sugar levels throughout the morning, whereas a breakfast of refined carbohydrates, like a doughnut, may trigger an insulin response and a drop in blood sugar in the middle of the morning.

You can speed up the rate at which you burn calories by eating smaller, more frequent meals and snacks. The more stable your metabolism and blood sugar levels, the more efficient you will be at burning calories and assimilating and utilizing nutrients. As we discussed earlier, when you eat, you're using energy (calories) through digestion, absorption, transport, and the metabolism of nutrients. This is called specific dynamic action (SDA), the energy required to utilize food. So if you don't eat or only eat once a day, your metabolic rate will slow down, because your body doesn't use energy (calories) for these processes. Your body uses more energy (calories) when you eat.

This may seem backward, but the more you deprive your body of food, the more it will hold onto whatever you ate by storing it as fat. Not eating for long periods of time causes glucose (blood sugar) to dip and creates mild, moderate, or even severe fatigue, anxiety, and personality changes, such as irritability, sadness, and mood fluctuations.

Controlled snacking can help you burn calories while it keeps your blood sugar stable and reduces fatigue. Snacking has gotten a bad reputation and is often associated with junk food and poor nutrition. Controlled snacking means having something nourishing to eat every couple of hours. It acts as an energy bridge between meals. The snack prevents a dip in blood sugar between meals, so you can stay feeling alert all day. Controlled snacking provides a constant and even supply of energy to your body. Snacking can give you a nutritional boost. A couple of quick, simple, and nutritious suggestions include cinnamon toast made with whole-wheat bread, carrots and zucchini dipped in seasoned yogurt, fresh fruit, popcorn with a splash of honey or whole-wheat crackers, and tuna.

Eating smaller, more frequent meals also allows your body more time to burn those calories for immediate energy or store them for energy in your liver and muscles as glycogen. Eating large amounts of food after allowing a longer period of time to pass between meals overloads your body with calories, which are converted to fat until they are needed. Overeating will overload your system with sugar and fat, and when these nutrients enter your bloodstream, glucose levels will rapidly rise, triggering the release of excessive amounts of insulin from your pancreas. Insulin plays a major role in how fat is stored in the fat cell. Insulin directs the storage of triglycerides (blood fats) inside the fat cells in the adipose tissue (fat tissue) for the purpose of storing fat to be used later when you skip a meal. Eating smaller, more frequent meals promotes a regular flow of stored triglycerides from your fat cells. Like your baby, you also benefit from small nutritious snacks that don't overwhelm your system.

Having a nourishing snack before bedtime will help you burn more calories while you sleep because the process of digestion, absorption, transport, and metabolism requires energy. Your body doesn't shut down when you sleep. Nutrition should be thought of as a twenty-four-hour process. Try to eat several snacks throughout your day and before bedtime.

You're probably thinking, *That sounds like a lot of work.* Well, it's not.

It is simply a new style of eating that you need to adopt after pregnancy, if you want to lose weight. Eating smaller, more frequent meals and snacks is one of the most effective ways for you to adjust to your new appetite and new metabolism after pregnancy.

A smart weight-loss program involves adapting to the following eating schedule: breakfast at 6:00 A.M., a snack at 9:00 A.M., lunch at 12:00 P.M., another snack at 3:00 P.M., dinner at 6:00 P.M., and a bedtime snack at 8:00 P.M. If you don't want to feel weak, tired, and grouchy, you have to be sure to eat. In chapter 13, you'll find over fifty recipes, including snack suggestions, and four week-long menu plans that make this new eating plan easy to incorporate into your busy daily schedule.

Step Six: Get Rid of the Bathroom Scale

Get rid of your bathroom scale; it is not an accurate weight-loss indicator. The scale doesn't offer you any predictability. Every day your weight can fluctuate dramatically, even when your body is in excellent condition. You'll get excited one week because you dropped a few pounds and disappointed the next week if your body is adjusting itself and the scale is not registering any weight loss. Getting upset because you haven't lost the weight you want to lose is self-defeating.

Do you use the scale as a way to seek approval or as a private form of self-punishment when you have overeaten? The bathroom scale doesn't make you aware of the emotional weight that you carry with you even after childbirth. When you step on the scale it doesn't tell you that you are carrying around ten pounds of frustration because you don't have the time to do the things you want to do, and ooops . . . about five pounds of guilt because you don't think you're as patient as other mothers. If emotional weight is not lost, the reason you were eating or not eating is still not addressed.

Don't rely on the scale to determine if you're successful or to provide you with a sense of accomplishment. If you want to gain control over eating and your body weight, get rid of the scale and listen to your own feelings. You can trust yourself.

When you first begin to lose weight, the weight that is lost initially is not fat but water and glycogen from your muscles and liver. Your body sees fat as survival, even though you see it as gross and ugly. Once your body begins to recognize a reduction in your caloric intake, it will begin to fight back and conserve fat stores, in fear of starvation. This is usually experienced by the dieter as a plateau period, which causes a great deal of anxiety. But this is the time when you're closer to losing fat than ever before. Still, at this point, most people give up or start severely restricting food, causing their body to fear starvation and hold onto fat. What you need to do is to continue eating lots of small meals and snacks that are nutrient dense—and stay off the bathroom scale.

Step Seven: Start Exercising Faithfully

If you want to lose weight after pregnancy, a regular exercise routine will have to become a natural part of your life. Often after pregnancy hormonal imbalances can cause fat stores to be used less as an energy source. So start with an easy exercise routine that you will stick to. Being faithful to a sensible level of moderate exercise every day is more beneficial to weight loss than sporadic high-intensity exercise.

Don't try to make radical changes you can't live with for long. Instead, start going out for regular walks. A sensible exercise program will give you peace of mind. I've seen too many anxious mothers go to extremes and overexercise. This happens because they are uncomfortable with their body weight and naturally want to change it as soon as possible to rid themselves of these bad feelings. So they buckle down, put their nose to the grindstone, take a deep breath, and start to force and hurry a process that can't be hurried. An overly vigorous exercise program after pregnancy will wear you out, and it's dangerous and counterproductive to losing weight. The more you push your body, the more it fights back. Moderate or even small amounts of exercise done faithfully is the best strategy.

When you're trying to make important personal changes in your life, pushing and hurrying the process is a catch-22. Eventually, you burn out, stop exercising, and get too tired to even think about making a positive change. It is this fatigue and disillusionment that make phony diet products so successful. The more tired you become, the more you search for a quick solution. Slow down and try to be a little easier on yourself.

On the other hand, if you haven't been a faithful exerciser, now is a good time to start. Trying to lose weight after pregnancy without exercise is difficult. Fat can only be removed from fat cells when it is burned in your muscles for energy. Fat can't be changed to a carbohydrate or protein. If your muscle mass is decreased through lack of exercise, some of your capacity to burn fat is lost.

Muscle contains enzymes that burn fat for energy. When you exercise, your muscles increase in size. Even small amounts of sustained slow exercise will increase muscle mass and create more fat-burning enzymes. Once fat is replaced by muscle tissue, you may notice an increase on the scale that indicates weight gained in lean muscle mass, not fat. Muscle may weigh more than fat, but it takes up one-fifth the space of fat. Overall, when there is an increase in your lean body mass, particularly the muscle tissues, there is a decrease in your body fat. So you may weigh more, but you'll lose inches and notice that your clothes are fitting better.

It is important to remember that internal changes in your body composition are taking place and that body fat is being lost, even if the scale shows no change. The scale tells you how many pounds you have lost, not how much fat. As I mentioned previously, weight loss may come from any one of three body sources: body water; lean tissue, such as muscle; and body-fat stores. When your diet is low in calories it will show a rapid weight loss on the scale due to decreases in body water and lean muscle tissue. On the other hand, weight loss that involves a moderate exercise program occurs at a much slower rate. Even though weight loss is slow, a good amount of the energy demands for exercise come from burning fat. This means the weight that is lost comes primarily from body fat, and not from water or lean muscle tissue.

Also, as long as you're lactating, your breasts will stay large and the scale will fluctuate an extra pound or two. In fact, during pregnancy you probably increased your muscle mass by carrying around those extra pounds for nine months. Think about how often you carry or lift your child. It is the most consistent weight-lifting program you'll ever be on. Your child slowly increases his or her weight, and you slowly increase your muscle mass and fat-burning ability. Muscle burns fat, no matter where it is on your body.

Walking is the best postpregnancy exercise. When you begin walking, start out slowly and gradually increase your walking time. You don't need to speed-walk. Once exercise becomes too intense, the fat can't continue to be used as an energy source and your body begins to use carbohydrates from the muscles and liver. Continuous regular exercise will increase the number of fat-burning enzymes in your muscles. You want to develop a metabolism that burns fat and stimulates muscle changes.

Your body has separate pathways for metabolizing fat and sugar. The pathway your body uses depends on how hard you work. Sporadic, high-intensity, vigorous exercise uses mostly sugar. Whereas continuous, regular exercise done at slow or moderate levels uses mostly fat. Choose a walking pace that's slow enough so that you can still carry on a conversation with your child but brisk enough that it will slightly affect the way you talk. Don't worry; this won't impair your child's speech development!

If you're breast-feeding, you should know about the study conducted in 1986 by the Adult Fitness Program at Indiana University, which found that babies do not like the lactic acid produced in their mothers' bodies during vigorous exercise. Lactic acid is the major cause of fatigue in the muscles. When muscle glycogen breaks down without the utilization of oxygen, it is called anaerobic glycolysis. ATP (adenosinetriphosphate), or energy, is produced rapidly, but lactic acid is the end product. Rapid weight loss should also be avoided when breast-feeding. This is because the toxins stored in fat cells are released into the breast milk and can be harmful to both you and your baby.

As mentioned earlier, the metabolic aftereffect of exercise will elevate your resting metabolic rate (RMR) 7 to 28 percent above basal metabolic rate (BMR), and the increase will last four to six hours. You're still benefiting from exercise even once you've stopped. Not a bad deal. Following are two specific exercise programs. Select the program that fits your metabolic type, and then exercise faithfully. It's important to keep your body hydrated during exercise. Water helps maintain proper body temperature and electrolyte balance, transports nutrients, lubricates muscles and joints, and aids in circulation and respiration. Before your next walk, don't forget to pack a water bottle for yourself! And remember to stretch for ten minutes before you walk.

Slow Metabolism

A. Walk 45 minutes three times a week for 1 month.

B. Walk 55 minutes four times a week for 3 months.

C. Walk 65 minutes three times a week for at least 8 months or until you reach your desired body size.

D. Once you've reached your desired body size, start to walk faithfully for 1 hour and 30 minutes twice a week. Continue this amount of walking as a natural part of your life.

Moderate Metabolism

A. Walk 55 minutes three times a week for 1 month.

B. Walk 60 minutes four times a week for 4 months.

C. Walk 65 minutes three times a week for at least 6 months or until you reach your desired body size.

D. Once you've reached your desired body size, start to walk faithfully for 1 hour and and 20 minutes twice a week. Continue this amount of walking as a natural part of your life.

3

"Which Basic Nutrients Does My Body Need?"

The Six Categories of Nutrients and How They Are Utilized

*H*ow pleasing it is that an activity as basic as eating has such wonderful appeal for all of your senses. Food can stimulate your appetite through color, shape, enticing aroma, flavor, and sound. When you enjoy the sensory pleasures of food, it's easy to appreciate the psychological contribution food makes to your life. But what about the physiological impact of food on your day-to-day existence?

Your ability to feel satisfied after eating a good meal is just one of the positive physiological effects of consuming nutrient-rich foods. Foods that contain more nutrients will provide you with a greater feeling of satisfaction than will foods that contain more flavor and fewer nutrients. A food with high nutrient density has a substantial amount of a specific nutrient or nutrients per serving or per a certain amount of calories. For instance, one hot dog contains 145 calories, 13 grams of fat, and no vitamin A. On the other hand, one-half roasted chicken breast contains 140 calories, only 3 grams of fat, and 18 International Units (I.U.) of vitamin A. The chicken breast has a higher nutrient density of vitamin A and contains fewer fat calories.

You must get a proper balance of nutrients from fewer food calories. The greater nutrient density a food has, the more satisfied you'll feel after eating. Remember this when you can't stop eating a bag of pretzels. By comparing the vitamin and mineral content of pretzels to the caloric content, you will understand why it is you're still hungry even after eating the whole bag. Pretzels are a poor source of protein, vitamins, minerals, and are mostly refined carbohydrates.

There Are Over Fifty Essential Nutrients

There are over fifty nutrients that are essential to your well-being. These can be grouped into six categories. Three of these categories provide the body with energy: carbohydrates, fats, and proteins (with carbohydrates being the primary source of energy). Fiber is also a form of carbohydrate that is a necessity in your diet. The other three groupings are minerals, vitamins, and water—all of which are vital to your body even though they do not serve as sources of energy.

Some foods, such as whole-wheat bread, may contain all six categories of nutrients, while others, such as table sugar, contain only one nutrient. Whole-wheat bread is still not a complete food since it does not contain all the essential nutrients. Ideally all your nutrients should come through a good diet of fresh, whole foods, including plenty of whole grains, fruits, and vegetables. When you have a baby, however, your priority is to keep life simple and your energy high. If you want to stay healthy and energetic you need to eat nutrient-dense foods. While drinking a soda may be pleasurable, a glass of nonfat milk is the nutrient-rich alternative that gives you calcium and protein in addition to water.

On the next page you'll find a chart that contains over fifty nutrients that are essential to your diet. All these nutrients are contained in varying amounts in the different foods you eat. This is why it is so important to eat a wide variety of foods.

No Two Foods Are Exactly Alike

No two foods are exactly alike in nutrient composition. However, certain foods are similar enough in nutrient content that they may be grouped together. The Food Guide Pyramid created by the United States Department of Agriculture in 1992, for example, groups foods according to nutrients in which they are rich.

ESSENTIAL NUTRIENT CHART

Carbohydrates/Fiber

Fats (essential fatty acids)	Protein (essential amino acids)	
Arachidonic	Isoleucine	Threonine
Linoleic	Leucine	Tryptophan
Linolenic	Lysine	Valine
	Methionine	Histidine
	Phenylalanine	

Minerals

Calcium	Iron	Selenium
Chloride	Magnesium	Silicon
Chromium	Manganese	Sodium
Cobalt	Molybdenum	Sulfur
Copper	Nickel	Tin
Fluorine	Phosphorus	Vanadium
Iodine	Potassium	Zinc

Vitamins

Fat Soluble	Water Soluble	
A (retinol)	B_1 (thiamine)	B_{12} (cyanocobalamin)
D	B_2 (riboflavin)	Biotin
E (tocopherol)	Niacin	Choline
K	B_6 (pyridoxine)	C (ascorbic acid)
	Pantothenic acid	Inositol
	Folic acid	Para-aminobenzoic acid

There are variations in the nutrient concentration of different foods within each group. A peach and a pear are both fruits, but the peach contains more vitamin A. So if you select a wide variety of foods from each group, your nutrient intake will be balanced. Finding a proper balance and mix of foods is extremely important to creating a healthy diet.

The Misconception About Carbohydrates

Carbohydrates are nutrients that provide energy for your body because they are quickly converted to glucose, which is your body's main fuel

THE USDA'S FOOD GUIDE PYRAMID

Food Groups	Meat, poultry, fish, dry beans, eggs, and nuts group	Milk, yogurt, and cheese group	Vegetable/ fruit group	Bread, cereal, rice, and pasta group
Nutrient Composition	Protein Thiamine Niacin Vitamin E Vitamin B_6 Vitamin B_{12} Iron Zinc Magnesium	Protein Calcium Riboflavin Vitamin A Vitamin D Vitamin B_{12} Phosphorus	Thiamine Niacin Riboflavin Protein Iron	Vitamin A Vitamin E Biotin Folic acid Iron Magnesium

source. Your brain, in particular, is fueled by carbohydrates. The central nervous system uses about 140 grams of glucose a day. Of course, glucose is not the only essential nutrient in the category of carbohydrates. Carbohydrates also include other sugars and the more complex starches, all of which are obtained only from plant foods.

Unfortunately many people still think that carbohydrates—wheat bread, pasta, potatoes, beans, peas, and other starchy foods—are fattening. This misconception about carbohydrates has spawned several fad diets that advocate eating only high-protein foods. The truth is, starchy foods are no more fattening than protein. Both contain the same amount of calories ounce for ounce. Carbohydrates can be simple (fruit, honey, syrup) or complex (grains, legumes, whole-grain bread or pasta), or they can be refined (wheat bread, cookies, sugar, soda, refined flour, pastry, dough-nuts, candy). Carbohydrates, simple or complex, are important nutrients that supply energy to the body's tissues and help burn fat.

When the body's carbohydrate stores become depleted, such as when a person is fasting or is on a very low carbohydrate diet, protein is broken down to supply the needed glucose. This protein will come from food sources, if available, or from the lean tissue, such as muscle and organs. Fasting is an ineffective and dangerous way to try to lose weight. Fasting may cause a rather rapid initial decrease in body weight, but this is primarily due to water depletion and decreases in lean body mass, not body fat.

Remember, muscle burns fat. The more muscle you have, the more fat you'll burn. Fats are "burned" in your muscle for energy. As your muscle gets smaller, your ability to burn fat decreases and metabolism slows down. The only way fat can be removed from fat cells is to be burned in your muscles for energy. As long as you have muscle tissue that needs energy, the fat molecules will move into your muscle and be burned.

If carbohydrates remain unavailable for several days, the body then attempts to conserve essential tissue protein by producing an alternative fuel source, called ketones, from the partial burning of fatty acids. Ketones serve as a glucose substitute that fuels some of the body cells. As the breakdown of fat continues, these ketones build up in the blood, causing an abnormal condition called ketosis. Research shows that it takes approximately 100 grams of carbohydrate a day to prevent ketosis in adults.

Complex carbohydrates supply the body with fiber, which is not found in fat or protein. Fiber, a form of carbohydrate found in plants, is not used by your body for energy. Nevertheless, it is a constituent of foods that helps your gastrointestinal system function smoothly. A fiber-rich diet is the best way to eliminate constipation and lower serum cholesterol. Complex carbohydrates are made up of long-chain sugar molecules, which are slowly broken down into smaller molecules of glucose during digestion. In other words, fiber slows the rate of absorption of sugar over a longer period of time and can reduce your craving for more sugar.

Fiber helps control weight in several other ways. It adds bulk to the diet and provides a feeling of fullness that can help prevent overeating. Because the digestive tract lacks the enzymes to break down fiber and use it for energy, it doesn't contain calories. That's right: Fiber contains no calories. Many of the so-called diet drinks, such as Slim Fast, are simply a mixture of various kinds of fiber and a few vitamins and minerals. However, this is an expensive way to get your fiber, vitamins, and minerals.

Your Body Sees Fat as Survival

Although fat is often thought of as bad, it's a vital nutrient your body must have to survive. Your body sees fat as survival, even though you see it as ugly. Fat is a concentrated form of energy that can be stored in your adipose (fat) tissue as an energy reserve. About half of the body's fat is deposited just beneath the skin, and the heart, kidneys, and other vital organs are surrounded by fat deposits, which protect them from injury. Adipose tissue insulates the body and protects you and your unborn child from physical trauma. This fat is the last to be converted to energy at times when calories are needed.

Many hormones are produced in the adipose tissue. Adipose tissue is important to regulating the production of female sex hormones. Either too much or too little fat can interfere with normal menstruation, ovulation, and fertility. A certain percentage of adipose tissue is necessary to have a baby. It is the enzyme aromatase in the adipose tissue that keeps estrogen levels high in overweight postmenopausal women and causes the development of breast tissue in some obese men.

It is now known that your fat-cell number can increase to accommodate extra weight gain. Adipose or fat cells can enlarge to store more and more fat. Fat cells never disappear, but they will shrink if excess fat is removed for energy. When you lose weight too quickly the shrunken fat cells send out a chemical signal to eat more and refill those fat cells. If you lose fat too quickly after pregnancy you'll find yourself feeling hungry and deprived, as your body desperately attempts to refill your fat cells. Dietary fats are just as important as fats that are stored in adipose tissue or the fats that circulate in the bloodstream. Dietary fats "carry" the fat-soluble vitamins and provide flavor as well as palatability. Fat increases your feeling of satiety or fullness from a meal because it's digested more slowly than proteins and carbohydrates.

The fatty acid compounds, such as linoleic acid, linolenic acid, and arachidonic acid (listed under the fat category in the Essential Nutrient Chart on page 33) are required for a variety of metabolic processes that are important during and after pregnancy. These essential fatty acids

(EFAs) are types of fat that you and your baby's body cannot produce and that must be part of your diet. As an example, linoleic acid contributes 7 percent or more of the calories in breast milk, depending on the mother's diet. Commercial formulas contain 10 percent. Oils like canola and soy are sources of these essential fatty acids.

Protein: Distinctly Different from Carbohydrates and Fats

Protein is distinctly different from both carbohydrates and fats because it contains another element: nitrogen. Nitrogen is incorporated in the structure of the subunits of protein. These subunits are called amino acids. The essential nutrients listed under the protein category on the Essential Nutrient Chart (page 33) are individual amino acids that your body must have for growth and maintenance.

Found in all your cells, proteins influence the distribution of fluids throughout your body. It is necessary for you to have enough carbohydrate and fat in your diet so that your body can use the proteins and various amino acids to build tissue protein for muscles, blood, enzymes, hormones, and so on. Both plant and animal foods are excellent sources of protein.

Minerals: Nutrients Your Body Cannot Manufacture

Minerals are nutrients that you cannot manufacture in your body; you must get them from the food you eat. Minerals are inorganic nutrients that serve a multitude of roles in your body, especially in skeletal maintenance and nerve conduction. The fact that so many different minerals are important in nutrition is a clear signal that a wide range of foods must be eaten to provide all these elements in appropriate quantities. Some minerals act as catalysts for the release of energy from carbohydrates, fats, and proteins, but the minerals themselves do not contribute energy. Minerals all work together just like vitamins to keep your body in check!

Vitamins: The Release of Energy from Food

Vitamins A, D, E, and K are nutrients and considered subgroups in the vitamin category. This is because these four vitamins have a characteristic in common—vitamins A, D, E, and K are fat rather than water soluble, as are the other vitamins listed in the Essential Nutrient Chart (page 33). The water-soluble vitamins include vitamin C and the B vitamins. None of the vitamins provide energy directly to your body, but many of them are needed for the release of energy from carbohydrates, fats, and proteins.

Water: A Remarkable Nutrient

Usually water is not considered a nutrient. Yet it is the most indispensable of all the six groups of nutrients. A person could die much more quickly from lack of water than from lack of any other nutrient.

Within your body, water is involved in many chemical reactions that release energy from carbohydrates, fats, and proteins. Water helps in the processes of absorption and transport of nutrients within your body. Every cell in the body depends on water to carry out essential functions. It is needed to produce the amniotic fluid that surrounds and protects the fetus during pregnancy. Even the evaporation of water from your lungs and skin is a vital part of controlling body temperature. In hot weather or during exercise the heat sensors in the skin and in the brain's hypothalamus stimulate the sweat glands to release perspiration and reduce your body's internal temperature.

You consume and excrete about 2½ to 3 quarts of water per day. Water balance is carefully regulated by your kidneys and by the thirst center of the brain's hypothalamus. Healthy kidneys will excrete at least 10 to 16 ounces of water each day to rid your body of toxic waste products. If you don't drink enough water, your blood volume decreases, causing a rise in the concentration of sodium in the blood. These changes are immediately sensed by the brain's thirst center, which triggers the sensation of thirst. If you drink too much water, then your body's blood volume increases, which causes a decreased concentration of sodium in the blood. These changes are again immediately sensed by your brain's thirst center, which sends out signals to suppress the release of the antidiuretic hormone, causing the kidneys to excrete the extra fluid.

Water is a truly remarkable nutrient and is available in generous amounts in many foods such as milk, fruit, and even vegetables, which contain 95 percent water. Meat is about 45 to 65 percent water, and bread, 36 percent water. When foods are broken down in your body they produce what is called *metabolic water*. It's the water in soda that quenches your thirst, and the sugar and salt that make you thirsty enough to keep drinking more. It's best to drink water when you're thirsty. When breast-feeding you must not only eat well, but most important, you must drink plenty of fluids. Drink when you feel thirsty, and always drink water before, during, and after exercise.

Why Every Mother Should Take a Supplement

Throughout this book I discuss the nutrients you need after pregnancy, and recommend that you take supplements. Think of a vitamin and mineral supplement as kind of a "natural" Band-aid, and use it in conjunction with healthy eating. The nutrient levels I recommend reflect the Recommended Dietary Allowances (RDAs) plus a little extra for the special needs of motherhood. The RDAs for most nutrients have been developed by the Food and Nutrition Board of the National Research Council, a committee funded in part by the federal government. This group is made up of scientists who evaluate the current research on nutrition to establish estimates of nutrient recommendations for protein, carbohydrates, fats, energy, eleven vitamins, and seven minerals.

The RDAs are recommendations, not requirements. The Nutrition Board states that the RDAs are intended to be met by a diet containing a wide variety of foods rather than by supplementation and that they apply to healthy populations, not to those people requiring special dietary needs. I believe the RDAs are too low and do not ensure optimum health. The optimum intake for vitamins and minerals is far greater than the RDA.

There is a significant difference between the level at which a nutrient is adequate to meet minimal growth and development needs and the level necessary for optimal health. For a person in good health, the optimum intake of vitamin C may be one hundred times the RDA; for the B vitamins and vitamin E, about twenty-five times the RDA; and for vitamin A, about ten times the RDA. These levels are also safe for those who are breast-feeding.

Even if you eat a variety of foods, it is difficult to maintain a complete balance of nutrients from day to day. If you are in good health, never lose a night's sleep, never get stressed out, have good digestion and assimilation, and live in an unpolluted environment, you probably would not need supplements. However, you probably don't eat and live in this ideal condition. Therefore, a vitamin and mineral supplement that is at or a little above the RDAs should absolutely be part of your daily nutrient regime. I recommend you take a combination vitamin and mineral supplement, and then take separate vitamin or mineral supplements when necessary. You should continue to take your doctor-prescribed prenatal supplement through your "recovery" period, and if you breast-feed you may need additional iron, B_6, folic acid, magnesium, calcium, and zinc.

Some people fear taking supplements—and we've all heard horror stories about people who have overdosed on certain vitamins and minerals. The margin of safety for vitamins and minerals is quite broad, and the reports of toxicity are greatly exaggerated. No lethal dose is known for most of the water-soluble vitamins. When the water-soluble vitamins such as C and B complex are taken in excess, they are excreted by the body. Most people take a super B vitamin supplement containing 50 milligrams of pyridoxine, or twenty-five times the RDA, with no adverse symptoms. Even the fat-soluble vitamins are excreted to some extent in the feces and the urine, but if you take excessive amounts of them, toxic levels can accumulate in storage areas such as the liver. It is estimated that a dose of 10,000,000 I.U. (International Unit) of the more toxic fat-soluble vitamin A might be lethal, but this is 4,000 times the RDA. The term *International Unit* is sometimes used instead of milligrams when referring to vitamins

A, D, and E. International Units are the measure of activity used rather than the weight dosage of these vitamins.

Most supplements are derived from synthetic sources, that is, laboratory products that have a molecular structure similar to that of a truly natural supplement. A truly natural supplement is one that is a concentrated food substance, which means it is extracted from plant or animal sources. Your body cannot differentiate between a natural source and a synthetic source, since their molecular structures are the same, and therefore they are used the same way in the body. Most vitamin C and B supplements are "co-natural," which means they're part synthetic and part natural. Sustained-release or timed-release supplements are designed to provide nutrients over a 6- to 12-hour period, and are not necessary if you take your supplements frequently. Vegetarian supplements contain all the necessary vitamins and minerals but are free of animal products and derivatives. Later in the book I will explain the function of different vitamins and minerals and how you can obtain these vital nutrients from food sources.

Vitamin and mineral supplements should be taken with food for best absorption. If not, they will leave your body within two hours instead of four or five, allowing less time for the body to use them. Another reason to take supplements with food is to prevent nausea, which often occurs when they are taken just with water or juice. Supplements should be kept in a dark, cool place with the lid closed tightly. Do not store them in the refrigerator since the moisture will build up inside the bottle after constant opening and closing.

Take a vitamin and mineral supplement in capsule, liquid, or straight powder form that is free of *excipients*—yeast, corn, wheat, lactose (milk sugar), sugar, salt, artificial sweeteners, fillers, binders, coatings, colorings, preservatives, or salicylates. Salicylates decrease the effectiveness of vitamin C and increase the need for vitamin K when used over a long time. These fillers and other substances compromise the bulk of a vitamin and mineral tablet. Side effects, such as headaches, upset stomach, and nausea are generally reactions to all the tablet fillers and binders, not to the vitamins or minerals themselves. Your supplement should contain a form of iron that is nonconstipating. Try a combination of ferrous sulfate and sodium fumarate or elemental iron from carbonyl.

Powders and liquids are assimilated very well and contain no excipients. Capsules are also very well assimilated, contain no excipients, and are easier to swallow. You'll find a list below of several quality nutritional supplement companies. Call for information and catalogs.

Richlife
222 N. Vincent Ave.
Covina, CA 91722
1-800-327-8355

Vitaline Formulas
722 Jefferson St.
Ashland, OR 97520
1-800-648-4755

Nature's Way
10 Mountain Spring Pkwy.
Springville, UT 84663
1-800-962-8873

Twin Laboratories
2120 Smithtown Ave.
Ronkonkoma, NY 11779
1-800-645-5626

Schiff Products
180 Moonachie Ave.
Moonachie, NJ 07074
1-800-526-6251

Wellness Health Pharmaceuticals
2800 S. 18th St.
Birmingham, AL 35209
1-800-227-2672

J. R. Carlson Laboratories, Inc.
15 College Ave.
Arlington Heights, IL 60004
1-800-323-4141

4

"I'm So Hungry All the Time"
Nutrients, Hormones, and Brain Chemicals
That Control Hunger and Satiety

"Will I ever lose my weight?" asks Cindy. "Why am I so hungry all the time?" Cindy, like most mothers, found it difficult to control her eating and felt anxious about not being able to lose her weight. Making matters worse, she would force herself to skip meals, then devour a pack of SnackWells "fat-free" devil's food cookies because there was nothing else around to satisfy her hunger. Meanwhile she worried about getting sufficient vitamins and minerals to breast-feed and felt more tired and irritable than ever.

Surprised at how familiar this sounds? The realities of life with a baby can be disturbingly different from your fantasies and hopes. You must adjust not only to a new baby, but to a new appetite, a new metabolism, and a new style of eating. That's a lot of adjusting. So it's not unusual that most mothers find feeding their babies and themselves more difficult than expected. The bottom line is that munching your way through a bag of processed chips or any processed food will never satisfy your hunger. Nor will skipping meals, liquid diets, or diet pills. It will only cause your hunger to return with a vengeance.

Remember, hunger is a basic drive—and you can't completely eliminate it. You can't convince yourself you're not hungry. You'll just become even hungrier. Instead, you must learn how to satisfy your hunger and stop trying to ignore it—or kill it. It is, after all, the hunger pain that makes your baby cry. There is a physiological basis for your hunger; it is not simply a psychological process of controlling your mind. It's your mind that is associated with the process of perceiving, thinking, remembering, and intelligent behavior. It's your brain that is the central organ of your nervous system, and the nerve signals that travel up and down the spinal cord link your brain to the rest of your body.

Nutrients: Brain- and Mind-Altering Substances

Your mind doesn't exist in a vacuum; it's linked to the chemistry of your brain. Therefore, hunger is a function of brain and mind. The nutrients found in the food you eat are brain- and mind-altering substances. Even your thoughts and feelings are brain and mind altering. The emotional and physical changes you experience after pregnancy can deplete your brain's output of neurotransmitters, disturb hormone levels and sleep, and affect the regulation of hunger and satiety.

For just a moment, I want you to think about how drawn you were to what was going on inside your body during pregnancy. In general, a woman will pay more attention to her body's hunger and satiety signals during pregnancy than at any other time in her life. After pregnancy, these signals change significantly. So it's important that you continue to pay attention and work with these new signals if you want to control your hunger and lose weight. Let's begin by discussing the neuroendocrine system, which is the nervous system (brain and spinal cord) and hormones from the endocrine system that work together to regulate hunger and satiety.

Your Brain's Chemistry and Hunger Control

Although it may seem logical to assume your stomach is the organ that controls hunger and satiety, it is not. The master control of hunger and satiety lies at the center of your brain in an area called the hypothalamus. The hypothalamus is the most powerful subdivision of the brain. This pea-sized structure is directly connected to the pituitary gland.

The pituitary is embedded in the bone of the skull under the hypothalamus. Through this connection, the hypothalamus regulates the

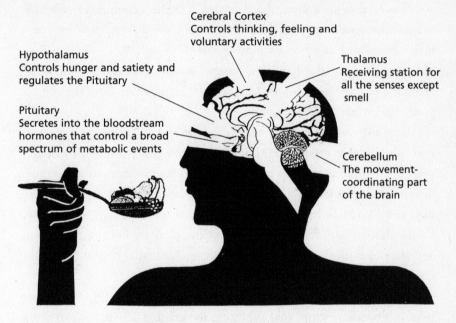

Figure 1. Systems in the Brain

Your ovaries produce the hormones estrodiol and progesterone, and are controlled by the hypothalamus and pituitary. After pregnancy these hormones, along with blood nutrient concentrations, fall and dramatically alter the hypothalamic-pituitary regulation of hunger and satiety. Estrogen will decrease hunger; progesterone will increase it.

secretion of hormones from the endocrine system and brain neurotransmitters that regulate hunger, satiety, and fat metabolism. In conjunction with the pituitary the hypothalamus also regulates water balance, body temperature, and sexual and reproductive functions. Under the control of the hypothalamus, the pituitary produces the hormone oxytocin, which is necessary for uterus contractions in childbirth, and prolactin, for breast-milk production.

During pregnancy the hormones estrogen, progesterone, and cortisol circulate in your blood in much higher levels than at any time in your life. After pregnancy the levels of these hormones fall drastically and disturb the balance of your brain's neurotransmitters responsible for regulation of hunger and satiety.

It has long been known that estrogen will decrease hunger, whereas progesterone will increase it. Hormonal excesses or deficiencies after pregnancy can alter hunger and satiety signals. Although breast-feeding does utilize calories, it will also increase hunger. It is the extra energy your body uses for breast-feeding and the lack of estrogen secretion from the cells in your ovaries that increase hunger.

After pregnancy you need to increase your intake of certain nutrients, not only for milk production, but to regulate hunger through balancing your brain's chemistry. It is not unusual for new mothers to experience hormonal dysregulation (a failure to react to the chemical signal to stimulate the thyroid), which can cause weight gain and fatigue. The nutrients absolutely necessary for the secretion of the pituitary hormones are zinc and vitamin E. Both these nutrients are found in higher concentrations in the pituitary than in any other part of the body.

The uniqueness and complexity of the brain is remarkable. There are over 100 billion neurons that constitute the brain. These neurons receive information from other nerve cells within and throughout the body, processing it and sending messages that affect every organ and cell.

A nerve impulse is an electric discharge that moves quickly along the fiber of a nerve cell. The fiber may end at a muscle, a gland, or another nerve cell, but there is always a tiny space between the end of the nerve fiber and the next cell. To bridge this gap, the nerve fiber releases small amounts of chemicals called neurotransmitters.

Events within your brain involve a chemical dialogue, a conversation in which neurotransmitters—serotonin, dopamine, norepinephrine, and acetylcholine—talk to each other. Reduction in hunger occurs when your brain has high levels of these neurotransmitters. Nutrients are needed by your brain for the production of these neurotransmitters, which are in turn modulated by hormones. It is the blood-brain barrier that allows nutrients from your bloodstream passage across its membrane into the cerebral-spinal fluid that bathes your brain and spinal cord.

In short, your digestive tract absorbs nutrients, and so does your brain. There are rapid and specific changes in your brain's composition even after eating a carrot stick. These biochemical changes that occur in your brain

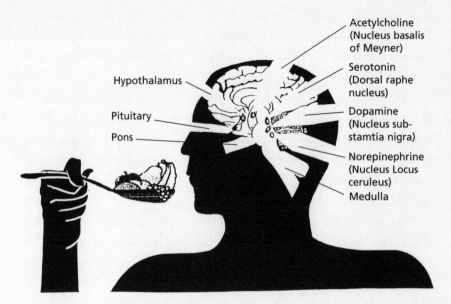

Acetylcholine
(Nucleus basalis
of Meyner)

Serotonin
(Dorsal raphe
nucleus)

Dopamine
(Nucleus sub-
stamtia nigra)

Norepinephrine
(Nucleus Locus
ceruleus)

Medulla

Hypothalamus

Pituitary

Pons

**Figure 2. The Neurotransmitters in the Brain that
Affect Hunger and Satiety**

Almost all the neurotransmitters responsible for hunger and satiety are present in a small group of neurons that are located primarily in the brain stem. Acetylcholine is the only major neurotransmitter that is not derived from an amino acid, but from the precursor nutrient choline. When choline is deficient in your diet, the function of your brain will be suppressed.

are directly related to the composition of the food you eat. Just as drugs are brain and mind altering, so are the nutrients in the food you eat, and the hormones that circulate in your bloodstream. Serotonin synthesis, for example, depends upon your brain's concentration of tryptophan, its precursor amino acid. When tryptophan is available, serotonin levels increase, producing signals that reduce hunger. Hunger is also reduced when the neurotransmitter norepinephrine is released into the hypothalamic neuron.

The brain's ability to regulate hunger and satiety is remarkable. But it can't do it alone. Without the proper protein, vitamins, and minerals, neurotransmitters are unable to function properly. Keep this in mind the next time you find yourself eating too many packaged processed foods. You're paying good money for products that are nutritionally inferior to fresh foods. Processed foods may be easy to prepare, but they lack the essential nutrients your brain requires to send the appropriate signals that you are full and need to stop eating. This is why it's so easy to overeat processed foods yet still feel hungry.

Certain drugs can reduce hunger by causing your brain to release the neurotransmitter norepinephrine from its stores. These drugs, however, cause your brain to use up its stores of norepinephrine, without stimulating it to produce more. Often the result is a depressive episode. Unlike drugs, vitamins, minerals, and protein trigger the release and production of norepinephrine rather than deplete the stores.

Now let's take a look at the specific nutrients that your brain requires to regulate hunger and satiety, such as protein, B_6 (pyridoxine), B_{12} (cobalamin), and zinc. I'll also explain why cold meals often don't satisfy your hunger like hot meals, and why too much sodium in your diet will cause you to overeat. At the end of this book there are recipes that are hot, satisfying, low in sodium, and contain all nutrients discussed in this chapter.

Protein and Hunger Control

It's a basic fact that all foods—vitamins, minerals, proteins, carbohydrates, and fats—are chemicals that control hunger by regulating your brain's chemistry. Though you wouldn't refer to common foods by their chemical names, some of them have complex names and structures. For example, if you had scrambled eggs for breakfast, you ate cysteine (amino acid), ovulbumin, conalbumin, ovomucoid, mucin, globulins, lipovitellin, livetin, cholesterol, lecithin, lipids, butyric acid, acetic acid, lutein, zeaxanthin, phosphates, and carotene.

Protein, for example, is a chemical compound needed by your brain if it's to send the appropriate signals about hunger and satiety. It sure would be handy if your brain released a tiny beep once satiety was reached to serve as a signal to stop eating. If you didn't stop eating, however, little by little this beep would grow louder. Not only would this be difficult for you to ignore, but it would make eating in a crowded restaurant an incredibly noisy experience.

Unfortunately your brain's signals are much more subtle and often go unheeded. One reason for this is that your mind perceives there's still food on your plate, so you continue to eat until your plate is empty, even though your brain reached satiety 2,000 calories before. This is just one example of how hunger and satiety are a function of brain and mind. Another reason for overeating is that you're trying to eat while you feed your child. Try eating when you're more relaxed and not so distracted. Too many distractions can cause you to eat too fast, and too much. Eating slowly and chewing food will encourage normal digestion and help eliminate or avoid constipation. You'll eat less and have a chance to taste what you're eating. Another reason you don't want to rush through eating is that food needs to be chewed thoroughly for efficient nutrient absorption.

Eat slowly and ask yourself, "Do I feel comfortable?" Don't wait until you have to loosen your clothing or to lie down because you're too full. Your brain is always sending you signals about hunger and satiety—listen to it. Listening to your body means eating smaller, more frequent meals and snacks. When you stuff yourself or skip meals you stop listening and override your own body process and its need for nourishment. Your stomach is only about the size of your fist, and resembles an expandable elastic bag that collapses when it is not inflated. There's no need to stuff it!

Let's take a look at the three amino acids (building blocks of protein) phenylalanine, tyrosine, and tryptophan and their effect on your brain's regulation of hunger and satiety. Phenylalanine is an essential amino acid, while tyrosine is normally listed as a nonessential amino acid. Both are of similar chemical structure so that when substantial quantities of tyrosine are contained in the diet the need for phenylalanine will decrease somewhat. The neurotransmitters dopamine and norepinephrine are synthesized from tyrosine. The dietary content of this amino acid and its precursor, phenylalanine, will directly decrease hunger by increasing brain concentration and neurotransmitter synthesis. Phenylalanine will also stimulate the hypothalamus to release the hormone cholecystokinin (CCK), which acts as an early "I'm full" signal to your brain, helping you eat less. CCK is a peptide hormone initially isolated from the small intestine and later shown to be found in the brain.

The CCK produced by your intestinal-lining cells is thirty-three amino acids long, and the CCK activity found in your brain is CCK-8, which is eight amino acids long. There is a widespread distribution of CCK-8 throughout your nervous system, including the cerebral cortex, the hypothalamus, the brain stem, and sensory nerves in the spinal cord. CCK is one of the many hormones that changes after pregnancy and needs to be regulated through the use of nutrients.

Another important neurotransmitter that regulates hunger and satiety is serotonin, which is synthesized from the amino acid tryptophan. When you eat an egg you're not only getting this amino acid but the additional bonus of two other nutrients: choline and lecithin (phosphatidylcholine). Both these nutrients are acetylcholine precursors and play an important role in regulating hunger and satiety. Your brain's conversion of choline or lecithin into acetylcholine requires vitamin B_5 (pantothenic acid), B_6 (pyrodoxine), and vitamin C. These vitamins are necessary for the conversion of all amino acid precursors to their appropriate neurotransmitters. The ability of neurons to synthesize a specific neurotransmitter depends upon the availability of nutrients in your diet.

No single amino acid or neurotransmitter is solely responsible for the regulation of hunger and satiety. Rather, they all interact with one another like the instruments in a symphony orchestra. As might be expected, the reduced production of any brain neurotransmitters is related to the low concentration of the necessary amino acid precursors in your diet. The decline in neurotransmitters after pregnancy is partly due to an inadequate supply of protein and to the dramatic fall in the hormones estrogen, progesterone, and cortisol. Without adequate levels of neurotransmitters an increase in hunger and weight gain is common.

The good news about the amino acids phenylalanine, tyrosine, tryptophan, and the vitamin choline is that they all increase the production and stores of neurotransmitters. If your meals are rich in these amino acids, you won't experience the letdown and rebound–eating binge problems that often plague dieters. This doesn't mean you should eat *only* foods that are high in these amino acids. Eating only protein will cause other amino acids, such as leucine, isoleucine, and valine, to compete, for instance, with tryptophan for specific carrier sites at the blood-brain barrier, and tends to reduce tryptophan transport. A well-balanced diet requires that you eat a blend of carbohydrates, proteins, and fats as well as vitamins and minerals.

After pregnancy it's important that you maintain your lean muscle tissue, and to do this it's essential you have sufficient carbohydrate and fat calories in order to create a protein-sparing effect. In other words, your carbohydrate and fat calories will be utilized for energy production, thus sparing utilization of protein as your energy source and allowing it to be used for its more important metabolic functions.

The best way for you to get a high-grade source of protein in your diet is to eat fresh food that is naturally high in protein. Processed foods, and most weight-loss products, use low-grade protein sources and are not nutritionally well-balanced. The amino acids phenylalanine and tyrosine, which are found in meat, eggs, and dairy products, are used to make dopamine, norepinephrine, and epinephrine, and are considered high-grade proteins. The amino acid tryptophan, which is found in milk and bananas and is used to make serotonin, is also a high-grade protein.

Skim milk contains just as much tryptophan as whole milk, but a lot less fat. Whole milk contains 3.25 percent milk fat, and skim milk must contain less than 0.5 percent milk fat. If you have trouble eating dairy products because you produce little or no lactase, which is an enzyme that digests lactose or milk sugar, you should try yogurt, acidophilus milk, or other cultured milk products. They are all excellent sources of protein and comparable to milk cup for cup. It's the beneficial bacteria in these products that convert lactose to lactic acid, making it easy for your body to digest.

Yogurt is a mixture of milk, skim milk, or cream that has been cultured with a beneficial bacteria called *lactobacillus acidophilus*. It is best to buy plain yogurt with no artificial sweeteners and then add your own fresh fruit and vanilla extract. Acidophilus milk was developed to create a way to promote the proliferation of beneficial bacteria in the intestines without the sour flavor of yogurt.

Also, there are commercially available lactose-free dairy products in most supermarkets. You can buy lactose enzymes (Lact-Aid) at any drug-store and add it to milk or take it before you eat dairy products that aren't cultured. Another nondairy alternative to milk is Eden Soy Milk, called Sunsoy.

Following you'll find a comprehensive list of foods that are high-grade proteins and contain the highest amounts of phenylalanine, tyrosine, and tryptophan. Eat a little more of all the foods I've listed and you can easily get enough of these three amino acids.

High-Grade Protein Sources

The amino acids tryptophan, tyrosine, and phenylalanine are building blocks of protein that affect your brain's regulation of hunger and satiety.

Sources of tryptophan: Milk, oatmeal, bananas, peas, spinach, broccoli, cauliflower, pineapple, nuts, beef, eggs, cheese

Sources of tyrosine and phenylalanine: Beef, poultry, fish, eggs, milk and cheese, beet greens, broccoli, corn, peas, soybeans, bananas, shredded wheat, whole-wheat pasta and bread, amaranth (grain), oatmeal

If you decide to purchase a combination protein supplement or to take amino acids separately, follow the directions listed on the label. There are also free-form amino acids that need no digestion and are absorbed directly into the bloodstream. When choosing amino acid supplements, look for products that contain USP (U.S. Pharmacopoeia) pharmaceutical-grade L-crystalline amino acids. Protein in animal and plant tissue are made from the L-forms of amino acids (with the exception of phenylalanine, which is also used in the form of DL-phenylalanine, a mixture of D- and L-forms). Amino acid supplements containing the L-forms seem to work best in the body.

It is safe to take amino acid supplements while breast-feeding—but not in excessive amounts. Taking dosages that greatly exceed the RDA will interfere with the absorption of other nutrients. The RDA for adults is between 100 and 500 milligrams for DL-phenylalanine or L-tyrosine and 250 milligrams for L-tryptophan. When you take amino acid supplements in dosages that greatly exceed the RDA you should be under the care of a doctor or nutrition counselor. Do not take amino acid supplements if you are taking MAO-inhibitor drugs for depression, have high blood pressure, or have PKU (phenylketonuria) or pre-existing pigmented melanoma.

I recommend you purchase amino acid supplements in capsule or straight powder form, and make sure they do not contain sugar, starch, salt, milk, preservatives, or chemical additives. Capsules are well assimilated, contain no excipients, and are easier to swallow than tablets. Amino acid liquids are also assimilated extremely well, and contain no excipients. Often it is the excipients that compromise the bulk of an amino acid tablet.

B_6 (Pyridoxine) and Hunger Control

Most mothers don't eat enough foods rich in vitamin B_6 (pyridoxine). Women seem to be especially prone to B_6 deficiency not only throughout prenatal development, but after pregnancy as well. Some pregnant women are unable to process carbohydrates properly, whether the carbohydrates are simple or complex sugars. This is referred to as gestational diabetes and two to three weeks of B_6 (pyridoxine) therapy during pregnancy usually relieves the symptoms of glucose intolerance. Nutritional research has also found that women on oral contraceptives who developed low levels of B_6 were unable to metabolize tryptophan. But by increasing their intake of B_6 (pyridoxine) the difficulties of metabolizing tryptophan were corrected.

Just a few years ago some infant-formula manufacturers used new processing techniques that removed B_6 (pyridoxine) content inadvertently during formula production. Infants, therefore, were being fed B_6 (pyridoxine)-deficient diets and having seizures. The B vitamins are utilized in all areas of your body as active coenzymes for numerous reactions. They are essential to metabolic production of energy from carbohydrates, fats, and proteins. I hope you're beginning to understand what powerful chemical substances nutrients are.

Plants are the main food source of B_6 (pyridoxine), and animals provide vitamin B_6 in the form of pyridoxal and pyridoxamine. B_6 is absorbed in your upper small intestine. B_6 (pyridoxine) has a very specific biological role in converting amino acids into neurotransmitters (serotonin) that control hunger and satiety. Vitamin B_6 is also necessary for fatty acid synthesis and maintenance of the insulating myelin sheath around nerves.

The RDA for B_6 is 1.6 milligrams and is extremely low. I recommend you eat more foods rich in vitamin B_6 and take a daily vitamin and mineral supplement that contains between 15 and 50 milligrams of B_6, although much higher daily amounts are still safe. Excessive dosages of B_6 in the 300- to 600-milligram range have been shown to decrease milk production and cause neurological damage. Again, purchase B_6 in capsule or straight powder form, and make sure it contains no yeast, corn, wheat, sugar, salt, artificial sweeteners, colorings, preservatives, or chemical additives. Following is a list of foods that are rich sources of B_6. From this list you can select the foods you like best and know how much B_6 you're consuming.

COMMON FOODS THAT ARE RICH SOURCES OF VITAMIN B_6

	Amount	Milligrams of B_6
Amaranth (grain)	½ cup	0.2
Avocado	½ slice	0.3
Barley	½ cup	0.3
Beef	4 oz.	0.4
Brussels sprouts	½ cup	0.2
Cauliflower	½ cup	0.3
Chicken	4 oz.	0.6
Duck	4 oz.	0.3
Fish	4 oz.	0.4
Lamb	4 oz.	0.2
Lentils	½ cup	0.2
Lima beans	½ cup	0.2
Okra	½ cup	0.2
Pinto beans	½ cup	0.2
Pork	4 oz.	0.4
Potato	1 medium	0.3
Quinoa (grain)	½ cup	0.3
Soybeans	½ cup	0.3
Spinach	½ cup	0.2
Sunflower seeds	1 oz.	0.3

| Turkey | 4 oz. | 0.6 |
| Whole grain | ½ cup | 0.3 |

B_{12} (Cobalamin) and Hunger Control

B_{12} deficiency is common after pregnancy and for people over forty years of age. Vitamin B_{12} is the largest complex molecule of all the vitamins. It's the only vitamin that contains a metal: cobalt. Besides cobalt, it contains carbon, oxygen, nitrogen, and phosphorus. B_{12} plays a vital role in controlling hunger and energy levels by regulating both carbohydrate and fatty acid metabolism.

As the main "anti-fatigue" vitamin, B_{12} is often taken along with folic acid, which is also a B vitamin. Both these B vitamins work together helping to increase energy, promote normal appetite, and prevent most anemias, provided there's adequate iron absorption. Although vitamin B_{12} is needed by all the cells, it is particularly important to the nervous system, digestive tract, and bone marrow. Vitamin B_{12} coenzymes aid in producing the DNA needed for red blood cells to mature.

The earliest symptom of B_{12} deficiency is anemia. The danger is that the anemia can disappear with adequate folic acid intake, and the B_{12} deficiency can be asymptomatic for a long time until there is more serious damage to the central nervous system. It's best to have B_{12} and folic acid blood levels measured before taking a folic acid supplement alone. Laxative use after pregnancy and overuse of antacids can also reduce absorption and deplete stores of B_{12}.

The highest concentrations of B_{12} are found in the heart, kidneys, liver, pancreas, brain, testes, and blood. A normal healthy person carries an average of a 600-day supply. Many people have problems absorbing B_{12} because they lack an enzyme responsible for its uptake and cellular acceptance. It is called the intrinsic factor, which is a mucoprotein that is secreted from the cell wall of the stomach during digestion.

The RDA for vitamin B_{12} is 2 micrograms. When you are breast-feeding, the RDA increases to 2.6 micrograms. A safe level is 10 to 20 micrograms daily. Most supplements contain higher dosages of 500 to 2,000 micrograms, which is still safe to take when breast-feeding. I suggest you eat several foods each day that contain B_{12}, and take a daily vitamin and mineral supplement. You can always take an additional B_{12} supplement separately if needed. For better absorption take a vitamin B_{12} sublingual (cyanocobalamin) or the nasal B_{12} supplement. It's best to get your blood level of B_{12} checked by your doctor before taking a supplement.

B_{12} is mainly present in animal products, but it can be found in milk products, breakfast cereals fortified with B_{12}, nutritional yeast, sea vegetables (kelp, kombu, hijiki, carragheen, nori, wakame), and miso. Following is a list of foods that are rich sources of B_{12}. From this list you can select the foods you like best and know just how much B_{12} you're consuming.

COMMON FOODS THAT ARE RICH SOURCES OF VITAMIN B_{12}

	Amount	Micrograms of B_{12}
Beef	4 oz.	2.0
Cheese	1 oz.	0.2
Chicken	4 oz.	0.3
Cod	4 oz.	1.0
Cottage cheese	½ cup	4.6
Duck	4 oz.	0.4
Egg	1	1.0
Egg white	1	0.2
Lamb	4 oz.	3.0
Lobster	4 oz.	3.0
Milk	½ cup	0.4
Pork	4 oz.	0.6
Salmon	4 oz.	6.0
Shrimp	4 oz.	1.0
Trout	4 oz.	4.0
Tuna	4 oz.	2.0
Turkey	4 oz.	0.4
Yogurt	½ cup	0.6

Zinc and Hunger Control

Your need for zinc is just as great after pregnancy as it was during pregnancy. Often morning sickness in pregnancy is the result of low zinc and B_6 levels, and supplementing these nutrients may help reduce symptoms. When observing zinc's biological influence on the metabolism it is astounding to conceive of a substance that is involved in so many processes in the body. Zinc is necessary for lactate and malate dehydrogenase, both important enzymes in energy production. Also, zinc is related to normal taste sensation.

Your body contains about 2.3 grams of zinc, which plays a role in over eighty enzymes. Zinc forms part of the insulin component secreted by your pancreas and is needed for the metabolism of carbohydrates and for protein synthesis in your body cells. Therefore, a deficiency of zinc can adversely affect hunger regulation. The depressed acuity of taste and smell are typical symptoms seen in early stages of zinc deficiency. Other signs of zinc deficiency are fatigue, oily skin, and hair loss.

Meeting the RDA for zinc is not easy to do, even if you're consuming 3,000 calories a day. The RDA for zinc is 12 milligrams. A safe level is between 12 and 30 milligrams, even when breast-feeding. It is estimated that only 20 percent of the zinc you eat actually gets absorbed. When you cook food, you diminish much of the zinc content. More important, when foods are processed, as in the refining of grains, much of the zinc is lost. Each day try to eat foods that contain zinc. I recommend you take a daily vitamin and mineral supplement that contains zinc gluconate or picolinate for better absorption. Don't forget you can take an additional zinc supplement if necessary. Make sure it is in a capsule or straight powder form and that it is yeast-free and contains no chemical additives or preservatives. Below I've listed foods that contain rich sources of zinc. You can easily select the foods you like best and know just how much zinc you're consuming.

COMMON FOODS THAT ARE RICH SOURCES OF ZINC

	Amounts	Milligrams of zinc
Barley	½ cup	3.0
Beef	4 oz.	5.8
Black-eyed peas	½ cup	3.0
Cereal, ready-to-eat	½ cup	1.6
Duck	4 oz.	3.0
Egg	1	0.5
Lamb	4 oz.	4.5
Legumes	½ cup	1.9
Milk	½ cup	0.5
Molasses	1 Tbsp.	1.0
Most fish	4 oz.	1.0
Oatmeal	½ cup	1.6
Pork	4 oz.	3.8
Poultry	4 oz.	3.6
Quinoa (grain)	½ cup	3.0
Seeds	1 oz.	1.4
Turkey	4 oz.	3.7
Wheat germs	1 Tbsp	0.9
Yogurt	½ cup	0.4

Sodium and Hunger Control

It's true: Too much sodium stimulates hunger. Both during and after pregnancy most mothers experience more salt cravings than they do sugar cravings. Your hunger after pregnancy might be triggered by an increase in thirst and the retention of body fluids. The regulation of food and water are closely related. When you're thirsty you're likely to be hungry too. During pregnancy, salt cravings are thought to occur because the mother's blood volume doubles, and therefore requires extra sodium to maintain the body's balance of the mineral. If you crave salt, retain water, or feel hungry all the time, you need to reduce your total sodium intake to about 1,500 milligrams each day.

Even though salt is essential for human life, a little goes a long way. Refined table salt is an unbalanced salt excessively high in sodium chloride and is stripped of other essential trace minerals such as magnesium, sulfur, and bromine. Not only is table salt unbalanced, it contains ferric ammonium citrate to make it free flowing, sodium carbonate to prevent it from turning purple, and dextrose (sugar) to stabilize the iodine. Yes, there's sugar in your salt. Unrefined salt is used by your body to regulate body fluid, cleanse mucus membranes, and normalize blood pressure.

Recent research has shown that sucrose (table sugar), especially in combination with salt, may produce larger increases in blood pressure than other dietary carbohydrates. Some good news is that breast-feeding may lower your blood pressure by acting as a diuretic, pulling extra fluid into your breast milk. The higher levels of prolactin that are present while you breast-feed can also help lower blood pressure.

Very little of your salt intake comes from the shaker. In fact, it accounts for only 6 percent of your overall sodium intake. Most of your salt comes from canned, bottled, frozen, processed, or fast food. Any products that are smoked or pickled have a high sodium content and should be avoided. Foods like hot dogs, luncheon meat, tuna (canned), sausages, and bacon should be avoided as well. Other high-sodium foods include condiments such as mustard, catsup, tamari, soy sauce, miso, barbecue sauce, chili sauce, Worcestershire sauce, bouillon cube, monosodium glutamate (MSG), and any onion, garlic, or celery salt. It is best to skip the condiments and focus on eating fresh foods, like vegetables, fruits, grains, low-fat dairy products, seafood, meat, and poultry.

Sodium Content, in milligrams per 3½-ounce serving	
Herring (kippered)	920
Herring (pickled)	875
Chinook Salmon (smoked)	785
Potato Chips	665
Pizza (cheese)	600
Hamburger (Whopper)	439
Tuna (canned)	355
Dungeness Crab	295
Shrimp (fresh)	147
Herring (fresh)	90
Swordfish (fresh)	90
Flounder (fresh)	80

Clams (fresh)	57
Cod (fresh)	54
Chinook Salmon (fresh)	47
Tuna (fresh)	37
Monkfish (fresh)	18

There are several ways you can add flavor without the salt. You'll be amazed at how herbs and spices enhance the natural flavor of food rather than mask it. Unlike salt, herbs won't cause you to retain water or make you feel hungry after eating. Try using the Everyday Herb Chart at the end of this book for an easy reference when cooking with different recipes.

Last, you need to read food labels. The Food and Drug Administration requires food processors to list the amount of sodium per serving. A product that claims "reduced sodium" on the label must contain 75 percent less sodium than a typical version of the food. "Low sodium" must have no more than 140 milligrams of sodium per serving; "very low sodium" has 35 milligrams or less; and "sodium free" contains less than 5 milligrams.

Hot Food and Hunger Control

Have you ever noticed how a cold meal often leaves you feeling hungry? There's a good reason for this. When hot food is eaten, the hunger center located in the hypothalamus responds quickly to the increase in body temperature (called a thermogenic effect) and decreases hunger. When you eat hot food satiety or fullness is reached sooner, due to an increase in the activity of the sympathetic nervous system, which serves as a signal to stop eating.

On the other hand, when cold food is eaten, satiety or fullness is not reached as soon, due to a decrease in the activity of the sympathetic nervous system, which serves as a signal to keep eating. Hot food will increase the activity of the sympathetic nervous system, keeping you alert and happy. A warmed baby bottle will satisfy your baby's hunger sooner than a cold bottle.

Hot food is also digested more easily than cold food. When hot food touches the nerve endings in your tongue and palate it stimulates the circulation of blood in the entire digestive system. There is even an increase in secretion of digestive enzymes and the release of a polypeptide hormone called cholecystokininin (CCK), which stops you from overeating.

If you want a hot meal that is nutritious, flavorful, and usually low in calories, try soup. Soup is a good choice when you're really hungry and are likely to eat too fast and too much. With all its liquid, soup takes up a larger volume of space in your stomach and can help control your appetite. Most soups are substantial enough to be considered a full meal-in-a-bowl. Add some bread to round out your meal. Soup is a good source of protein, vitamins, and minerals and can be sprinkled with some pine nuts or sunflower seeds on top to make it a complete protein. Try some of the soup recipes at the end of this book.

"Will I Ever Stop Feeling Depressed and Anxious?"

Fighting Depression and Anxiety with Nutrients

"Several weeks after my daughter was born I felt like I was falling apart," one mother recalls. "All of a sudden I felt self-critical, easily irritated, and confused." Another mother recalls never shedding a tear until four months after her son was born. But she, too, suddenly felt anxious and forgetful, and would cry for no reason at all.

Have you ever felt like that? If so, it is important that you realize that varying degrees of postpartum depression and anxiety are normal and temporary. It's estimated that 500,000 women each year in the United States experience postpartum depression that is partially due to hormonal changes. Postpartum depression can occur anytime in the first year of your child's life.

It's stressful to be continuously exposed to a new baby with no relief. Most mothers feel like they're being pulled in a million different directions—and usually are. The added responsibility of motherhood can seem overwhelming and can contribute to depression and anxiety. During those first several months with a new baby, the isolation alone can cause you to feel anxious and depressed. These feelings can worsen when you isolate yourself for too long. If hormones have never thrown off your emotions before, this temporary loss of control can be tremendously disturbing and frustrating. You can feel happy and peaceful one moment and find yourself in the depths of despair the next.

You might think that you'll be able to cope. After all, mothering is supposed to be a pleasant, rewarding, and fulfilling experience. But telling yourself you shouldn't be depressed or ignoring your feelings will only make things worse. Denying your emotions will only make you feel "numb." This numbness soon spreads to every aspect of your life.

Depression and Overeating

When you're depressed it's necessary for you to identify your feelings and then accept them. Otherwise, you'll never achieve the emotional freedom you need to be yourself. The more you fight your true emotions, the more you turn to or away from food for comfort and control. Emotions were meant to be expressed. If they are not expressed, fear, happiness, love, doubt, and anger can all be displaced onto food.

When you're depressed, overeating is fueled by an emotional hunger as well as a physical hunger. If you find yourself still eating even after a full meal, ask yourself if your hunger has a physical or emotional component. Then ask yourself, "Why am I overeating? What am I looking for, and will I find it in the refrigerator?" Many times you may be mistaking thirst for hunger, or fatigue for hunger.

Caring for yourself emotionally and physically is truly the greatest contribution you can make to your family. Allow yourself to be more open and less inhibited about your feelings and needs. There's nothing wrong with depending on others.

Depression and Preserving Your Self-Esteem

Asking for help is essential to preserving your self-esteem. Asking for help doesn't make you morally weaker than another mother who does everything herself. You may need help at the moment, but this doesn't suggest a lifelong weakness in your character.

Self-esteem refers to your psychological "wholeness," how you think and feel about yourself. Self-esteem gauges how capable you think you are, how much you like yourself, and how much you trust your insights and judgments. Your self-esteem is composed of two parts, the interior and the exterior. When life gives you more than you can handle, understanding this concept can help you get through difficult times.

By the time you are an adult your interior self-esteem is unbelievably powerful—it reflects the "real you." It consists of firm attitudes and beliefs about yourself you have formed over the years. On the other hand, your exterior self-esteem consists of attitudes and beliefs that change in direct relation to what you experience from day to day. After the birth of your baby you may experience some very real losses and low feelings that affect your exterior self-esteem—the loss of your old life and the time you had for yourself. You may also experience conflicting feelings about how you feel about motherhood, yourself, and your friends. Thoughts about yourself may be disoriented, and you may feel lonely and empty. When you feel like you're falling apart, remember, your interior self-esteem is still intact. Eventually, as you work through your feelings, the real you will emerge in one piece.

Look at Yourself Through the Eyes of Someone Who Cares

Each time you bring a new life into the world you will always have to adjust how you feel about yourself and your life. Trying to get back to the life you once had before your children were born is unrealistic, and will only cause pain and frustration. When you're anxious or depressed it's difficult to see that your personality has changed, or that you're being too self-critical, or that you're trying to be supermom. So it's important to look at yourself through the eyes of someone who cares. This will help you to make a shift in your perspective so you don't get stuck in a distorted image of yourself and your life. You may learn that what you thought were weaknesses are instead normal or are actual strengths. You need to redefine what "normal" is. Normal is when you feel peaceful and comfortable about your imperfections. Within time, your normal coping mechanisms will return and you'll feel good again.

It's important that you slow down and do something fun for yourself. Stay in touch with your friends. Buy yourself a new outfit and get out of the house. Save your energy and don't overdo the housework. Instead, try to eat, rest, and sleep as much as possible, so you can enjoy being with your baby. Doing this will make being a mother a much more fulfilling and enjoyable experience.

Depression and Anxiety: It's Not All in Your Mind

Anyone who has ever been depressed will tell you that no one wants to be depressed. The depression and anxiety that you might be feeling after the birth of your baby is not all in your mind. It is a function of the brain and mind. Remember, your mind doesn't exist in a vacuum; it's linked to the chemistry of your brain. When your nervous system does not work, neither your mind nor your body will function well. If you don't have the right brain chemicals, hormones, and nutrients present in the right amounts, your thoughts and feelings may be distorted.

Your thoughts and emotions are the result of chemical processes going on within your brain. Proper nutrition can help bring about a normalization of your brain chemistry along with your mood. That cup of coffee you have in the morning and the aspirin you take for a headache are all brain- and mind-altering substances. Even chocolate contains caffeine, beta-phenylethylamine, and theobromine, which are all habit-forming substances. Theobromine is similar to caffeine and acts as a diuretic, stimulates the heart, and dilates blood vessels.

Nutrient and hormone imbalances can greatly effect the production of brain neurotransmitters, which are responsible for ensuring that nerve impulses complete the jump from one neuron to another. In other words hormonal changes and even sleep deprivation can trigger an imbalance in neurotransmitters. For example, after pregnancy, the hormones estradiol and progesterone, along with blood-nutrient concentrations, drop and alter the hypothalamus-pituitary regulation of several brain neurotransmitters that affect moods, feelings, and behaviors.

The hormonal changes after pregnancy are dramatic. For example, when the pituitary releases prolactin for milk production around the third day after childbirth, this may cause an imbalance in other hormones, and can deplete the brain's output of the neurotransmitters norepinephrine, dopamine, and serotonin. Too much or too little of these three neurotransmitters as they journey through the brain may be the reason for anxiety disorders and some types of depression.

Antidepressants: Food-Drug Interactions

Antidepressant medications work by restoring a normal balance to several neurotransmitters and by altering the activity of specific neurotransmitters. There is also a variety of other treatment options, including psychotherapy, self-help groups, and nutrition. Whenever a medication is prescribed for you, ask your doctor or pharmacist about possible interactions it may have with certain foods. Certain foods may alter a drug's therapeutic performance, the body's metabolism, or its ability to utilize nutrients in a way that over time can lead to nutritional deficiencies.

Probably the most dangerous food-drug interactions involve a class of antidepressants known as *monoamine oxidase inhibitors* (MAO) and the amino acid tyramine, found in pickled products, aged cheese, red wine, fermented and aged foods and beverages, as well as in the yeast extract found in most processed foods and some seasonings. Also, *do not* take amino acid supplements if you are taking MAO-inhibitor drugs.

The combination of high-tyramine foods and MAO inhibitors such as phenelzine (Nardil), tranylcypromine (Parnate), or isocarboxazid (Marplan) can cause a sudden rise in blood pressure, severe headaches, and even death. There are also MAO inhibitors and tricyclic antidepressants, such as amitriptyline (Elavil) and imipramine (Tofranil), which stimulate appetite as a side effect.

Some medications are better absorbed when taken with food. On a full stomach the delivery of a drug to its absorption site is delayed, which is desirable for slow dissolving so it doesn't pass through the intestine and never enter the bloodstream. Always ask your doctor or pharmacist if you should take your medication on a full or empty stomach. None of these antidepressant medications should ever be taken with alcohol.

Depression: Nutrition and Balancing Brain Chemicals

Your body manufactures neurotransmitters and many other brain chemicals from nutrients. The presence of the amino acids L-tyrosine, L-phenylalanine, L-tryptophan, and other nutrients such as choline, B_5, niacin, folic acid, vitamin E, zinc, and bioflavonoids are all useful in the treatment of depression and anxiety.

In addition to adding these nutrients to your diet, you will need to regulate your blood sugar. If your diet is high in simple carbohydrates (refined sugar), your blood sugar levels will fluctuate dramatically. After a meal there is always a rise in blood sugar, a process controlled by the secretion of insulin. When you don't eat for long periods of time, blood sugar is prevented from falling to low levels by the release of glucose from liver glycogen and by the manufacture of new glucose from amino acids and glycerol in your liver.

Keeping blood sugar levels stable is important to your brain because it is highly dependent on blood sugar as fuel. When your blood sugar falls below critical levels, your body takes steps to raise the glucose levels by turning off insulin secretion and by releasing catecholamines, glucagon, glucocorticoids, and growth hormones, all of which affect the amounts of blood sugar released. Should your blood sugar level fall lower than 40 mg/dl, brain function may be impaired, resulting in symptoms of confusion, memory loss, fatigue, and blurred vision. The normal range for blood sugar levels is 65 to 110 mg/dl.

Eating foods that are good sources of soluble fiber will regulate your blood sugar so you can think clearly and start to feel better. Soluble fiber will slow the rate of absorption of sugar over a longer period of time while lowering absorption of cholesterol and fat. The chart on page 173 gives you a list of foods that contain soluble fiber. The U.S. Department of Agriculture recommends you daily eat six to eleven servings of grains, which contain soluble and insoluble fiber. Now let's take a closer look at other nutrients—"brain foods" that can help you battle depression and anxiety.

Choline or Lecithin: Emotional-Control Nutrient

Choline is referred to as the "memory vitamin" and is present in all living cells. Your body can synthesize choline from the amino acid glycine. When choline is depleted, fat metabolism and utilization may be decreased and lead to fat accumulations. The ability of some neurons to synthesize a specific neurotransmitter like acetylcholine depends upon the availability of precursor components like choline.

Choline is one very important precursor component of the neurotransmitter acetylcholine. Acetylcholine is one of several brain neurotransmitters that control emotions and feelings. When choline is lacking in your diet, your brain can't function efficiently. The blood flow into the brain and the subsequent synthesis of acetylcholine are complex processes. If the millions of chemical shifts are to take place between neurons there needs to be a consistent and abundant supply of acetylcholine available to the region of your brain called the limbic system.

Choline or Lecithin (phosphatidylcholine)
Acetlycholine

The limbic system consists of a set of structures that are in the core of your forebrain. This system is directly connected to all parts of the brain and spinal cord, and plays a key role in the expression of emotions and feelings at a chemical level. Acetylcholine is also used by your brain's system to control the penetration of outside stimuli. In other words, choline provides a type of stimulus barrier. Without enough acetylcholine, outside stimuli, such as the sound of a crying baby, will come pouring in. You may experience headaches, irritability, fatigue, memory loss, and problems concentrating.

The richest source of phosphatidylcholine is in lecithin, which is usually found in soybeans and eggs. Choline is combined with fatty acids, glycerol, and phosphate to make lecithin. I recommend you eat more food rich in choline and take a daily vitamin and mineral supplement in capsule or straight powder form. You can also take lecithin granules or a liquid choline chloride and add them to cereal, salad, or fruit juice. Make sure the lecithin you purchase is 95 percent phosphatides. Choline chloride will not cause diarrhea like choline bitartrate and does not contain the fat found in lecithin granules. No RDA has been established, but I'd suggest taking 200 milligrams daily. Choline is also found in fish, liver, eggs, cabbage, cauliflower, garbanzo beans, green beans, rice, soybeans, peanuts, split peas, and wheat germ.

Folic Acid and the Formation of Choline

Often the first symptom of low folic acid levels is depression. Folic acid deficiency is fairly common after pregnancy and may be misdiagnosed as hormonal. The symptoms of a folic acid deficiency are similar to those of B_{12} (cobalamin) deficiency anemia. A folic acid deficiency can result in a condition called megablastic anemia, in which an usually large proportion of the red cells do not mature normally. Anemic conditions in mothers are easily developed if dietary or supplemental folic acid levels are not adequate. Depression is often a common side effect of taking birth control pills because they reduce absorption of this folic acid by 50 percent.

Folic acid is involved in the formation of choline, which, as we've discussed, is essential for controlling emotions and anxiety levels. Folic acid is needed for the conversion of phenylalanine to tyrosine and glycine to serine, and in the formation of porphyrin for hemoglobin. Folic acid, like the other B vitamins, is needed on a daily basis because storage is limited. The RDA for folic acid is 180 micrograms. I recommend you take a daily vitamin and mineral supplement that contains between 180 and 400 micrograms, even when breast-feeding. Take it in capsule or straight powder form, and make sure it is free of yeast, corn, wheat, and sugar. You should also eat more foods that contain folic acid, such as fish, milk, eggs, wheat germ, whole grains, barley, beans, peas, endive, brewer's yeast, oranges, bananas, avocados, tomatoes, corn, soybeans, lentils, and rice.

Pantothenic Acid (B_5): Help for Fatigue and Depression

The most common symptoms of B-vitamin pantothenic acid deficiency are fatigue and depression. Pantothenic acid is a water-soluble vitamin. It is an essential component of a compound called acetyl CoA, which plays a central role in energy and tissue metabolism within the cells.

Pantothenic acid is referred to as the antistress vitamin that helps with the stress-induced exhaustion and blues often experienced after pregnancy. Pantothenic acid, like choline, contributes to the synthesis of acetylcholine, the brain neurotransmitter that controls emotions and feelings. A by-product of the bacteria flora of the digestive tract, pantothenic acid can be depleted by the use of antibiotics.

Pantothenic acid serves as a major energy source for the adrenal glands; therefore deficiency of pantothenic acid can cause adrenal exhaustion. Pantothenic acid is important to the production and release of cortisone and other adrenal hormones from the adrenal glands to help counteract stress.

You have two adrenal glands, one located above each kidney. Each gland is composed of two parts. There is the inner core, called the medulla, which secretes the hormone epinephrine and has a wide range of "emergency" effects on your temperature, blood, and muscle. The outer core, called the cortex, produces the hormones cortisol and aldosterone, and controls carbohydrate, protein, mineral, salt, and water metabolism. All these hormones and nutrients act to preserve your physical and mental well-being.

There is no RDA for pantothenic acid that is defined by age. A daily intake of 4 to 7 milligrams is recommended for adults of all ages. Try to eat several foods each day that contain pantothenic acid, and take a multiple vitamin and mineral supplement that contains between 25 and 50 milligrams of B_5. These dosages are safe to take when breast-feeding. Take your supplements in a capsule or straight powder form that is yeast-free and contains no preservatives or chemical additives.

Pantothenic acid is found in eggs, fish, meat, poultry, blue cheese, whole grains, lentils, corn, peas, avocados, cauliflower, sweet potatoes, green beans, sunflower seeds, and peanuts.

Niacin (B₃) and Its Source

Niacin is used to support a variety of metabolic functions and has been beneficial for treating depression and anxiety. A by-product of the amino acid tryptophan, niacin is an important vitamin for the synthesis of the sex hormones, such as estrogen and progesterone. Niacin in the form of nicotinic acid helps in the regulation of blood sugar, stimulates blood flow in the capillaries, and lowers cholesterol.

Niacin in the form of nicotinic acid can produce redness, warmth, and itching of the skin. This reaction, called the niacin "flush," is harmless. This reaction occurs when dosages of 50 milligrams or more are taken and results from the release of histamine by the cells, which causes blood vessels to dilate. You should purchase niacin supplements in the form of niacinamide, which will not produce this reaction. Niacinamide won't lower cholesterol like nicotinic acid will. People on high-blood-pressure medicine who have ulcers or diabetes should be careful when taking higher dosages of nicotinic acid.

The first signs of a niacin deficiency are decreased energy and skin that becomes dry, red, and sensitive when exposed to the sunlight. The RDA for niacin is 15 milligrams. Eat more foods that contain niacin and take a vitamin and mineral supplement each day that contains between 15 and 50 milligrams of niacin, which is safe to take if you're breast-feeding. Avoid supplements that use yeast, corn, wheat, salt, artificial sweeteners, binders, fillers, preservatives, or salicylates.

The best food sources of niacin are beef, milk, veal, pork, lamb, turkey, tuna, swordfish, shrimp, peanut butter, whole-wheat bread, cream of wheat, rice, bananas, peaches, tomatoes, broccoli, and peas.

Vitamin E (Tocopherol) and the Production of Hormones and Neurotransmitters

Vitamin E is a fat-soluble vitamin that plays an important role in the functioning of the nervous system. More concentrated in the pituitary then in any other part of your body, vitamin E is an essential nutrient for the production of hormones and neurotransmitters. It functions as an antioxidant, protecting the structure of cell membranes from damage, and red blood cells from disintegrating. With vitamin E available, oxygen is bound by it rather than left free to oxidize vitamins A and C or polyunsaturated fatty acids. The first sign of vitamin E deficiency may be loss of red blood cells because of fragility caused by the loss of membrane protection.

Vitamin E holds in place neurotransmission synapses between brain cells that are important for controlling moods, feelings, and behaviors. After pregnancy, a vitamin E deficiency can adversely affect mood and may contribute to or cause depression and anxiety. Headaches may sometimes be helped with vitamin E treatment.

The RDA for vitamin E is 8 milligrams. I recommend you take a multiple vitamin and mineral supplement that contains between 8 and 12 milligrams of vitamin E. Vitamin E palmitate and acetate are water-soluble forms of vitamin E that work best in the body and are safe to take when breast-feeding.

Try to eat more foods that contain vitamin E, such as wheat-germ oil, whole-wheat flour, seeds, almonds, walnuts, dried beans, corn oil, safflower oil, peanut oil, hazelnuts, and green leafy vegetables.

Zinc (Zn) and the Secretion of Pituitary Hormones and Brain Neurotransmitters

Zinc is a mineral that is needed in all metabolic functions. It is present in high concentrations in the pituitary, and affects the secretion of pituitary hormones and brain neurotransmitters. Zinc is a constituent of your body's enzyme systems and is needed for the transport of carbon dioxide from the blood into the lungs for expelling. Your body contains about 2.3 grams of zinc, which plays a role in over eighty enzymes. Zinc is a component of insulin and is needed for the metabolism of carbohydrates and for protein synthesis in the cells of your body.

After pregnancy, a zinc deficiency can adversely affect your mood. Zinc needs to be in balance with copper, so an excessive copper to zinc ratio may be the cause of depression and irritability. Taking birth control pills usually causes elevated copper levels and the need for additional zinc. Depression is often a common side effect of taking birth control pills. Your body is approximately ten parts zinc to nine parts copper. The suggested zinc to copper ratio is about 15:1.

The RDA for zinc is 12 milligrams. A safe level to take even when breast-feeding is between 12 and 30 milligrams of zinc per day. For better absorption I suggest you take a daily vitamin and mineral supplement that contains zinc gluconate or picolinate. Meat and seafood are much better sources of available zinc than vegetables. On page 58 there is a list of foods that are rich in zinc. Try to include several foods that contain zinc in your diet each day.

Vitamin C and Bioflavonoids: A Powerful Combination

Bioflavonoids are water-soluble substances and are members of the group of compounds called flavonoids. Bioflavonoids are found in foods along with vitamin C, particularly in the pulp of citrus fruits. Bioflavonoids enhance the absorption of vitamin C. Oranges, grapefruits, and lemons are good sources of bioflavonoids, and the pulpy portion of the fruit contains ten times the amount of bioflavonoids as that in strained juice.

Rutin is one of the bioflavonoids that has recently gained attention for treatment of depression. The buckwheat plant, both the leaf and grain, is a good source of rutin. Other bioflavonoids include citrin, quercetin, flavones, and flavonals. As a group, these bioflavonoids help build resistance to infection, relieve water retention in the tissues, and work to keep the capillary blood vessels strong. They also transport oxygen and nutrients to the organs, tissues, and cells, and then pick up carbon dioxide and water, and carry them through the veins and back to the heart.

No RDA has been established for bioflavonoids, but for every 500 milligrams of vitamin C, you should get at least 100 milligrams of bioflavonoids. You can purchase a vitamin C supplement that contains all the bioflavonoids, or purchase bioflavonoids separately. If you take a vitamin C supplement, take it in a capsule or straight powder and make sure it contains the bioflavonoids. Capsules and straight powders rarely contain fillers and binders and are assimilated very well. Some good food sources of bioflavonoids are apricots, cherries, plums, black currants, grapes, green peppers, lemons, tomatoes, broccoli, cantaloupe, papaya, oranges, and grapefruit.

Amino Acids and Depression:
Phenylalanine, Tyrosine, and Tryptophan

Several of the brain's most important neurotransmitters are known as catecholamines, which include dopamine, norepinephrine, and epinephrine. They are produced within your brain by a sequence of chemical conversions of phenylalanine and tyrosine. Some forms of depression and anxiety are the result of low levels of dopamine, norepinephrine, and ephinephrine. The essential amino acids phenylalanine and tyrosine are used by your brain to make dopamine and norepinephrine and are both effective in relieving depression and anxiety.

Eating foods that contain protein increases the amount of tyrosine in the blood, causing tyrosine levels in the brain to increase. The increase in brain tyrosine will, in turn, increase the levels of catecholamines. Tryptophan is another important amino acid needed by your brain to produce serotonin, the neurotransmitter used in the treatment of depression. When your depression and anxiety can be reduced to tolerable limits, you can think clearly and deal with the stress after pregnancy. All three amino acids—tryptophan, tyrosine, and phenylalanine—are essential for normal brain functioning and for combating depression and anxiety.

Supplemental amino acids are available in combination with various multivitamin formulas as protein mixtures, and in a number of amino acid formulas. There are also free-form amino acids that can be purchased separately or as a complex. I recommend using free-form amino acids because they need no digestion and are absorbed directly into the bloodstream.

When choosing amino acid supplements, look for products that contain USP (U.S. Pharmacopoeia) pharmaceutical-grade L-crystalline amino acids. Protein in animal and plant tissue is made from the L-forms of amino acids (with the exception of phenylalanine, which is also used in the form of DL-phenylalanine, a mixture of D- and L-forms). Amino acid supplements containing the L-forms are more compatible with human biochemistry.

For best results, choose amino acid supplements in capsule or powder form. Individual amino acids should not be taken for longer than two months. Some amino acids can be toxic when taken in high dosages of over 2,000 milligrams per day. If you are taking antidepressants known as monoamine oxidase inhibitors (MAO), do not take amino acid supplements. Amino acid supplements should be used with caution and under the supervision of a physician in cases of high blood pressure. Phenylalanine supplements should not be used if you have PKU (phenylketonuria) or with pre-existing pigmented melanoma. Consult your doctor if you take dosages of any amino acid that greatly exceed the RDA. The RDA for adults is between 100 and 500 milligrams for DL-phenylalanine or L-tyrosine and 250 milligrams for L-tryptophan.

On page 52 you'll find RDA information and a list of foods that are high in the amino acids tyrosine, phenylalanine, and tryptophan.

"What Vitamins and Minerals Do I Need?"

Vitamins and Minerals for Breast-feeding and Weight Loss

*T*he special attention that you gave yourself during pregnancy doesn't stop after birth, but some of the requirements do change. You must continue to "listen" to the messages your body sends you about its needs—for more rest, or certain foods, or exercise—and then make changes. By paying attention to your body's needs and then responding accordingly, you can prevent small problems from becoming big ones.

Mothers are often misinformed or not informed at all when it comes to weight loss and breast-feeding. And it's not hard to see why. Deciding whether to breast-feed or lose weight is usually not discussed openly. Both involve very personal and emotional decisions. After all, it is your body and your baby, and only you can decide what to do.

This chapter will help you select foods that are rich in the vitamins and minerals your body needs for breast-feeding and weight loss. By making good food selections you can lose weight without compromising your milk production.

Things You Should Know
if You Breast-feed or Bottle-Feed

Breast-feeding alone doesn't automatically mean you'll lose weight. In fact, mothers who are breast-feeding often gain weight because they are hungrier. If you're nursing, you feel and look different from a mother who is not nursing. Your hormonal state differs because your body is producing a high level of the hormone prolactin.

If you're undecided about whether to breast-feed, remember that it is easier to try it for the first few days of life, and then switch to partial or complete bottle-feeding. Although health professionals will encourage you to breast-feed, if you cannot or do not want to breast-feed, don't feel guilty. You can still have a close relationship with your baby if you bottle-feed. Whether you breast-feed or bottle-feed, sit down, relax, and enjoy holding your baby for thirty to forty minutes at each feeding. If you breast-feed you should nurse for at least ten minutes per breast at each feeding.

If you plan to go back to work within a few weeks of the birth, bottle-feeding may be an easier method. Most babies can drink cow's milk formula without any problems. The technologic advances in commercially prepared infant formulas have already reproduced many of the beneficial effects of breast milk. Commercially prepared formulas are made from either cow's milk or soybeans, with nutrients added to imitate the composition of breast milk. Breast milk provides approximately 20 calories per ounce, which is 40 percent carbohydrate, 10 percent protein, and 50 percent fat. As you can see, fat calories are an extremely important nutrient for both you and your baby.

Occasionally after bottle-feeding your baby might have gas, loose stools, or an unpleasant stool odor. If this happens frequently ask your pediatrician about trying another type of formula that contains less protein than cow's milk formula. There are two types of protein found in cow's milk formula, casein and whey. Cow's milk formula contains much more casein protein than breast milk does. The casein protein can form a large curd in your baby's stomach that is hard to digest. Whey protein forms a small, soft, digestible curd in the stomach. Whey protein compromises 60 percent of breast milk protein, but only 20 percent of cow milk protein. You can purchase infant formulas that contain whey protein instead of casein.

The high lactose (milk sugar) content of breast milk benefits your baby in several ways because it increases calcium and iron absorption. Commercial formulas add lactose to their product to imitate the carbohydrate content of breast milk. Breast milk also contains enzymes that are activated by bile salts in the intestine that digest the fat in breast milk easily. This enzyme, called milk lipase, can break down most of the milk fat in only half an hour and allows essential fatty acids to be absorbed easily. These polyunsaturated essential fatty acids are the most important source of energy for you and your baby. This is why some of the saturated milk fat has been removed from infant formulas and replaced with vegetable oil, which is higher in polyunsaturates than the fat in cow's milk.

Drink Plenty of Water

Water is a vital nutrient. Drinking plenty of water or fluid is necessary when breast-feeding or losing weight. You need to take in extra fluids to replace the 23 ounces used to produce milk every day and to meet your own body's needs. Plenty of water is also needed when you're losing weight, because it will protect you when your diet is lacking in carbohydrates. When carbohydrate levels are low, fat will be broken down for energy faster than your body can use it, and your liver will release ketones into the blood. To get rid of the overload of ketones, your body draws large amounts of water from the tissues.

This water loss, through urination, can cause dehydration, muscle weakness, and loss of valuable vitamins and minerals. Ketones cause sleeplessness, suppress the appetite, and cause bad breath (acid breath). This is one reason why plenty of water is required when losing weight. Always drink plenty of water when you're thirsty, and stick with drinking milk or juice, or eat some fruits or vegetables, which are 95 percent water.

Good Foods Make Good Milk

If your diet is too low in calories or contains an inadequate supply of vitamins and minerals it can negatively affect the nutrient concentration and production of your breast milk as well as inhibit weight loss. And remember, good foods make good milk. So try to eat a healthful diet of fresh, whole foods rich in the vitamins and minerals that will help you produce enough milk and still lose weight. If you breast-feed, don't stuff yourself with food in fear you may not be able to produce enough milk. Simply eat a variety of foods, and then eat enough so that you feel good—not full.

Occasionally something you eat may bother your baby. Certain foods can enter breast milk and upset your baby as soon as two hours after you eat. If you suspect a food or drink is causing a problem for your baby, eliminate it from your diet for two weeks. Usually you'll see an improvement in your baby's behavior in as soon as one to two days. Babies have difficulty tolerating gassy foods, such as milk products, as well as strong vegetables—broccoli, cauliflower, onions, brussels sprouts, cabbage, corn products, beans, and wheat. It's also best to avoid spicy garlicky foods and, of course, processed foods that contain colorings and flavorings. Often your baby will outgrow the intolerance as he or she grows older. Some babies like the taste of spicy foods and will actually breast-feed longer.

All Vitamins and Minerals Work Together

All vitamins and minerals work together and have the same biological effect for both you and your baby. When you breast-feed, your baby is dependent primarily on your milk for practically all nutrients until solid foods are provided. For example, both you and your baby need zinc, a mineral needed to pull vitamin A from storage in the liver. Another example is calcium, which is absorbed better when taken with vitamin D and magnesium. Vitamins and minerals contain no calories and provide no extra energy. But without them you would be unable to transform food into the energy your body needs for milk production and weight loss.

The vitamins that you need are classified as fat soluble or water soluble. The fat-soluble vitamins include the B vitamins (thiamine, riboflavin, niacin, pantothenic acid, folic acid, biotin, vitamin B_6, vitamin B_{12}, and vitamin C or ascorbic acid). Inadequate intake of these vitamins can negatively affect the nutrient concentration and production of breast milk, and inhibit weight loss. Vitamins do not provide energy, nor do they construct or build any part of your body. They are needed for body maintenance and for transforming food into energy.

Your body has no nutritional use for excess vitamins, and some vitamins can be stored only for short periods and are then excreted. When a vitamin enters the body it will travel through the bloodstream to a specific body cell, and then form part of the enzyme complex within the cell. The cell, however, has a limited ability to produce these enzymes, and once that capacity is reached, the vitamin cannot be used. It will then be excreted in the urine, especially a vitamin that is water-soluble. The fat-soluble vitamins are likely to be stored, although they are still excreted to some extent in the feces and urine.

Minerals serve a multitude of roles in your body, especially in skeletal maintenance and nerve conduction. All foods, whether from plant or animal sources, contain minerals. Minerals influence the acid-base balance of your body, regulate body fluids, and play an essential role in the formation of bones and teeth. Like other nutrients, minerals are absorbed in the intestines and transported in the blood to other parts of your body.

The classification of minerals is based on their occurrence in the body, as either macronutrient or micronutrient minerals. Macronutrients, such as calcium, phosphorus, magnesium, sulfur, sodium, potassium, and chloride, are present in the body in larger amounts than micronutrients, such as iron, manganese, copper, iodine, zinc, fluoride, chromium, cobalt, molybdenum, and selenium.

On the following pages we will explore the function that specific vitamins and minerals have in relation to breast-feeding and weight loss. As you read this chapter, don't forget that all vitamins and minerals function best when they work together.

The Fat-Soluble Vitamins

Vitamin A (Retinol): Protection Against Infection for You and Your Baby
Vitamin A is needed for breast-feeding and weight loss. This was the first true vitamin to be discovered, and it wasn't until later that beta carotene

and provitamin A were detected in plant structure and seen to be identical to the preformed or animal version of vitamin A, called retinol.

Vitamin A is important in carbohydrate metabolism, the synthesis of glycogen for the storage of body energy, and the way cholesterol is used in your body. Vitamin A is also necessary for bone growth, ovarian function, and the formation of tooth enamel. It helps protect you and your baby against infection by promoting normal secretions of mucus from the epithelial cells that line body surfaces. Vitamin A is essential for the normal function of the retina. It combines with the red pigment of the retina (opsin) to form a substance called rhodopsin, which is needed for sight in partial darkness.

Although all forms of vitamin A can be absorbed, retinol is the dominant form absorbed through the wall of the small intestine. Conversion of provitamin A or beta carotene to vitamin A also occurs in the intestinal wall. It's your liver that serves as the main storage area for vitamin A until it is needed in the body, and it can hold enough of this vitamin to meet your requirements for several months. Since vitamin A is fat soluble, it is excreted with bile salts in the feces.

The RDA for vitamin A is 800 micrograms, which increases to 1,300 micrograms during the first six months of breast-feeding and then decreases to 1,200 micrograms for the second six months of breast-feeding. I encourage you to eat more foods rich in vitamin A and to take a daily vitamin and mineral supplement that includes vitamin A. If you use a supplement that contains amounts that far exceed the RDA, you'll increase the vitamin A content of your breast milk to unsafe levels and cause toxic symptoms in your baby. Hypervitaminosis A is a condition resulting from an excessive intake of vitamin A. Symptoms include loss of appetite, headaches, diarrhea, nausea, blurred vision, irritability, and cracking skin. If these symptoms occur, discontinue the supplement and allow your body to return to normal storage levels of vitamin A.

If you eat an enormous amount of carrots or other vegetables high in beta carotene or provitamin A, your skin may turn yellow. It's not very attractive, but it's certainly not a toxic reaction. This happens when more carotenes are eaten than can be converted to active vitamin A.

Particularly rich sources of provitamin A or beta carotene include: sweet potatoes, yellow squash, spinach, Swiss chard, apricots, carrots, tomatoes, broccoli, papaya, peaches, pumpkins, cantaloupe, and kale. The preformed or animal version of vitamin A includes: milk, cheese, cottage cheese, eggs, ice cream, halibut, swordfish, and beef.

Vitamin D (Calciferol) for Muscle Development and Weight Loss

Although it is considered a vitamin, vitamin D has a molecular makeup that more closely resembles that of the hormones cortisone and estrogen than that of a vitamin. Clearly the biological benefit of vitamin D is as much hormone-related as it is vitamin oriented. Vitamin D is considered a hormone because of its ability to regulate the activity of an enzyme called L-hydroxylase, which is needed to convert vitamin D in the body to its active form, calcitriol. Blood levels of vitamin D and calcium will determine the amount of L-hydroxylase production needed.

Vitamin D_2 is marketed under the names ergocalciferol, calciferol, and viosterol. The form of vitamin D that is of animal origin is called cholecalciferol, or vitamin D_3. While it is found in dietary sources, vitamin D is produced when sunlight irradiates 7-dehydrocholesterol, a compound present in your skin. The ultraviolet rays cause a modification in the chemical structure and form vitamin D_3, which passes from the skin into the bloodstream.

Primarily active vitamin D facilitates the absorption of calcium and phosphorus from specific cells in the small intestine. But vitamin D also regulates your body's levels of amino acids, which are important to muscle development and weight loss. When vitamin D is inadequate, amino acids are excreted in the urine, and your body is unable to build the muscle needed to burn fat.

The RDA for vitamin D is 5 micrograms, which increases to 10 micrograms when breast-feeding. A baby will consume about 0.3 to 0.6 micrograms in a full day's supply of breast milk. Deficiency of vitamin D is rarely a major problem. Instances of toxic intakes of vitamin D have been due to the excessive use of a supplement, not food. The symptoms of an excessive intake of vitamin D include loss of appetite, excessive thirst, vomiting, weight loss, high blood calcium levels, and calcium deposition in soft tissues.

Try to get your vitamin D from food sources, and take a daily vitamin and mineral supplement that contains vitamin D. Some rich sources of vitamin D include: milk, salmon, tuna, beef, vitamin D-fortified margarine, butter, eggs, swordfish, and mackerel.

Vitamin E (Tocopherol): Important Antioxidant

Vitamin E is an essential vitamin that is important to you and your baby. If you want to lose weight and stay healthy, vitamin E *must* be included in your diet. The antioxidant properties of vitamin E protect the oxidation (oxygen metabolism) of hormones from the pituitary and adrenal glands. Oxygen is essential to life, but, as it passes through the cells of the body, it breaks down and forms substances called *free radicals*. Free radicals attack cell membranes and disrupt their normal functioning. Vitamin E protects the body from free radicals, especially during weight loss, when fats are being burned. With vitamin E available, oxygen is bound by it, rather than remaining free to oxidize other vital nutrients.

This is not the only function vitamin E has. This vitamin is a factor in maintaining cell membranes and therefore helps to prevent the liberation of red blood cells. The synthesis of some enzymes involved in oxygen production require vitamin E.

The average diet today contains much less vitamin E than it did fifty years ago. The RDA for vitamin E is 8 milligrams, which increases to 12 milligrams during the first six months of breast-feeding and then decreases to 11 milligrams for the second six months of breast-feeding. Your baby will take in about 1.4 to 2.3 milligrams of vitamin E in your breast milk each day.

Take a daily vitamin and mineral supplement that contains the palmitate and acetate forms of vitamin E that are water soluble. They are easier to digest than the fat-soluble vitamin E and are safe to take when breast-feeding. Don't forget to eat several foods that contain vitamin E each day.

Some good sources of vitamin E include: almonds, hazelnuts, peanut oil, corn oil, safflower oil, walnuts, wheat germ, whole-wheat flour, margarine, dried beans, and green leafy vegetables.

The Water-Soluble Vitamins

Vitamin B$_1$ (Thiamine): The Regulation of Appetite

When scientists began studying B vitamins, B$_1$, the vitamin now called thiamine, was the first B vitamin to be isolated and identified as a unique substance. There are more deficiencies of thiamine than any other vitamin in the water-soluble group. The major reason for the depletion of B$_1$ is that manufacturing techniques and processing destroy most of this water-soluble nutrient in packaged foods.

Drinking too much coffee and tea also destroys thiamine. A quart of coffee consumed over a three-hour period eliminates most of your body's store of thiamine. It's the caffeine and a factor in plant metabolism called cholorogenic acid that does the damage. Because caffeine is a diuretic, it stimulates the formation of urine and the removal of water along with thiamine from the body.

Following the ingestion of coffee, soda, or other caffeine-containing beverages, the blood levels of caffeine peak within twenty to thirty minutes. Then the caffeine is quickly distributed to the body tissues roughly in proportion to their water content. There are many physiological effects of caffeine. In general caffeine is a stimulant, and may have a direct effect on some tissues or act indirectly on the nervous system.

One to two cups of coffee can contain approximately 100 to 300 milligrams of caffeine. In dosages of 50 to 200 milligrams, it may cause increased alertness, but in dosages of 300 to 500 milligrams, it can cause nervousness and muscular tremors. Caffeine will stimulate the release of adrenaline and increase heart rate. It will also increase the amount of free fatty acids in the blood, which are energy sources for muscle tissue. Caffeine raises blood sugar levels and stimulates the secretion of gastric acids. This is why some people may get an upset stomach after drinking coffee.

If you are a coffee drinker, try to have your last cup of coffee not later than six hours before bedtime to ensure a serene night's sleep.

One of the most "obvious" sources of caffeine is chocolate. It, too, contains several stimulating substances, which is why chocolate dependence is so very common. You probably know a few chocolate addicts. Chocolate contains caffeine, beta-phenylethylamine, and theobromine, which are habit-forming chemicals. Theobromine is similar to caffeine, in that it stimulates the heart, dilates blood vessels, and acts as a diuretic. If you are a heavy coffee drinker or chocolate addict you may be depleting your body of thiamine.

The more sugar you and your baby eat, the greater your need for thiamine. Thiamine promotes and regulates your appetite. It plays an essential role in weight loss because it is part of the coenzymes that function in normal metabolism to release energy. Over the years there have been numerous dieters who have gone into cardiac arrest because of excessive fasting, which promotes dangerously low thiamine levels.

A deficiency of thiamine can result in lower thiamine concentrations in breast milk, and inadequate growth is a possible indicator of thiamine malnutrition. Beriberi is a thiamine-deficiency condition that is characterized by loss of appetite, fatigue, nausea, vomiting, irritability, and depression in the early stages. These symptoms are the result of elevated levels of pytuvic acid, a consequence of limited thiamine pyophosphate activity.

The RDA for thiamine is 1.1 milligrams. When breast-feeding the RDA increases to 1.6 milligrams per day. Remember, thiamine is critical to the production and quality of your breast milk. Make sure the B-vitamin supplement you take is between 25 and 50 milligrams of thiamine. It should contain no yeast and be in capsule or straight powder form. These dosages are safe to take if you are breast-feeding. I recommend you purchase a yeast-free daily vitamin and mineral supplement that contains thiamine, and eat more foods that are rich in thiamine. Some good sources of thiamine are poultry, pork, fish, nuts, legumes, milk, cheese, wheat germ, whole-grain products, sunflower seeds, garbanzo beans, kidney beans, and brewer's yeast.

Vitamin B₂ (Riboflavin): Oxygen for Your Cells

Riboflavin is the second of the B vitamins that is important to you and your baby. Present in minute amounts in all plant and animal cells, it provides the oxygen that enables cells to breathe. Riboflavin is closely related to two other water-soluble vitamins, B_6 (pyridoxine) and vitamin C, and plays a key role in the metabolism of each of these nutrients.

Riboflavin is important to the nutrient concentration and production of breast milk as well as to weight loss. Riboflavin is required for carbohydrate and fat metabolism, and regulates the breakdown of protein in the body. Specifically, it is needed to activate vitamin B_6 so that the conversion of the amino acid tryptophan into niacin can occur. Symptoms of riboflavin deficiency are cracks at the corner of the mouth, cracking and soreness of the lips, and sensitivity to light.

The RDA for riboflavin is 1.2 milligrams. If you are breast-feeding, the RDA increases to 1.8 milligrams for the first six months and then decreases to 1.7 milligrams for the second six months of breast-feeding. I encourage you to eat more foods rich in riboflavin and take a combination vitamin and mineral supplement each day that contains between 25 and 50 milligrams of B_2. These dosages are safe to take if you are breast-feeding. Avoid supplements that use yeast and excipients. The best sources of riboflavin are beef, veal, pork, lamb, fish, chicken, eggs, milk, beans, oatmeal, whole-wheat bread, shredded wheat, cream of wheat, peanut butter, nuts, potatoes, green vegetables, and oranges.

Vitamin B₃ (Niacin): Fatty Acid Synthesis and Regulation

The release of energy from food is dependent upon the function of several enzyme systems. Two of the coenzymes that are important to metabolism contain niacin, in the form of nicotinamide. These coenzymes nicotinamide adenine dinucleotide (NAD) and nicotinamide adenine dinucleotide phosphate (NADP) are necessary for the many chemical reactions occurring in tissue respiration, which is important to the release of energy during metabolism.

NAD is important to weight control because it functions as a coenzyme necessary for regulating blood sugar and fat. Niacin is a vital component of the GTF (glucose tolerance factor). GTF is also important to regulating blood sugar, and is made of niacin, glutamic acid, glycine, cysteine, and chromium. A deficiency of niacin can result in lower niacin concentrations in your breast milk and negatively affect milk production and weight loss. Your body, however, can convert tryptophan to niacin if it needs to keep up supplies.

The RDA for niacin is 15 milligrams, which increases to 20 milligrams if you are breast-feeding. Start eating more foods that contain niacin and remember to take a daily vitamin and mineral supplement that contains niacin. Make sure it is yeast free and contains no preservatives. The best sources of of niacin are beef, milk, veal, pork, lamb, turkey, tuna, swordfish, shrimp, peanut butter, whole-wheat bread, cream of wheat, rice, bananas, peaches, tomatoes, broccoli, and peas.

Vitamin B_6 (Pyridoxine): Metabolism of Protein and Fat, and Insulin Utilization

Women seem to be especially prone to B_6 deficiency, particularly throughout prenatal development and after pregnancy. Vitamin B_6 is stored in the fetus during gestation in quantities sufficient to provide the newborn in the event that dietary sources of the vitamin are low in the first part of infancy. Each B vitamin works independently and plays a very specific biological role. B vitamins are utilized in all areas of your body as active coenzymes for numerous reactions.

Vitamin B_6 is involved in the metabolism of protein and fat, and in insulin utilization. If your diet is deficient in B_6 it can inhibit weight loss and negatively affect the B_6 concentration and production of your breast milk. The higher your protein intake, the greater your need for B_6. Infant formulas usually contain the correct amount of B_6 per gram of protein to prevent symptoms of a vitamin B_6 deficiency.

The RDA for B_6 is 1.6 milligrams, which increases to 2.1 when breast-feeding. There are three dietary sources of B_6: pyridoxine, pyridoxal, and pyridoxamine. Plants are the main food sources of pyridoxine, and animal foods provide vitamin B_6 in the form of pyridoxal and pyridoxamine. All these forms are used well in your body. I recommend you take a combination vitamin and mineral supplement that contains B_6 and eat more foods rich in B_6. Most vitamin and mineral supplements contain between 15 and 50 milligrams of B_6, which is safe to take when breast-feeding. Keep in mind that you can always take vitamins and minerals separately if you need more.

Vitamin B_{12} (Cobalamin): The Nervous System, Digestive Tract, and Bone Marrow

Vitamin B_{12} has two outstanding characteristics that are important to you and your baby. It is the largest molecule of all the vitamins, and right in the middle of the complex ring structure is a single atom of cobalt. This explains why B_{12} is named cobalamin.

The large size of this vitamin molecule makes it difficult to absorb through the intestinal wall, and needs the help of the intrinsic factor. The intrinsic factor, a mucoprotein secreted in the stomach, combines with B_{12} in the small intestine and binds this vitamin to the intestinal wall for absorption. Often a B_{12} deficiency occurs because of the lack of the intrinsic factor rather than a dietary lack of the vitamin. Yogurt and acidophilus milk contain beneficial bacteria that promote the growth of the intrinsic factor.

You carry an average of a 600-day supply of B_{12}. Vitamin B_{12} is needed by all cells, but it is particularly important in the nervous system, the digestive tract, and the bone marrow. Vitamin B_{12} coenzymes aid in producing the DNA needed for red blood cells to mature.

Vitamin B_{12} is functionally similar to folic acid, and both are involved in the metabolism of fats, proteins, and carbohydrates. Problems of the central nervous system are often the result of poor carbohydrate metabolism. If your diet is deficient in B_{12}, it can negatively affect the B_{12} concentration and production of your breast milk, and inhibit weight loss. Your baby needs around 0.3 to 0.5 micrograms each day. A strict vegetarian who consumes no animal or dairy products is not getting enough vitamin B_{12} and will need to take a supplement.

The RDA is 3 micrograms, which increases to 4 micrograms if you are breast-feeding. Even if you eat animal or dairy products you should still take a vitamin B_{12} supplement. I suggest you take a daily vitamin and mineral supplement that contains between 10 and 20 micrograms of B_{12}, even when breast-feeding. For better absorption, take a B_{12} sublingual (cyanocobalamin) or a nasal B_{12} supplement separately if you need more. Make sure it is free of yeast, sugar, or preservatives.

It's necessary for you to eat animal foods and dairy products because they are good sources of cobalamin, whereas plant foods contain none. Soy milk and breakfast cereals are fortified with B_{12}. On page 56 you'll find a comprehensive list of foods containing B_{12}.

Biotin and Fatty Acid Metabolism

Biotin is synthesized by beneficial intestinal bacteria called lactobacillin and is then absorbed into your bloodstream. Taking antibiotics, especially sulfa, will diminish this biotin-producing intestinal bacteria. Without this beneficial intestinal bacteria, vital nutrients necessary for weight loss are not absorbed. Also, the branched-chain amino acids leucine, isoleucine, and valine, which must be present for muscular development and growth, are dependent on biotin. Thirty-five percent of your muscles are made up of the branched-chain amino acids. These three amino acids must be present for muscular growth and development to take place. A deficiency in any one of them will cause muscle loss and reduce your ability to burn fat.

Biotin is essential to weight loss. It is needed for the release of energy from carbohydrates, for the production and burning of fats, and for the breakdown of amino acids. Biotin is needed for the transformation of tryptophan to niacin, which is necessary for controlling appetite. Biotin is involved in the production of pancreatic amylase for digestion of carbohydrates. If your diet is low in biotin, weight loss is difficult and the quality of your breast milk is compromised. Biotin deficiency is sometimes seen in babies when biotin-deficient formula is used or when there's a problem with intestinal biotin synthesis.

No RDA has been established for biotin, but a daily intake of 30 to 100 micrograms is considered safe for everyone over eleven years old. Most multiple vitamin and mineral supplements contain 300 micrograms of biotin. Take a supplement that is yeast free and in capsule or powder form. You can always take a biotin supplement separately if you need more. Particularly rich sources of biotin include eggs, meat, milk, cereal, legumes, nuts, and yeast.

Folic Acid and the Manufacture of Red Blood Cells
Folic acid is essential to you and your baby. Folic acid helps your body manufacture red blood cells. It is part of a coenzyme that aids in various intracellular reactions in your body. Folic acid is required for the synthesis of the essential nucleic acids RNA and DNA, and is vital to the growth and regenerative process of cellular makeup, especially during fetal development. This is why prenatal supplements contain this vital nutrient. You need to keep a rich supply of folic acid in your diet to maintain the folic acid level of your breast milk and still have enough necessary for losing weight.

Folic acid is involved in the formation of choline, the conversion of phenylalanine to tyrosine and glycine to serine, which are essential to hunger control. A folic acid deficiency can result in a condition called megablastic anemia in which an unusually large proportion of the red cells do not mature normally. Anemic conditions in mothers are easily developed if dietary or supplemental folic acid levels are not adequate. Anemia can cause severe fatigue and inhibit weight loss.

The Recommended Dietary Allowance of folic acid for pregnant women is twice as high as that for anyone eleven years old or over. During the last trimester of pregnancy, in particular, there is an apparent stress situation placed on the maternal supply of folic acid to meet the sharply increasing demand of the fetus. Folic acid, just like the other B vitamins, is needed on a daily basis because your body's ability to store it is limited. The RDA for folic acid is 180 micrograms, which increases to 280 micrograms for the first six months of breast-feeding and then decreases to 260 micrograms for the second six months of breast-feeding.

Make sure you are eating foods rich in folic acid, and take a daily vitamin and mineral supplement that contains approximately 400 micrograms of folic acid, which is safe to take when breast-feeding. It should be in capsule or straight powder form, and free of yeast, corn, wheat, and salt. Some good food sources of folic acid are fish, milk, eggs, wheat germ, whole grains, barley, beans, peas, endive, brewer's yeast, oranges, bananas, avocados, tomatoes, corn, soybeans, lentils, and rice.

Pantothenic Acid (B_5) in Energy and Tissue Metabolism

Like the other B vitamins, pantothenic acid is water soluble. It is an essential component of a compound called acetyl CoA, which plays a vital role in energy and tissue metabolism within the cells, making it an important element of weight loss. And it's also involved in the release of energy from carbohydrates, fats, and proteins. Almost all energy-related metabolic reactions in your body and your baby's body require CoA. The synthesis of some very important compounds in the body require CoA. For example, porphyrin for hemoglobin formation, steroid hormones, fatty acids, and cholesterol are dependent on CoA for their synthesis.

A regular diet of processed food or the use of antibiotics can lead to a B_5 deficiency. A deficiency of B_5 can cause headaches, fatigue, poor muscle coordination, nausea, and muscle cramps. While there is no RDA for pantothenic acid (B_5) that is defined by age, a level of 4 to 7 milligrams daily is recommended for all adults, and breast-feeding increases your need by one-third. An inadequate supply of pantothenic acid can cause low pantothenic acid concentrations in your breast milk and negatively affect milk production.

Take a B_5 supplement that contains between 25 and 50 milligrams per day. Most multiple vitamin and mineral supplements contain these levels, which are safe to take when breast-feeding. Make sure all the B vitamin supplements you take are in capsule or straight powder form and free of yeast, corn, wheat, lactose (milk sugar), sugar, salt, artificial sweeteners, preservatives, or chemical additives.

Some good food sources of pantothenic acid are meat, fish, eggs, lobster, blue cheese, soybeans, peanuts, sunflower seeds, corn, avocados, brewer's yeast, and whole-grain products.

Vitamin C (Ascorbic Acid):

Main Component of Connective Tissue

One of the most recognized roles of vitamin C is in the formation of collagen. Throughout the body, collagen is the main component of the connective tissue that cements the cells and tissue together. After pregnancy the formation of collagen is essential to your recovery and weight loss. Without adequate collagen, wounds do not heal properly and tend to keep breaking open. Vitamin C is important to maintain the elasticity and strength of normal capillary walls.

It has also been observed that the protein structure of bone and teeth form abnormally when there is a vitamin C deficiency. Vitamin C enhances iron absorption, which is vital to you and to your baby. Iron is absorbed and utilized more efficiently when it occurs as the ferrous (reduced) iron, a process that is aided by the presence of vitamin C. The conversion of folic acid to the active form of the vitamin is also aided by the presence of vitamin C.

Vitamin C is essential to weight loss because it is required for the metabolism of the amino acids tyrosine and phenylalanine. When vitamin C is lacking, the conversion of tyrosine to the hormone thyroxine is suppressed, and your metabolism slows down. And when the conversion of phenylalanine to adrenaline is suppressed, it causes a disruption in the regulation of hunger.

Because your body cannot manufacture vitamin C, it must be obtained through your diet or in the form of supplements. The RDA for vitamin C is 60 milligrams, which increases to 95 for the first six months of breast-feeding and then decreases to 90 milligrams for the second six months of breast-feeding. You can safely take up to 3,000 milligrams of vitamin C daily, even when breast-feeding. I recommend you take esterified vitamin C (ester-C) in straight powder form because it is the most effective form of vitamin C.

Esterified vitamin C is combined with minerals such as calcium, magnesium, potassium, or zinc. This creates a form of vitamin C that is nonacidic and that contains vitamin C metabolites identical to those produced by your body. Esterified vitamin C enters your bloodstream and tissues faster than standard vitamin C, and it also stays in your body tissues longer.

Vitamin C is found in citrus fruits, asparagus, avocados, cabbage, broccoli, tomatoes, potatoes, green peppers, spinach, brussels sprouts, chard, watercress, kale, beet greens, onions, turnip greens, alfalfa, collards, radishes, green peas, sweet peppers, apples, papayas, mangoes, persimmons, pineapples, strawberries, grapefruit, and cantaloupe.

Now that the fat-soluble and water-soluble vitamins have been discussed, we can move on to the final part of this chapter—the importance of macro- and microminerals to weight loss and breast-feeding.

The Macro- and Microminerals

Calcium (Ca): The Most Abundant Mineral in Your Body
The most abundant mineral in your body is calcium. An inadequate supply of calcium can cause low calcium concentrations in your breast milk and inhibit weight loss. Calcium comprises between two to three pounds of your overall body weight, and 99 percent of that calcium is stored in your skeletal structure. In fact, 20 percent of the calcium in bone is replaced annually. It is because of this continuing need to replace calcium that you have a requirement for calcium of 800 milligrams daily.

Calcium plays a critical role in the structure of both bones and teeth. After pregnancy your teeth and gums need special attention. This is because throughout your pregnancy your baby uses most of your stored calcium, and this can lead to brittleness and decay of your own teeth. Calcium is essential to the normal formation of blood clots and plays an important role in the digestion of fat by activating pancreatic lipase, one of the enzymes that split fatty acids from glycerol in the small intestine. Even vitamin B_{12} requires calcium to be absorbed through the intestinal wall.

Perhaps the most dramatic function of calcium is its role in the maintenance of the heartbeat. Calcium in the interstitial fluid regulates the contractions of the heart and other muscles. Calcium functions in the nervous system by making the neurotransmitter acetylcholine available. Acetylcholine is needed for normal brain functioning and for battling depression and anxiety. Hormones are also involved in the regulation of your calcium balance. When your blood calcium level goes above a certain level, your thyroid gland secretes the hormone calcitonin, which blocks the action of the parathorome, preventing release of calcium from your bones. Even the sex hormone estrogen slows the breakdown of bone by stimulating the thyroid gland to secrete the hormone calcitonin.

Calcium is absorbed with varying efficiency, primarily in the upper part of the small intestine. Some absorbed calcium is excreted in urine, and a small amount is lost in perspiration and feces. Your body is remarkably adaptive and absorbs calcium more efficiently when you breast-feed. This is because lactose, the sugar in breast milk, favors calcium absorption.

Lactose is also a natural sugar found in dairy products that helps to improve calcium absorption. If you have trouble eating dairy products because you produce little or no lactase (the enzyme that helps you digest lactose or milk sugar), you should try yogurt, acidophilus milk, or other cultured milk products. These are all excellent sources of protein that are comparable to milk cup for cup. Yogurt is a mixture of milk, skim milk, or cream that has also been cultured with a beneficial bacteria called *lactobacillus acidophilus*. It is best to buy unsweetened yogurt that contains no flavorings, and then sweeten it with fresh fruit. A nondairy alternative to milk is Eden Soy Milk, called Sunsoy.

There are also commercially available lactose-free dairy products sold in most supermarkets. You can purchase lactose enzymes (Lact-Aid) at any drugstore and add it to milk or take it before you eat dairy products that aren't cultured.

Calcium is best used by your body when the ratio of calcium to phosphorus in your diet is approximately equal (a 1:1 ratio). When you drink soda, which is a carbonated beverage that contains phosphate, the values of calcium to phosphorus shift to a ratio of 1:4. Stay away from carbonated beverages, and instead drink low-fat milk. Inadequate calcium intake in women who have undergone numerous pregnancies may lead to osteoporosis (porous bones). Osteoporosis is a condition in which the total amount of bone is reduced and is associated with a calcium and fluoride deficiency.

The RDA for calcium is 800 milligrams, which increases to 1,200 when breast-feeding. I recommend you eat more foods rich in calcium, and take a calcium supplement that contains a calcium gluconate or carbonate in capsule or straight powder that is free of yeast, corn, wheat, sugar, salt, artificial dyes, colors, or flavors. Most daily vitamin and mineral supplements contain calcium. For some people calcium chloride and calcium carbonate can cause constipation, bloating, and gas. If this becomes a problem for you, switch to a calcium lactate or gluconate.

Milk and milk products are outstanding sources of calcium. There are good nondairy sources of calcium, such as broccoli, kale, mustard greens, spinach, sunflower seeds, sweet potatoes, almonds, garbanzo beans, pinto beans, rutabagas, bok choy, oranges, and salmon.

Phosphorus (P): High-Energy Compound

The mineral that occurs in the second greatest quantity in your body is phosphorus, in the form of phosphate. During the first year of life, the recommended ratio of calcium to phosphorus is 1.5:1. After the first year, the recommended ratio is 1:1, and this ratio is suggested throughout the remainder of life, even when breast-feeding. The RDA for phosphorus is 800 milligrams, just like calcium, and increases to 1,200 milligrams when breast-feeding.

Phosphates are essential to the normal functioning of several of the B vitamins involved in energy production. This mineral is vital to the utilization of carbohydrates and fats for energy production and in protein synthesis for the growth, maintenance, and repair of all tissues and cells. These are just a few of the many functions that make phosphorus important to losing weight.

Phosphorus is part of the high-energy compound found in your muscle cells that is needed for exercise and muscle development. The more lean muscle mass you have, the more fat you'll burn. The use of antacids for long periods of time can decrease absorption of phosphorus and cause loss of calcium from bones and muscle weakness. On the other hand, high consumption of meat and soda increase phosphorus intake and can cause an imbalance in the ratio between calcium to phosphorus. You need to regulate the balance of calcium to phosphorus in your diet for optimum nutritional health and weight loss.

Phosphorus is a component of the phospholipids, which are fat molecules essential to the formation of cell membranes. Lecithin, the best-known phospholipid, helps in fat emulsification and is important to weight loss. Phosphorus is found in lecithin supplements. You can take two tablespoons of lecithin granules or one lecithin capsule each day. Lecithin is safe to take if you're breast-feeding. Try to incorporate phosphorus-rich foods in your diet each day. Your daily multiple vitamin and mineral supplement should also include 800 milligrams of phosphorus. Animal proteins are the best sources of phosphorus and these include: cheese, milk, meat, fish, poultry, and eggs. Plant sources include grains, nuts, legumes, oatmeal, soybeans, pinto beans, and tofu.

Magnesium (Mg): Metabolic Catalyst

Magnesium is an indispensable mineral to both breast-feeding and weight loss. It is involved in every major biological process in the body and is a vital component of the water that flows in and out of cells. Magnesium activates a number of enzymes, and is involved in the regulation of protein synthesis, body temperature, and muscle contractions. It's the magnesium in the extracellular fluid that bathes nerve cells helping to conduct nerve impulses that relax muscles following contractions.

Substantial quantities of magnesium are stored in the skeletal system, which serves as a reserve during short periods when your dietary intake is deficient. The magnesium found in the cells of soft tissue catalyzes virtually hundreds of metabolic reactions that result in changes in energy states necessary to losing weight. Adequate magnesium also promotes the retention of calcium in tooth enamel, and through its role in releasing thyroxine, helps regulate your metabolic rate. Magnesium works along with the other electrolytes—calcium, sodium, potassium, and chloride—to maintain body fluids and the acid-base balance of the blood. Moderate deficiencies of magnesium may lead to calcification of soft tissue and are common in illnesses associated with protracted vomiting, diarrhea, or kidney disease.

The RDA for magnesium is 280 milligrams, which increases to 355 milligrams for the first six months of breast-feeding, then decreases to 340 milligrams for the second six months of breast-feeding. I recommend you take a daily vitamin and mineral supplement in capsule form that contains magnesium and eat several magnesium-rich foods each day. You can always take a magnesium supplement separately if you need more. Some good food sources of magnesium are beef, lamb, pork, turkey, veal, flounder, salmon, shrimp, crab, almonds, peanuts, pistachio nuts, walnuts, spinach, potatoes, beans, bananas, and oranges.

Potassium (K): Major Electrolyte

Potassium is an extremely significant body mineral necessary to both cellular and electrical functioning. Potassium is vital to the regulation of various body processes, including maintenance of normal water balance, conduction and transmission of nerve impulses, muscle contractions and heart action, and functioning of enzymes. As a major electrolyte inside the body cells, potassium works in close association with sodium and chloride to maintain body fluids and the acid-base balance of the blood.

Maintaining consistent levels of potassium in the blood and cells is critical to body function. A potassium deficiency can cause fluid retention (bloating) and fatigue, stimulate hunger, and cause sleep difficulties. Early symptoms include dry skin or acne, muscle weakness, slow reflexes, insomnia, irregular heartbeat, and loss of gastrointestinal tone. If you take diuretics or drink too much coffee you're depleting your body of potassium and other vital minerals. During and after diarrhea, potassium replacement may also be necessary because low potassium may impair glucose metabolism and lead to elevated blood sugar. Studies have shown that a high-sodium diet with low potassium intake may elevate blood pressure. Therefore, the elevation or depletion of potassium can cause many problems, and in the most extreme cases, even death.

There is no RDA for potassium, though it is thought that at least 3,000 milligrams per day are needed. Potassium is found in a wide range of foods. Many fruits and vegetables are high in potassium and low in sodium. Potassium supplements are available separately, and usually contain 99 milligrams per tablet or capsule. Potassium can also be purchased in a multiple vitamin and mineral supplement.

Each day try eating several foods that contain potassium. These include: bananas, oranges, cantaloupe, raisins, prunes, apricots, cabbage, broccoli, cauliflower, squash, tomatoes, mushrooms, asparagus, potato, 1 cup milk, 1 egg, 1 cup oatmeal, molasses, and apricots.

Chromium (Cr) and the Maintenance
of Normal Glucose Levels

Chromium plays an important part in the metabolism of fats, proteins, and the nucleic acids DNA and RNA. Chromium is an essential nutrient for both you and your baby, and it works with insulin to maintain normal glucose levels (blood sugar). Maintaining normal glucose levels is important to losing weight. After you eat, your body transforms carbohydrate into energy in the form of glucose. It's chromium that helps glucose move from the bloodstream into the cell. If glucose does not enter the cells, the excess circulating sugar can cause damage to the cells.

Chromium is vital to GTF (glucose tolerance factor) production and is found in the center of GTF. GTF improves the uptake of glucose in the cells so it can be metabolized to provide energy. The more sugar you eat, the more you need GTF to work with insulin. GTF is made of niacin, glutamic acid, glycine, cysteine, and, of course, chromium. Food processing reduces the level of chromium in foods. Even mild deficiencies of chromium can disrupt weight loss and produce other symptoms, such as fatigue and anxiety. No RDA has been established for GTF. About two tablespoons—or six tablets of brewer's yeast—per day is one of the best sources of chromium and GTF.

The RDA for chromium has not been established for breast-feeding mothers, but nutritionists suggest a safe daily range of 50 to 300 micrograms. Many vitamin and mineral supplements contain about 100 to 150 micrograms of chromium. Chromium is best absorbed by the body when it is taken in a form called chromium picolinate. Chromium picolinate promotes the burning of fat and increases muscle tissue. If you have diabetes, do not take chromium or GFT supplements without consulting your doctor. Make an effort each day to eat foods that contains chromium.

Foods that contain chromium include wheat germ, whole-grain products, brewer's yeast, milk, cheese, beef, chicken, eggs, fish and seafood, fruits, and vegetables.

Fluoride (F): For Strong Bones and Teeth

This essential mineral, found in your bones and teeth, is needed for resistance to tooth decay and for strong bones. Fluoride is needed throughout life to maintain the strength of teeth and bones. Maintaining strong bones is important to exercise and weight control. The actual amount of fluoride present in the body varies from one person to another, depending on the fluoride intake in the diet.

A day's supply of fluoridated water contains about 1 milligram of fluoride. Breast milk contains about 16 micrograms of fluoride per liter. Fluoride at a controlled level of 1 part per million (ppm) in drinking water from infancy reduces tooth decay by 60 to 70 percent. Fluoride is added to toothpaste and mouthwash to prevent tooth decay. Too much or too little fluoride can cause the discoloring of teeth. Large amounts of fluoride can cause joint pain, swelling, and digestive problems. About 3 milligrams of fluoride per day is eliminated through the kidneys. The remaining fluoride is stored in your bones.

The fluoride content of plant sources varies greatly, depending on the fluoride content of the soil in which they were grown. Since most foods do not contain enough fluoride to provide the necessary protective benefits, the public health officials have promoted the need for fluoridated water in communities across the country.

The RDA for fluoride is 1.5 to 4 milligrams per day, even when breastfeeding. Check to see if your daily multiple vitamin and mineral supplement contains fluoride. If not, I suggest you eat more food that is rich in fluoride. Foods that contain fluoride are fish, milk, egg yolk, drinking water (if fluoridated), sardines (because of their bones), dehydrated food (because of water used for rehydration), and tea.

Iodine (I): For Regulating Metabolic Energy

Iodine itself is a poisonous gas. However, the salts or negatively charged ions of iodine (iodides) are soluble in water. The absorption of carbohydrates, protein synthesis, cholesterol production, and conversion of carotene to vitamins are functions that involve the presence of iodine. Iodine is important to weight loss because it helps your body metabolize excess fat.

Iodine is absorbed from the stomach into the bloodstream. About 8 milligrams of iodine are concentrated in the thyroid gland in your neck, with the remaining iodine distributed throughout all your cells. Your thyroid manufactures two iodine-containing hormones, thyroxine and triodothyionine, which are important to weight control. Both these hormones are released into the bloodstream either as the free hormones or combined with albumin (protein) in your blood. These iodine-containing hormones regulate the metabolic energy of the body and set your basal metabolic rate.

Goiter, which is an enlargement of the thyroid gland that results from a lack of iodine, is the most well-known ailment associated with iodine deficiency. This enlargement occurs as the thyroid increases its cell size to try and trap more iodine, and as a result the whole gland increases in size and creates a swelling in the neck. Also, a child can be born with a very serious condition called cretinism if his mother had a severely iodine-deficient diet during pregnancy. It is a serious and nonreversible problem that can be avoided with proper prenatal iodine intake.

Your dietary intake of iodine is greatest during pregnancy and while breast-feeding. Remember, the amount of iodine in your breast milk depends on your dietary intake of iodine-containing foods. Each day try to eat foods that contain iodine. The RDA for iodine is 150 micrograms, which increases to 200 micrograms when breast-feeding. Excessive iodine intake (over thirty times the RDA) can cause diarrhea and vomiting. I recommend you take a daily multiple vitamin and mineral that contains iodine in a capsule or straight powder that is free of preservatives and chemical additives.

Some good sources of iodine are iodized salt, saltwater fish, shellfish, salmon, shrimp, haddock, cod, lobster, oysters, seaweed, mushrooms, garlic, sesame seeds, spinach, lima beans, and asparagus.

Iron (Fe): When You Lose Fat, You Lose Iron

Iron is a part of the overall process called respiration, or the burning of energy from the food you eat to produce biological energy. A key function of iron is in the formation of *hemoglobin*, the oxygen-transporting protein in blood. It transports oxygen to the cells, and carbon dioxide away from the cells. When this process is hindered by an iron deficiency, the result is symptoms of fatigue, headaches, and shortness of breath. Besides being part of hemoglobin, iron is stored in the liver, spleen, and bone marrow, where it can be drawn on to supply extra iron for hemoglobin production. Iron is also found in another oxygen-transporting protein, called *myoglobin*. Myoglobin carries oxygen from the blood to the enzymes in your muscle cells to produce energy for muscular activity.

Iron is a necessary mineral important for weight control and breast-feeding. Iron from the red blood cells is saved and returned to the bone marrow to be used over again in synthesizing new red blood cells. Initially, an iron-deficient diet results first in the reduction of stored iron, then in the reduction of hemoglobin concentration in red blood cells. When iron stores are depleted, the body cannot make enough hemoglobin to fill its new red blood cells, causing the cells to become smaller and less able to carry oxygen from the lungs to your tissues where it is needed. This condition causes severe fatigue, and is known as *iron deficiency anemia*.

The fat that you burn during weight loss has a rich blood supply. Fat has several miles of capillaries for every pound, so when you lose fat, you also lose iron. Strenuous exercise and heavy perspiration also deplete iron from your body. During the last few months of pregnancy, a mother transfers 500 to 700 milligrams of iron to her growing baby. Then, after delivery, more iron is depleted through blood loss, often causing severe fatigue for mothers. It can take several months to replenish the lost iron.

The RDA for iron is 15 milligrams even while breast-feeding. When breast-feeding, your baby takes in about 1 to 2 milligrams per day. Iron from animal sources is absorbed better than iron from plant sources. Iron absorption from the intestinal tract is a slow process that takes between two to four hours and is poorly absorbed. Make sure your daily multiple vitamin and mineral contains an iron that is nonconstipating. Try an iron supplement that contains ferrous gluconate or ferrous fumarate, which do not cause constipation. It should also be free of yeast, corn, wheat, binders, coatings, coloring, preservatives, or chemical additives. Make an effort to eat more iron-rich foods each day.

Foods that contain iron are beef, veal, pork, lamb, chicken, eggs, swordfish, tuna, shrimp, oysters, prunes, raisins, figs, grapefruit, spinach, beet greens, peas, lima beans, potatoes, whole-grain bread, rye bread, oatmeal, rice, and shredded wheat.

Selenium (Se): Important Antioxidant Compound

Selenium can keep you in good health while you lose weight. Selenium is a mineral that your baby needs to obtain through your breast milk. It usually appears in breast milk at a concentration of 20 micrograms per liter. Breast milk has several times more selenium than cow's milk.

Selenium is present in all tissues of the body, with the greatest amount found in the hair, liver, and kidneys. It is important as an antioxidant compound, which means it appears to stimulate antibody formation and has anticarcinogenic (cancer-fighting) effects. In low levels, selenium aids in slowing the rate of cancer growth. Its functions are similar to those of vitamin E. In fact, vitamin E is required primarily as a means of protecting selenium in your body.

Some toxic effects of ingesting too much selenium may include loss of hair, edema, brittle nails, and discolored teeth. The RDA for selenium is 55 micrograms, which increases to 75 micrograms when breast-feeding. If you take a supplement, it's wise to take it along with vitamin E since the antioxidant effect of selenium and E are synergistic. The best way to obtain both these nutrients is to to take a multiple vitamin and mineral supplement that is yeast free. The amount of selenium found in plant foods varies depending on the mineral content of the soil in which the food was grown. For example, grains grown in selenium-depleted soil will have a low selenium content. Eat more plant and animal foods that contain selenium, such as bran, broccoli, cabbage, celery, milk, chicken, seafood, egg yolk, tuna, cucumbers, garlic, mushrooms, onions, wheat germ, and whole-grain products.

Zinc (Zn) and Its Relation to Insulin Function

Zinc is another nutrient that is essential to weight loss and to maintaining good health for you and your baby. It is important for the normal growth and development of the immune system. Zinc is also closely associated with the functioning of insulin, an important hormone that regulates carbohydrate metabolism. Zinc, which is found in the hemoglobin of red blood cells, protects them from destruction and is necessary to produce the protein needed to make DNA, RNA, and sex hormones.

Vitamin A could not be pulled out of storage from the liver without the help of zinc. Your stomach needs zinc to produce the hydrochloric acid needed for proper digestion of foods. The RDA for zinc is 12 milligrams, which increases to 19 milligrams for the first six months of breast-feeding, then decreases to 16 milligrams for the second six months of breast-feeding. Meeting your requirement is not easy to do, even if you consume 3,000 calories a day.

Take a zinc supplement that is between 15 and 30 milligrams. For better absorption look for a multiple vitamin and mineral supplement that contains zinc gluconate or picolinate. You can always take additional zinc as a separate supplement if needed. Make sure it is free of yeast, corn, wheat, sugar, salt, artificial sweeteners, dyes, colors, or flavors. On page 58 there is a list of foods containing zinc that you can choose from.

"I'm So Exhausted, But I Just Can't Sleep"

How Eating Patterns, Hormones, and Sleep Affect Weight Loss

I have to get more sleep! Millions of mothers make this complaint, but don't know what to do about it. Almost all mothers at some time or another will suffer from sleep-loss blues. Do you fall asleep within five minutes after your head hits the pillow? Or do you find yourself dozing at times when you want to be awake and alert? If you're a new mother or have recently had a sick child, you may find that you have little time for sleep.

Sleep-Loss Blues: Affects the Way You Think and Feel

Even though sleep may seem to be a waste of time or even a luxury, it's as biologically necessary as food and water. Sleep deprivation is cumulative. It takes its toll before you notice the effect because you learn to adjust to your sleeplessness. Sleep experiments have shown that five or six nights of shortened or interrupted sleep can adversely affect the way we think and feel. When sleep deprivation is extreme it may take weeks of satisfying sleep to make up for what was lost during the week.

Research suggests that the longer you sleep, the longer the duration of the REM (rapid eye movement) stage. REM sleep is generally interpreted as a sign of dreaming, and is needed to process emotions and memories important to your psychological well-being. Fetuses as young as twenty-three weeks experience REM sleep. Nondream sleep, or NREM, is just as important.

Upon going to sleep you usually enter nondream sleep. There are four stages of nondream sleep, through which you progress in set order during the first thirty to forty-five minutes of sleep. After that you move between them as you sleep, and spend a greater amount of time in stages two and three. About every ninety minutes during the course of your sleep there's a rapid transition from the deeper and more restful stages (three and four) to a rhythm that resembles that of stage one or two. This sleep pattern is associated with dreaming or REM. Periods of REM tend to be very short during the first hours of sleep, and grow in length as you sleep.

Your Sleep Quota: Biologically Necessary for Losing Weight

Sleep-deprivation can interfere with weight loss, and cause exhaustion and severe depression. You need about six to eight hours of sleep a night to function efficiently. Babies average sixteen hours, and toddlers need about twelve hours. In other words, everyone has a sleep quota. If your night hours are interrupted by crying, feeding, and diapering, and your days are devoted to your children, you're probably not getting your full sleep-quota of six to eight hours. This daily wear and tear can sap your stamina, and the less energy you have, the less capable you are at handling stress and your emotions. Getting a restful sleep not only is refreshing, but is biologically necessary to losing weight.

Your metabolism doesn't stop when you sleep, it just slows down. As morning approaches, the complex daily rhythms begin to speed up, hormone levels change, and your body begins to wake up. About one hour after the onset of sleep a major burst of growth hormone is released from the anterior pituitary gland, which stimulates muscle growth and fat burning. Growth-hormone production is regulated by the brain through the hypothalamus. Throughout the day your body experiences seemingly random releases of growth-hormone. In fact, growth-hormone secretion occurs after exercise. Certain proteins (arginine and L-dopa) cause growth-hormone release, whereas high levels of blood sugar suppress growth-hormone production.

Eating Patterns: How They Affect Sleep and Weight Loss

Overeating or eating foods high in sugar before you sleep will elevate your blood sugar level for several hours and suppress growth-hormone production. Overeating also overloads your digestive system and increases your heart rate, making it difficult for you to fall asleep.

On the other hand, you shouldn't go to bed hungry either, because the discomfort of a gurgling stomach also can keep you awake. If you want to sleep peacefully have a light snack before bedtime that won't overload your digestive tract. Try not to let a long period of time pass between meals. Start eating smaller, more frequent meals or healthful snacks. For example, before you take a nap or go to bed for the night, have a half of a tomato and riccota sandwich, or a cup of wild rice with pecans, or even a strawberry-oatmeal bar. You'll find recipes for all of these nutritious snacks in chapter 13. A frequent pattern of eating promotes sleep, which is necessary for weight loss and increases the burning of fat in the body.

Weight Loss and Sleeping Pills: Make It Difficult to Sleep

Once you get into your fat-burning state and begin to lose weight, you may have difficulty sleeping. This difficulty occurs because of the metabolic fat-burning state called *ketosis*. This is when fat is being broken down for energy faster than your body can use it. When this happens, your liver releases ketones into your blood, causing acid blood and hyperalertness, which makes it difficult to sleep. A slow, gradual weight-loss pattern will help you avoid this problem. And once again, eating snacks or smaller, more frequent meals will keep your body chemistry in balance so you sleep well and still continue to burn fat.

Taking sleeping pills won't help you lose weight. Sleeping pills do not produce real sleep and can give you a terrible hangover. They interrupt natural sleep patterns by suppressing REM, which makes sleep less restful. You should consult your doctor before taking sleep medication, especially if you're breast-feeding. The stronger sleeping pills available by prescription are going to really knock you out, but they do not produce a natural sleep and may cause respiratory failure as well as interfere with the release of growth hormone (GH) important to burning fat. The more sleep medication you use, the more disturbed your sleep. This vicious cycle is called drug-dependent insomnia. It's better for you to drink a 4-ounce glass of warm milk before you go to bed—it's rich in the nutrient tryptophan, a sleep-inducing amino acid.

Tryptophan in milk is used by your brain to make the neurotransmitter serotonin, which is responsible for your ability to sleep. Appetite suppressants, for instance, work by temporarily increasing your brain's production of serotonin. However, once you deplete your brain's supply of serotonin, you will have difficulty sleeping until your brain regenerates more serotonin. Also, when serotonin levels are low, you are more likely to overeat carbohydrates.

Melatonin: The Sleep Hormone

The hormone melatonin is also involved with your ability to sleep. It, too, is synthesized from the amino acid tryptophan via a series of steps catalyzed by enzymes present only in the pineal gland. The pineal gland sits in the center of your brain and is about the size of a pea.

Serum melatonin levels in your blood are influenced by light-dark cycles. Under normal conditions the pineal gland secretes the hormone melatonin at night and not during the daytime. Sunlight and bright room light will suppress nighttime melatonin secretion. There's a direct pathway from the retina of your eye to the site closest to your brain's biological clock in the hypothalamus. In other words, light that is received by your retina suppresses melatonin secretion, and darkness enhances its secretion. So if you rest during the daytime, make sure your room is as dark as possible. Black out windows, and use clocks and radios that do not emit light. Even your baby's night-light could interfere with his or her ability to fall asleep. Use either a blue or red light bulb in your baby's night-light—these colors don't disrupt sleep.

Upon awakening, turn on the lights or pull up the shades and try to get sunlight. Sunlight is necessary for your mental health, but it's not what you need when you are trying to get some sleep. Lack of sunlight can severely effect mood as seen in cases of SAD (seasonal affective disorder), which occurs in many people as the days grow shorter. The symptoms of SAD include depression, weight gain, and even sleeplessness. Both light and dark cycles are needed for maintaining good health.

Melatonin supplements *should not* be taken if you are breast-feeding. Although no toxic levels of melatonin have been found, further research is still needed. The following foods are high-grade proteins and contain the highest amount of tryptophan from which melatonin is synthesized: milk, beef, eggs, oatmeal, bananas, peas, spinach, broccoli, cauliflower, pineapples, and nuts.

Four Sleep-Promoting Nutrients

One of the four nutrients vital to your ability to sleep is pantothenic acid (B_5). It is pantothenic acid that activates the proper neurotransmitters for sleep. Before bedtime take a vitamin B complex as directed on the label, plus an extra 50 milligrams of pantothenic acid. If you want more information on pantothenic acid and its metabolic importance to weight loss, turn to page 92.

Another sleep-promoting nutrient is a B vitamin, a phospholipid called inositol. It enhances sleep without suppressing rapid eye movement (REM) or causing respiratory failure like some sleep medications. Inositol in the form of phosphatidylinositol is found in lecithin. Inositol is a necessary component of your cell membranes, and serves as an important conductor of nerve impulses essential to sleep. It is especially important in preventing excess fatty acid from accumulating in the liver.

There is no established RDA for inositol. Inositol is present in both plant and animal foods. I do not recommend you take separate inositol capsules. Instead, take lecithin granules or capsules, which contain a much better balance of inositol, choline, and linoleic acid. Take two tablespoons of lecithin granules or one lecithin capsule at bedtime.

PANTOTHENIC ACID
meat, chicken, fish, eggs, blue cheese, nuts, sunflower seeds, avocados, dates, green beans, peas, cauliflower, sweet potatoes, corn, whole-grain products

INOSITOL
grapefruit, cantaloupe, oranges, limes, green beans, flax seeds, whole wheat, rice, oats, nuts, wheat germ, lecithin, molasses, grapefruit, peanuts, cabbage

CALCIUM
milk and milk products, broccoli, kale, mustard greens, spinach, sunflower seeds, sweet potatoes, almonds, garbanzo beans, pinto beans, rutabagas, bok choy, oranges, salmon

MAGNESIUM
beef, lamb, pork, turkey, veal, flounder, salmon, shrimp, crab, almonds, pistachio nuts, walnuts, peanuts, spinach, potatoes, beans, bananas, oranges

Calcium and magnesium taken in dosages of 1,000 milligrams each at bedtime relax the muscles and promote sleep, and are safe to take when breast-feeding. If you want to learn more about these two important minerals, turn to pages 94 and 97.

One hour before bedtime try eating foods that contain these four sleep-promoting nutrients. Listed below are foods that contain pantothenic acid, inositol, calcium, and magnesium.

Drugs That Interfere with Your Sleep

Many prescription and over-the-counter drugs, including antihistamines, allergy drugs, antibiotics, high-blood-pressure drugs, caffeine, chocolate, and alcohol, can interfere with your natural sleep patterns. If you have trouble sleeping after starting any medication, talk with your doctor. Some medications may contain caffeine, so you need to ask about the best time to take a drug so that it will not interfere with your sleep.

If you're a coffee drinker, try to have your last cup of coffee not later than six hours before bedtime. Caffeine is legally classified as a drug. It is a bitter, white substance of organic nature found in several types of plants. One to two cups of coffee can contain approximately 100 to 300 milligrams of caffeine. Following the ingestion of coffee, soda, or other caffeine-containing beverages, the blood levels of caffeine peak within 20 to

30 minutes. Then the caffeine is quickly distributed to the body tissues roughly in proportion to their water content. The physiological effects of caffeine are many. In general, caffeine is a stimulant, and may have a direct effect on some tissues or act indirectly on the nervous system. Caffeine as well as coffee oils like cafestol and kahweol can raise your blood cholesterol.

In dosages of 50 to 200 milligrams caffeine may cause increased alertness, but in dosages of 300 to 500 milligrams it can cause nervousness and muscular tremors. Caffeine will stimulate the release of adrenaline and increase heart rate. It will also increase the amount in the blood of free fatty acids, which are potential energy sources for muscle. Caffeine raises blood sugar levels and stimulates the secretion of gastric acids. This is why some people may get an upset stomach after drinking coffee. Finally, caffeine is a diuretic. It will stimulate the formation of urine and the removal of water from the body.

Another source of caffeine is chocolate. It too contains several stimulating drugs, which is why chocolate dependence is so very common. Chocolate contains caffeine, beta-phenylethylamine, and theobromine, which are all habit-forming drugs. If you are a chocolate or coffee addict try to have your last serving no later than six hours before bedtime. Avoid eating foods that contain the amino acid *tyramine*, which increases the release of norepinephrine, a brain stimulant that will keep you awake. Avoid tyramine-containing foods such as chocolate, cheese, eggplant, spinach, ham, sausage, and wine close to bedtime.

When it comes to alcohol, moderation is the answer to a good night's sleep. If you're not pregnant or breast-feeding, a moderate daily alcohol intake of one drink will not disrupt sleep patterns. A drink is defined as 12 ounces of beer, 5 ounces of wine, or 1.5 ounces of whiskey. Some research indicates that alcohol raises levels of high-density lipoprotein (good cholesterol) and reduces the chances of heart disease. However, too much alcohol stimulates liver synthesis of triglycerides (blood fats) and increases the production of low-density lipoproteins (bad cholesterol) that transport cholesterol through the blood and deposit it in the arteries.

A program of regular exercise, such as walking, can also raise HDL levels, improve sleep quality, and help you live a healthier and happier life. Your goal is to establish a set of healthy eating habits and to follow them consistently. These habits will then help you establish a healthy sleep cycle that promotes weight loss.

"I Know My Baby Needs Fat, But Do I?"

How Much Fat Is Necessary for Hormone Regulation and Weight Loss

*A*re you afraid you'll never lose weight unless you cut out *all* the fat from your diet? Are you contemplating spending the rest of your life nibbling on carrot sticks? Relax. Such drastic changes won't be necessary. In many cases, those who eat the most low-fat foods actually consume more calories than those who eat no low-fat foods. A low-fat cookie, for instance, is usually higher in carbohydrates and often contains more calories than the cookie that is higher in fat. There is also a tendency to overeat low-fat products because they just aren't as satisfying as their higher-fat alternatives.

Fats are important nutrients, and should not be eliminated from your diet. Often a mother will eliminate all fat from her diet in a desperate attempt to lose her embarrassing abdominal bulge and stretch marks. This will only make losing fat even more difficult, since you need fat to burn fat. The burning of fat is a complex process. No diet pill or weight-loss drink can change the way fats function and burn in the body. If you try to fight this complex body process it will only cause you frustration. You must work with your body if you want to lose weight. Let's begin by learning about fats and how they are classified and function.

What Are Fats?

Fats, also known as *lipids*, comprise a number of different compounds found in the body in the form of both solid fat and liquid oils. The three major types are triglycerides, sterols, and phospholipids. The fats of major interest are the triglycerides, for theirs is the primary form in which fats are eaten and stored in your body. Triglycerides are composed of two different compounds—fatty acids and glycerol. One of the components of fat are fatty acids, which are chains of carbon, oxygen, and hydrogen atoms that vary in the degree of saturation with hydrogen. All fatty acids are classified as saturated, monounsaturated, or polyunsaturated. All foods contain a mixture of these fats, but in varying proportions. Saturated fats, such as butter and fats from meat, are solid at room temperature. Unsaturated fats, such as vegetable oil, are liquid at room temperature.

Generally, animal foods are higher in saturated fats and vegetable foods are higher in monounsaturated and polyunsaturated fats. Preferably, the fat in your diet should contain more of the unsaturated fats. For example, 4 ounces of salmon contain 15.6 grams of fat primarily from polyunsaturated fats, whereas 4 ounces of lean beef bottom round contain only 8.2 grams, but they are primarily saturated fat.

The American Heart Association recommends that no more than 30 percent of all calories consumed in one day come from fat. Of that 30 percent, they suggest that less than 10 percent come from saturated fat, with the remainder from monounsaturated and polyunsaturated fats.

Some Common Fatty Acids

Saturated	Monounsaturated	Polyunsaturated
Butyric	Oleic	Linoleic
Myristic		Linolenic
Palmitic		Arachidonic
Stearic		

• Butyric, myristic, palmitic, and stearic are saturated fatty acids that are *not* beneficial to losing weight. Your liver uses saturated fats to manufacture cholesterol. Therefore, foods that are high in saturated fats raise blood cholesterol the most. Saturated fats are found in varying amounts in animal foods, such as red meat, and whole-milk products, such as cheese and ice cream. Saturated fats are found in many popular foods, such as commercially baked cookies, cakes, crackers, cereals, and candies. These foods contain one or more saturated vegetables oils—palm, palm kernel, and coconut.

This doesn't mean you have to eliminate these foods or avoid saturated fats completely. Simply try to eat any commercially baked goods in moderation and never eat them when you're hungry. Choose lean cuts of red meat, like beef eye round, top round, or tenderloin. Try leg of lamb or top round. Pork tenderloin, center loin chop, boneless sirloin chop, or veal-leg cutlets are also a good choice.

A manufacturing process called *hydrogenation* adds hydrogen atoms to unsaturated fats, making them more saturated. Saturated fats are loaded with all the hydrogen atoms they can carry. Unsaturated fatty acids do not have all the hydrogen atoms they can carry. Unsaturated fatty acids (good fat) contain one or more double bonds in the *cis* configuration. But when unsaturated vegetable oils are hydrogenated, various amounts of the *cis* form are converted to a less healthful *trans* configuration. Therefore, hydrogenated fats like vegetable shortening and margarine function the same way saturated fats do in your body. Once vegetable oil is hydrogenated it becomes a solid, and it is no longer an unsaturated fat. It is now a saturated fat that is less healthful. *Trans* fatty acids also interfere with the conversion of linoleic acid to arachidonic acid, which is important to losing weight. *Trans* fatty acids also reduce the production of prostaglandins, which are produced by every cell in the body and control such things as hormones and inflammation.

• The monounsaturated fatty acids are effective in lowering serum cholesterol and the bad LDL cholesterol while maintaining the good HDL cholesterol levels. Monounsaturated fatty acids are found in olive oil, canola oil, and high-oleic safflower and sunflower oils. Canola oil is produced from a special plant bred from the rapeseed, a member of the mustard seed family. Canola is one of the oils lowest in saturated fats and one of the few vegetable sources of omega-3s. Monounsaturated fatty acids are found in certain plant foods like avocados, olives, almonds, and peanuts. Peanut oil is 46 percent monounsaturated, and olive oil is 81 percent monounsaturated

• Linoleic, linolenic, and arachidonic are polyunsaturated fatty acids. These fatty acids are found in soybean oil, corn safflower oil, sunflower oil, and certain fish oils. All seeds and nuts are rich in polyunsaturates. Eating foods that contain these polyunsaturated fatty acids can significantly increase the level of essential fatty acids in your breast milk. Linoleic acid contributes 7 percent or more of the calories in breast milk (depending on your diet), and most commercial formulas contain over 10 percent. Infants lacking these essential fatty acids in their diet will lose weight and develop eczema.

Unlike saturated fats, polyunsaturates lower your blood cholesterol level. Vitamin E is also found in most vegetable oils, and is needed to protect the polyunsaturated fatty acids from becoming rancid. When vegetable oils are used to fry foods, the vitamin E is destroyed, and so are the health benefits. To keep your cardiovascular system healthy and your blood fats low, you need to maintain a balance between the polyunsaturated fatty acid content of your diet and the vitamin E that protects it.

You Need Fat to Burn Fat: The Essential Fatty Acids

Nearly 60 percent of the calories you burn during rest is provided by the metabolism of fat. To burn these fat calories, you need a balance of essential fatty acids. Linoleic (an omega-6 fatty acid), arachidonic (an omega-6 fatty acid), and linolenic (an omega-3 fatty acid) are known as the *essential fatty acids*. These essential fatty acids promote weight loss and reduce blood cholesterol levels. Linoleic acid cannot be produced by your body and therefore must be obtained from your diet. However, both arachidonic acid and linolenic acid can be synthesized in your body if linoleic acid is supplied in your diet. It is difficult for your body to burn fat and lose weight when there is a deficiency of linoleic acid and prostaglandins. Without the essential fatty acids your body can't manufacture prostaglandins. Prostaglandins are hormonelike substances that regulate a wide range of functions in your body, including hormone production after pregnancy,

The Conversion of Essential Fatty Acids (EFAs)
(Important to fatty acid metabolism)

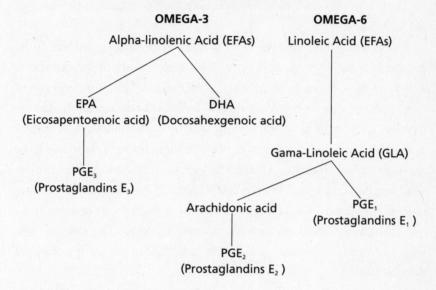

fat burning, and muscle contractions of the digestive tract and uterus for childbirth. Essential fatty acids can help you lose weight by regulating many important body processes.

Your body makes gama-linoleic (GLA), an omega-6 fatty acid, from linoleic acid, and from this GLA your body forms the prostaglandin E_1 (PGE_1) series, which is important to the fat-burning process. GLA also makes the essential fatty acid arachidonic, from which your body forms the PGE_2 (prostaglandins E_2). PGE_2 is one type of prostaglandin that stimulates production of the thyroid, which is, as I've mentioned, so important to the regulation of body metabolism and the burning of calories.

Arachidonic acid has some special properties besides those of its companion fatty acids, linoleic and linolenic. For example arachidonic acid, an omega-6 fatty acid, is needed to regulate the conversion of carbohydrates into fats. A low level of arachidonic acid in your liver will increase the conversion of carbohydrates into fats, even *without* an excess of carbohydrates. In other words, your body converts a disproportionate amount of the food you eat into fat. It is your liver that manufactures glucose from carbohydrates, but it has a limited capacity for storing carbohydrates. So when there's an excess, your liver converts carbohydrates into fats. This process, called *lipogenesis*, is a biological process that no diet pill will change.

A deficiency of arachidonic acid in the muscle also contributes to lipogenesis. Your liver can store about 300 calories worth of carbohydrates, and your muscle can store between 1,000 and 2,000 calories worth of carbohydrates, but only if your muscle can efficiently absorb the carbohydrates. A low level of arachidonic acid in your muscle, a condition associated with insulin resistance, prevents muscle from absorbing large amounts of carbohydrates. Unabsorbed carbohydrates from your muscle will then be sent to your liver, and if it's already full, these carbohydrates will be converted into fat. Some of this fat will then be converted into essential fatty acids and synthesized into prostaglandins. The rest will continue the metabolic journey, and will be either burned for energy or stored for later use.

The omega-6 fatty acids can be found in breast milk, lean meat, nuts, pumpkin seeds, sunflower seeds, soybeans, sunflower oil, sesame seed oil, safflower oil, corn oil, soy bean oil, and cottonseed oil.

Eicosapentoenoic acid (EPA) and decosahexaenoic acid (DHA), which are usually found together, are omega-3 fatty acids that produce the prostaglandin E_3 series (PGE_3). In addition to regulating metabolism, they have anti-inflammatory benefits. The omega-3 polyunsaturated fatty acids can be found in canola oil, linseed oil, walnut oil, wheat-germ oil, hickory nuts, beech nuts, walnuts, pumpkin seeds, wheat germ, sea vegetables, leafy green vegetables, salmon, cod, mackerel, sardines, herring, lake trout, shrimp, oysters, bass, flounder, tuna, and anchovies.

As you have seen, not only are some fats "good" for you, but the essential fatty acids—omega-3s and omega-6s—are a vital part of every system in your body. If you eat more of the essential fatty acid–rich foods, you can help your body regulate hormones and burn fat. If you want the health benefits of these fatty acids, one way to get them is by eating fish at least twice a week.

If you want to take fish-oil supplements that contain EPA and DHA, make sure they are in capsule form and contain vitamin E to prevent oxidation. EPA and DHA supplements should not contain vitamin A or vitamin D, which are stored in your body and could be toxic if taken in concentrations that are too high. EPA and DHA are available in capsule form in a commercial product called MaxEPA. The oil that comes from the seeds of the evening primrose plant contains GLA. Evening primrose oil capsules are a nontoxic source of GLA and often come in combination with vitamin E and beta carotene. These supplements are available at health food stores and you should follow the dosage prescribed on the bottle. If you're breast-feeding the safest way to get these fatty acids is from eating fish, not taking fish oil capsules.

Cholesterol: Another Important Fatlike Substance

Another important fatlike substance that is essential to good health is cholesterol. Cholesterol is not a fat, but a wax or sterol. Your liver and intestine synthesize cholesterol from saturated fat, a process that requires twenty different enzymes. About 80 percent of the body's cholesterol is used by your liver to form bile acid, which is necessary for the digestion and absorption of fats. Most of the hormones of the adrenal cortex and several hormones of the ovaries (progesterone and estrogen) and testes (testosterone) are derivatives of cholesterol. It is now scientifically proven that the female sex hormone estrogen decreases cholesterol.

Cholesterol is essential to you and your baby, and is needed for proper brain development. Much of your brain is composed of cholesterol. Breast milk has a higher cholesterol content than formula. Studies have shown that the cholesterol content of breast milk will stay constant in the range of 100 to 150 milligrams per liter of milk no matter how much cholesterol a mother consumes. The recommendation for adults is to eat no more than 300 milligrams of cholesterol per day, and the same rule applies when breast-feeding. One egg provides around 250 milligrams, almost meeting the RDA.

The American Heart Association states that the average total plasma cholesterol level of 180 to 200 mg/dl (milligrams of cholesterol per deciliter of blood) in an adult indicates a low risk of cardiovascular disease. Although total cholesterol is an important indicator of risk, an even more precise measurement is the LDL cholesterol level. You may have heard the terms *high-density lipoproteins* (HDL) and *low-density lipoproteins* (LDL). Lipoproteins are necessary because all cholesterol is insoluble in water and therefore cannot be transported in a pure state via the bloodstream. It must first be combined with fat and protein (lipoprotein) in order to become soluble. The LDLs (bad cholesterol) transport cholesterol through the blood and deposit it in the arteries. HDLs (good cholesterol) do the opposite, taking cholesterol away from the lining of the arteries.

This is why doctors recommend lower fat consumption and a moderate alcohol intake to control LDL levels and serum cholesterol. To maintain good health, you want to have low levels of total cholesterol, LDL cholesterol, very-low-density lipoprotein (VLDL) cholesterol, and triglycerides (blood fats) as well as a low cholesterol ratio, while keeping a high level of good, protective HDL.

Most people are confused about identifying the foods that contain cholesterol. It is found in animal foods such as meat, beef, veal, pork, lamb, poultry, shrimp, lobster, oysters, egg yolks, milk, cheese, butter, and other dairy products. The cholesterol content of lean trimmed red meat is not that much higher than that of chicken or fish. Caffeine, as well as coffee oils like cafestol and kahweol, can raise your blood cholesterol. Cholesterol is also manufactured in your body from the breakdown of carbohydrates and protein.

The American Heart Association recommends a daily intake of up to 6 ounces of cooked poultry, fish, or lean red meat. Food from plants like vegetables, grains, and nuts do not contain cholesterol. Although alcohol contains no fat or cholesterol, it still contains calories. Alcohol is a simple carbohydrate that is broken down even faster than sugar. Too much alcohol stimulates liver synthesis of triglycerides (fats) and increases the production of VLDL, or very-low-density lipoproteins, the substance that transports triglycerides.

Yet a moderate daily alcohol intake of one drink can reduce your chances of heart disease. A drink is defined as 12 ounces of beer, 5 ounces of wine, or 1.5 ounces of whiskey. Some research indicates that alcohol raises levels of high-density lipoproteins (HDL), the "good" cholesterol. Regular exercise like walking also can raise HDL levels.

Mother Nature Says You Must Have Some Fat on Your Body

It is necessary to have some fat in your diet and on your body. While you were pregnant your body took good care of both you and your baby by becoming more efficient at storing fat. If you want to lose weight, and keep it off, the extra fat you stored during pregnancy must be lost gradually. Fats are much too important to the overall health of your body. If you lose fat too quickly, your body will work hard at trying to gain it back.

Fats are essential for the utilization of other nutrients and for the production of hormones. A fat-free, high-carbohydrate diet can cause fatigue, dry skin, brittle nails, and recurring yeast infections. A fat-free meal will leave you feeling hungry and unsatisfied. It is the fat content of your meal that gives you a feeling of long-lasting satisfaction. When fatty food is eaten it requires four to six hours of digestion just to empty out your stomach. And as long as you have food in your stomach your appetite is suppressed, so you don't feel hungry.

It is also necessary to have some fat on your body for reserve. If body fat gets too low, you may experience irregular or painful menstrual periods. In some cases ovulation will stop altogether and your body won't be able to resume its reproductive function until an acceptable amount of fat is restored. The reason for this reproductive change is that the reproductive hormone estrogen is stored in fat cells as well as ovaries. It's estrogen that prepares the mucus-membrane lining of the womb for the fertilized egg, and the breast cells and glands for milk production. So when you lose fat, you lose some estrogen as well.

This is why Mother Nature is so resistant to you losing too much fat too quickly. If you try to lose weight too quickly, you're going to have a fight on your hands. Another reason Mother Nature is so resistant to losing fat too quickly is because fat serves as the vehicle for carrying the fat-soluble vitamins A, D, E, and K. If fats are not present, these fat-soluble vitamins cannot perform their vital functions.

L-Carnitine: For Burning Fat

The amino acid L-carnitine is also needed by the body in order to burn fat efficiently, and permits other amino acids to be used by the cells for energy. During the metabolic process, L-carnitine is utilized to transfer long-chain fatty acids across the membrane of the mitochondria within each cell. This enables the long-chain fatty acids to be burned for energy and not be stored as fat. L-carnitine is synthesized in your liver and kidneys, and is then transported through the bloodstream to the skeletal system and muscles, where it accumulates in the muscle cells. If there isn't enough L-carnitine within the cells, the fatty acids are poorly metabolized and blood fats become elevated.

Abdominal Bulge and Stretch Marks

Fat accumulation is not the only reason why your abdomen bulges. The other reason is that pregnancy caused your lower abdominal area to stretch and your lower back to be pulled, which tilted the pelvis forward, causing your buttocks to stick out and your lower abdomen to bulge. Therefore, improving your posture will help strengthen your abdominal muscles and flatten your stomach. Also, eating the "right types" of fats in moderation will help you burn fat.

Stretch marks are due not only to fat deposits, but to elevated estrogen and progesterone levels. Elevated estrogen levels along with the increase in blood vessels during pregnancy are responsible for the reddish veins under the surface of the skin. Most pregnant women get stretch marks, to a greater or lesser degree according to how rapidly or dramatically they gained weight. Stretch marks show up in the area of the body where you stretch the most—the thighs, tummy, and breasts. During pregnancy, all these areas are pulled beyond the norm by the expanding uterus and by extra deposits of fat and fluid. Once progesterone levels drop after pregnancy, the stretch marks will diminish.

How to Purchase Oils and Margarines

If you want to purchase the most healthful oils it's important that the label reads either *expeller pressed* or *mechanically pressed*. These terms indicate that the oil has only been pressed at low temperatures and not solvent-extracted. Hexane, the most common chemical used in solvent extraction, is a highly volatile, toxic petroleum derivative, traces of which remain in the oil at the end of the process. The oil is heated at high temperatures to evaporate the toxic solvent, but nutrients and flavor are lost during this process. The label also should say "unrefined." An unrefined, mechanically pressed oil has a strong natural flavor and aroma that indicate its source.

When you're selecting a margarine or spread, look for one with at least twice as much polyunsaturated as saturated fat. If the label does not include a breakdown of fats, don't buy the product. Those that are lowest in saturated fat are sunflower, corn, and safflower oil. If the words *hydrogenated oil* or *partially hydrogenated oil* are listed first, the product is probably more saturated. The process called hydrogenation is used to make oil solid, and to prolong its shelf life by adding hydrogen molecules. Margarines and vegetable shortening, commercial peanut butter, palm oil, and some candies are all hydrogenated, and so are solid at room temperature. Diet margarine and margarine with water listed as the first ingredient have one-third less fat than the average margarine and are good choices.

When you're cooking with fats or oils don't use excessive heat. This is because overheating affects the digestibility of fats by transforming the glycerin component of fat into a potentially toxic substance called acrolein. This is why deep-fried foods may irritate your stomach and cause flatulence and heartburn hours after you've eaten them.

9

"Just How Much Protein Do I Need in My Diet?"

Why and How Much Protein Is Required for Breast-feeding and Weight Loss

Life begins as one tiny cell, which multiplies itself several billion times before birth. As this multiplication occurs, the twenty-two amino acids and four nucleotides that make up the protein in your body form various combinations, which are the basis of individuality. All heredity depends upon protein and the nucleotides of DNA and RNA. The information that nucleic acids convey ranges from your baby's eye color and height to more complicated matters like intelligence, talent, and even temperament.

You need protein and so does your baby. It is the main component of all living matter. Proteins are constantly being replaced twenty-four hours a day throughout your entire life. Your muscles, organs, bones, cartilage, skin, antibodies, enzymes, hormones, and neurotransmitters are made from protein. Proteins are large molecules composed of long chains of amino acids linked together. The sequence of amino acids functions like a language. The informational content of these sequences is a function of the varying number and order of twenty different amino acids. For example, prolactin, the pituitary hormone necessary for milk production, is made of 198 amino acid links, whereas cholecystokinin (CCK-8), a brain hormone that controls hunger, is 8 amino acids long. There are also protein molecules called enzymes that start your metabolic process and must be present for the chemical reactions that are important to losing weight. These enzymes allow calories from proteins, fats, and carbohydrates to be stored and then burned for energy.

Eating protein-rich foods can help you lose weight because they require a lot of energy to burn and can raise your basal metabolic rate by as much as 10 percent. Protein also takes a while to digest, so they make you feel fuller longer. Proteins do not stimulate your body's insulin production, and that means your blood sugar doesn't drop and you don't feel as hungry later on.

Protein: Building Muscle and Burning Fat

It is important to remember that after pregnancy internal changes in your body composition are taking place very rapidly. Therefore your body needs a good supply of protein (the building material) to help you recover from the physical stress of healing, postpartum depression, sleep deprivation, and hormone and brain chemical changes. The RDA for protein for adults is 65 grams and when breast-feeding you need an extra 12 to 15 grams of protein each day. A high-protein diet may contain up to 200 grams per day, or four times the RDA. When breast-feeding you secrete about 11 grams of protein in your breast milk each day. If you don't eat enough protein and are breast-feeding, the protein for your baby will be drawn from your muscle. As we have learned, muscle burns fat. The more muscle you have, the more fat you'll burn.

Fats are burned in your muscle for energy. Fat cannot be changed to a carbohydrate or a protein. Fat can only be removed from fat cells when it is burned in your muscles for energy. This is because muscle contains fat-burning enzymes that fat must move into in order to be burned and used for energy. As your muscle gets smaller—through lack of exercise or protein deficiency—your ability to burn fat decreases and your metabolism slows down. You want to prevent significant losses of lean body mass, particularly muscle tissue. Thirty-five percent of your muscles are made up of the branched-chain amino acids leucine, isoleucine, and valine. These amino acids must be present in your body in order for your muscles to grow. A deficiency in any one of them will cause muscle loss and reduce your ability to burn fat.

Some good news is that regular exercise, such as walking, will increase muscle growth and provide more enzymes to burn fat. When you exercise, the muscles increase in size so they can handle the demands of exercise. At the same time, body-fat stores will slowly begin to diminish as fat is burned for energy. Once fat is replaced by muscle tissue you may notice an increase on the scale which indicates weight gained in lean muscle mass, not fat. Muscle may weigh more than fat, but it takes up one-fifth the space of fat. So you may weigh more, but be inches smaller and notice that your clothes are fitting better. Overall, there is an increase in your lean body mass and a decrease in your body fat.

After pregnancy, weight loss may come from any one of three body sources: body water; lean tissue, such as muscle; and body-fat stores. If you're eating a healthy diet and not severely restricting calories, weight loss as seen on the scale will be gradual and initially come from body water and then body fat. If your diet is too low in calories, weight loss as seen on the scale will be rapid and come from body water and lean muscle tissue, but not from body fat. On the other hand, weight loss as seen on the scale through an exercise program and healthy eating will occur at a much slower rate. This is because body water levels remain relatively normal after replacement of water lost through exercise, and because muscle tissue increases. Even though weight loss is slow, a good amount of the energy used for exercise comes from the burning of fat, and not from water or protein from lean muscle tissue. If you want to lose your weight by using up your fat stores, you must eat well, exercise, and be patient with your body.

Carbohydrates: Prevention of Protein Breakdown in Muscle Tissue

Now you know that both exercise and protein will help you to develop and maintain lean body mass. But did you know that eating enough carbohydrates prevents the breakdown of protein from lean muscle tissue? Carbohydrates have a protein-sparing effect. If you're not getting enough carbohydrates in your diet, your liver will convert protein into glucose for energy. However, your energy supplies should be derived primarily from carbohydrates and fats, not from protein sources. Protein is mainly a building material, not a primary energy source. Protein should be reserved for cell growth, repair, and development and maintenance of lean muscle mass.

After pregnancy, especially if you're breast-feeding, you need a good balance of both carbohydrates and protein to stay healthy and lose weight. Any protein overload, like any excess carbohydrate, is converted to fat and stored. A high-protein diet will strain your kidneys and liver. It can destroy lean muscle and lower your metabolism. This destruction of muscle is actually caused by the loss of water from your muscle. So high-protein diets are dangerous and can often lead to dehydration, electrolyte imbalance, and loss of lean muscle mass. What you see on the scale is water loss, not fat loss.

If you eat a variety of foods you naturally get a healthful balance of both carbohydrates and proteins. Seeds such as sunflower, pumpkin, and sesame are good sources of both protein and carbohydrates. Most nuts are primarily fat, but almonds, pistachios, and pine nuts are high in carbohydrates as well. The entire vegetable family is a rich source of complex carbohydrates, vitamins, minerals, and fiber. All yellow and orange vegetables, such as carrots, yams, squash, and sweet potatoes, are good sources of complex carbohydrates as well as vitamin A (beta carotene). Fruits are also excellent sources of complex carbohydrates and nutrients, but are higher in sugar than vegetables. Many grains and grain products (whole-wheat bread, cereal, and pasta), oats, barley, brown rice, and millet are good sources of complex carbohydrates.

Some Excellent Sources of Protein

Foods that contain all eight of the essential amino acids are called *complete protein foods*. For protein to be absorbed and used by your body, all eight essential amino acids must be present in a certain proportion, actually in about the same proportion in which they occur in eggs. Eggs contain the richest source of the amino acid L-cysteine and come closest to matching the protein found in the body, whereas protein found in fruits, vegetables, and grains are incomplete; that is, they have insufficient amounts of one or more of the eight essential amino acids. These eight amino acids include: threonine, valine, tryptophan, lysine, methionine, histidine, phenylalanine, and isoleucine.

Virtually all animal and animal products (beef, veal, pork, lamb, fish, eggs, milk, and cheese) supply a sufficient amount of all eight essential amino acids and thus provide complete proteins. Beef is an excellent source of protein, niacin, iron, B_{12}, riboflavin, and zinc, whereas fish and poultry are good sources of protein and vitamins A and C, but are deficient in iron, vitamin B_{12}, and zinc. Your body needs these vital nutrients, especially after pregnancy. A deficiency of these nutrients can interfere with breast-milk production and weight loss.

Although meat (beef, veal, lamb, and pork) and poultry are excellent sources of protein, vitamins, and minerals, it's not necessary to eat large portions to get enough protein. A 3- to 4-ounce serving of cooked lean meat, poultry, or fish is all you need. By preparing your own meals you'll save money and reduce your fat intake considerably. I recommend you consume at least two servings (3 ounces each) of lean beef each week. You should also include at least 3 eggs in your diet a week.

It is the quality of the meat and how it's prepared that gives it flavor. An extra-lean piece of beef can have more flavor than one marbled with fat. Good-quality lean beef is consistently bright to deep red in color. For grinding, choose lean meat and poultry that contain no visible fat. When you're choosing a lean cut of beef or veal, the cut with the most fat or marbling is given the highest grade—"Prime"—followed by "Choice" and "Select." On the average, a cut of beef graded "Select" has 5 to 20 percent less fat than the same cut of Choice, and 40 percent less fat than Prime.

Unlike beef, fish is lower in saturated fat and contains a rich source of polyunsaturated omega-3 fatty acids. It is an excellent source of protein and is as easy to prepare as chicken or beef. When buying frozen fish, make sure it is solidly frozen, with no soft spots. The package should be tightly wrapped, with no ice-crystal deposits on the inside of the package. The ice crystals hurt the cells in the flesh of the fish and dry it out. Quality fish can certainly be frozen, but quick freezing is the key to preserving fish and seafood. This does not destroy flavor or nutrient content like the omega-3 fatty acids.

Cheese, eggs, milk, and yogurt are also good nonmeat protein sources. Milk has about 9 grams of protein per cup whether it's skim or whole. Even the skin that forms on pudding is a protein, called casein, and the substance that burns at the bottom is another protein, called whey. And it is the casein found in milk that is used to make cheese, yogurt, cottage cheese, sour cream, and buttermilk.

If you have trouble eating dairy products because of the protein or lactose, try taking one of the over-the-counter lactase supplements before consuming milk or other dairy products. You can also try yogurt, acidophilus, or other cultured milk products. These products contain live, beneficial bacteria that "predigests" lactose, the sugar in milk, to lactic acid, making it easier to digest. Try eating some yogurt before eating regular dairy products—it can help your body digest the lactose. Stick with small servings to be on the safe side. Most cheeses (except cottage cheese) have only a trace of lactose, especially hard cheeses like Parmesan and Romano.

Low-cholesterol cheese is another protein source. In this type of cheese, butter fat is replaced with vegetable oil, so you get the same amount of fat and protein as in the original cheese. In other words, this type of cheese is low in cholesterol but still high in fat. Imitation cheeses that are made from soy milk or tofu are also high in fat and sodium. Extra salt is added to make up for the flavor lost with the butter fat, and sodium phosphate is used as an emulsifier. There is a tasty cheese available at most supermarkets called Soya Kaas, which comes in mozzarella and Cheddar flavors and contains no cholesterol and very little fat.

Low-fat cheese is your best choice. Cheese that is low in fat is still an excellent source of protein. A truly low-fat cheese should contain 3 grams of fat or less per ounce. Try part-skim ricotta cheese, 1 percent cottage cheese, and low-moisture mozzarella, Swiss, and feta. These soft and semi-soft cheeses are higher in water content and lower in fat. Cheddar, a hard cheese, is higher in fat in comparison to Swiss and mozzarella. And keep in mind that the cream cheese you spread on a bagel contains the same amount of fat as butter, and has little nutritional value.

Plant Foods: An Excellent Source of Protein

Plant-derived foods can be excellent sources of protein if eaten in complementary combinations that supply adequate amounts of all essential amino acids. For instance, the amino acids that are deficient in a vegetable can be provided by a grain product, another vegetable, or an animal-derived protein. And if you eat chicken or dairy products, this will go a long way toward completing the protein in your grains or beans. Soybeans, for example, are low in the amino acid tryptophan but high in lysine. To enhance their nutritional value you can combine them with complementary proteins like nuts, grains, and seeds that are low in lysine but high in tryptophan.

Other legumes, like lentils, chick-peas, and various kinds of beans, are low in certain amino acids but high in others. So you can combine them with grains, nuts, and seeds to form complementary protein of high nutritional value. Grains and cereals make excellent complements to legumes because they are high in tryptophan and low in isoleucine and lysine.

Remember, when you combine grains, seeds, and legumes, you can easily obtain animal-protein quality. On the other hand, believing that any meat is a good protein source is simply wrong. Cured ham contains only 15 percent protein; hot dogs and bologna only 7 percent; while sunflower seeds contain more than 27 percent protein.

Both beans and other legumes contain toxins, such as lectins and trypsin inhibitors, that can inhibit digestion, but these toxins become harmless when they're cooked or sprouted. All grains and some legumes contain in their outer husk a substance called phytic acid, which can cause a zinc and calcium deficiency. Grains should therefore be sprouted, baked with yeast, or cooked thoroughly.

There's also a way to reduce the gas-producing properties of beans, a problem that is discouraging when you're trying to trim down. Therefore, during preparation soak the beans, discard the water, then boil the beans in a large quantity of fresh water. This eliminates some of the indigestible complex sugars that pass into the large intestine, where they are fermented into gas. Soybeans, cabbage, broccoli, brussels sprouts, cauliflower, and eggplant are all gas-producing. You don't want to stop eating these nutrient-rich foods. So your best approach for eating these gassy foods is to eat small amounts at a time. Another suggestion is to remove the cover for one minute when you're steaming these vegetables, which releases some of their gas-producing properties.

It's best to stay away from deep-fried or overcooked protein foods. Excessive heating of any protein, whether of animal or plant origin, may cause what are known as cross-linkages. Cross-linkages make it difficult for protein-digesting enzymes to break protein down into simple amino acids so they can be absorbed. Even milk and milk products are especially sensitive to heat and should not be heated above the boiling point. Keep this in mind the next time you warm your baby's bottle.

It's best to rely on the protein found in the foods you eat that contain a balance of vitamins and minerals, and not on a diet protein drink. Diet protein drinks contain low-quality protein and use an improper balance of vitamins and minerals. Biotin, for example, a B vitamin that is present in most protein foods and is important to the metabolism and utilization of protein, is not found in diet drinks.

Following you'll find a list of food sources that are rich in protein. You can select foods from this list to meet the Recommended Daily Allowance of 65 to 80 grams of protein each day. You don't have to combine complementary foods at the same meal to get a complete protein; you can eat them apart or even later in the day.

COMMON FOODS THAT CONTAIN HIGH-QUALITY PROTEIN

Protein	Amount	Grams of Protein
Grains and Grain Products		
Rice, white, enriched	1/2 cup	3.0
Rice, brown, long-grain	1/2 cup	3.0
Wild rice	1/2 cup	6.0
Bulgur wheat	1/2 cup	3.0
Bread, white, rye, sourdough	1 slice	2.0
Bread, whole-wheat	1 slice	2.0
Corn muffin	1 average	3.0
Ready-to-eat cereals	1 ounce	3.0–5.0
English muffin	1 average	4.5
Wheat germ, sprinkled on breakfast cereal, yogurt, or salad	3 Tbsp.	9.0
Amaranth—not a true grain and not deficient in the amino acid lysine, so when eaten with wheat, rice, or barley it provides a complete protein	1/2 cup	14.0
Barley, pearl	1/2 cup	13.0
Kasha—roasted, hulled buckwheat kernels that are cracked into coarse or fine granules	1/2 cup	13.0
Millet—deficient in the amino acid lysine and should be eaten with beans and other legumes that are rich in lysine	1/2 cup	4.0
Oat bran	1/2 cup	3.0
Quinoa (keen-wah)—like other nontrue grains it is not low in the amino acid lysine	1/2 cup	13.0
Couscous—cooked cracked rye, with fruit, can be eaten as a pilaf or hot cereal	1/2 cup	13.0
Fresh pasta	1/4 cup	5.0

Protein	Amount	Grams of Protein
Egg noodles	1/4 cup	5.0
Spaghetti, whole-wheat or enriched	1/4 cup	5.0
Legumes, Nuts, and Seeds		
Chick-peas (garbanzo beans)	1/2 cup	9.0
Pinto beans	1/2 cup	8.0
Lentils	1/2 cup	9.0
Black beans	1/2 cup	9.0
Lima beans	1/2 cup	8.0
Navy beans	1/2 cup	9.0
Black-eyed peas	1/2 cup	6.0
Soybeans or soybean products,	1/2 cup	17.0
tempeh, tofu, miso, split peas	1/2 cup	8.0
Great northern beans	1/2 cup	8.0
Kidney beans	1/2 cup	9.0
Adzuki beans	1/2 cup	8.0
Walnuts, black	1 ounce (about 15)	7.0
Almonds	1 ounce (about 25)	6.0
Sunflower seeds	1 ounce (3 Tbsp.)	6.0
Pumpkin seeds, shelled	1 ounce (3 Tbsp.)	7.0
Pistachios	1 ounce (about 50)	6.0
Pine nuts/Pignoli	1 ounce (3 Tbsp.)	7.0
Peanuts, dry roasted	1 ounce (about 30)	8.0
Sesame seeds	1 ounce (3 Tbsp.)	5.0
Almond butter	2 Tbsp.	5.0
Cashew butter	2 Tbsp.	6.0
Peanut butter	2 Tbsp.	8.0
Tahini	2 Tbsp.	5.0
Fruits and Vegetables		
Alfalfa sprouts, raw	4 ounces	3.5
Artichoke	4 ounces	3.0
Broccoli, raw	1/2 cup	3.6
Broccoli, frozen, chopped, boiled w/o salt	1/2 cup	3.0
Brussels sprouts, boiled w/o salt	1/2 cup	3.5
Cauliflower, raw	1/2 cup	3.0

Protein	Amount	Grams of Protein
Corn, whole-kernel, low-sodium if canned	1/2 cup	3.1
Kale leaves, boiled, w/o salt	1/2 cup	4.5
Asparagus	6 spears	2.5
Potato, baked, with skin	1 average	6.0
Spinach, frozen, chopped, boiled w/o salt	1/2 cup	3.0
Avocado, raw, pitted	4 ounces	2.5
Banana	1 average	1.5
Orange, peeled	1 average	1.4
Prunes, dried	about 5	1.2
Raisins, seedless	3 ounces	3.2
Raspberries, red	3 ounces	1.5
Watermelon*	1 slice	3.3

Dairy and Eggs

Milk, whole 3.5% fat	1 cup	9.0
Milk, 1% or 2%	1 cup	10.0
Milk, skim or nonfat	1 cup	9.0
Buttermilk, cultured from skim milk	1 cup	9.0
Soy milk	1 cup	8.9
Kefir, less tart than plain yogurt	1 cup	8.0
Yogurt, skim-milk	1 cup	8.0
Acidophilus milk	1 cup	9.0
Lactose-reduced milk	1 cup	9.0
Egg	1 medium	6.0
Provolone	1 ounce	8.0
Muenster	1 ounce	7.6
Gouda	1 ounce	8.0
Mozzarella (part-skim)	1 ounce	7.8
Ricotta (part-skim)	1 ounce	6.0
Soycheese	1 ounce	6.0
Cottage cheese, 2% fat	1 cup	7.8
Feta cheese	1 ounce	6.0
Romano, grated	1 ounce	9.0

*Most other fruits have less than 1 gram of protein.

Protein	Amount	Grams of Protein
Meat and Poultry (cooked)		
Beef sirloin, broiled, choice grade	3 1/2 ounces	31.9
Beef flank, braised, choice grade	3 1/2 ounces	30.3
Extra lean ground beef	3 1/2 ounces	24.0
Beef chuck, braised, choice grade	3 1/2 ounces	29.8
Beef rump, roasted, choice grade	3 1/2 ounces	28.9
Lamb leg, roasted, choice grade	3 1/2 ounces	28.5
Lamb loin, broiled, prime grade	3 1/2 ounces	27.8
Veal leg, roasted, choice grade	3 1/2 ounces	27.0
Veal loin, broiled, choice grade	3 1/2 ounces	26.2
Pork loin, broiled, medium fat	3 1/2 ounces	30.4
Pork shoulder, roasted, medium fat	3 1/2 ounces	29.0
Chicken, light meat, roasted w/o skin	3 1/2 ounces	31.4
Chicken, dark meat, roasted w/o skin	3 1/2 ounces	27.8
Turkey, roasted, w/o skin	3 1/2 ounces	29.0
Cornish hen, roasted w/o skin	3 1/2 ounces	29.0
Fish and seafood		
Lingcod, broiled	3 1/2 ounces	28.0
Brook trout, baked	3 1/2 ounces	19.0
Yellow fin tuna, broiled	3 1/2 ounces	17.0
Pink salmon, broiled	3 1/2 ounces	20.3
Swordfish, broiled	3 1/2 ounces	27.8
Bass, baked or broiled	3 1/2 ounces	19.0
Bay and sea scallops, steamed	3 1/2 ounces	23.2
Halibut, broiled	3 1/2 ounces	25.0
Haddock, broiled	3 1/2 ounces	25.0
Flounder, baked	3 1/2 ounces	30.0
Perch, baked	3 1/2 ounces	11.0
Shrimp, broiled or steamed	3 1/2 ounces	28.0

10

"How Can I Get Rid of My Yeast Infection?"

Vitamins and Essential Fatty Acids That Help Prevent or Eliminate Yeast Infections

*I*t is the lucky mother who has never suffered an agonizing itch that she can't scratch in public. Most women are highly susceptible to the development of yeast infections, especially during and after pregnancy. This is due to the changes and imbalances in their estrogen and progesterone levels. Yeast infections can even cause hormone imbalances. When yeast infects the vagina, it results in vaginitis, which is characterized by a thick white discharge, intense pain, and burning on urination. Other symptoms include swelling in the vagina to varying degrees as well as fatigue, headaches, and even depression.

Vaginitis is the generic term that means inflammation and infection of the vagina. The symptoms are itching and inflammation of the vulva and the vaginal opening and an abnormal vaginal discharge. There are many causes for vaginitis. It may result from the use of feminine deodorant sprays, commercial douche preparations, spermicidal creams, soap, or even laundry detergent. More often, however, the cause is infection by the organisms *Candida albicans*. Candida is a prolific yeast that lives primarily in the gastrointestinal tract and genital area. As its numbers grow, this friendly yeast changes to a fungus, which bores its rootlike structures into the vaginal area or gastrointestinal tract.

The normal physiological environment of your vagina is hostile to *Candida albicans*. It is the lactic-acid producing Doderlein's bacilli (beneficial bacteria) in the vagina that are responsible for the lowered pH that protects against pathogenic invaders such as *Candida albicans*. But anything that disturbs the natural balance between the Doderlein's bacilli and the pathogenic microorganisms, such as hormonal changes after pregnancy, will decrease the acidity of your vagina, killing off Doderlein's bacilli. Frequent use of antibiotics and corticosteroid drugs also decrease the acidity of your vagina, destroying beneficial bacteria that keep candida under control.

Treatment with Antifungal Preparations

Once it has been determined by a doctor that the vaginitis is the result of *Candida albicans*, it can then be treated with antifungal preparations. These include prescription and over-the-counter drugs. For example, Nystatin (Mycostatin) and Gyne-lotrimin are antibiotic and antifungal agents that can be obtained by prescription, and now Monistat is available over the counter. When inserted into the vagina in suppository or cream form, these drugs specifically attack candida organisms by changing their structure.

These drugs are highly effective when they are use throughout the entire recommended course of treatment, which is anywhere from seven days to two weeks, depending on which drug you use. It's important that you complete the yeast treatment. Stopping after a few days because the itching has disappeared is an invitation for a recurrence. If you do not respond well to any of these antifungal preparations, there is a stronger antifungal drug called Nizoral. Nizoral (ketoconizole) is highly effective in treating most yeast problems, but can be irritating to the liver and should not be taken when breast-feeding. A new Nizoral-related drug, Diflucan (fluconazole), is now available, and is a slight improvement over Nizoral, but it, too, must be watched closely by your doctor and should not be taken when breast-feeding.

Reestablish Normal Bacterial Flora

As I mentioned previously, antibiotics given for an infection elsewhere in the body as well as birth control pills and corticosteroids suppress and kill off beneficial bacteria in the vagina and gastrointestinal tract. Yeast problems are often the result of these commonly prescribed drugs. Long-term antibiotic treatment after pregnancy will cause yeast to proliferate in the vagina and intestines, often leading to flatulence and destruction of vital nutrients. To help restore the normal balance of healthy flora in the intestine and vagina, you need to replace the yeast with several strains of beneficial bacteria.

There are several strains of beneficial bacteria—*Lactobacillus acidophilus, Lactobacillus bulgaricus, Streptococcus thermophilus*, and *Bifidobacterium bifidum*—that should be taken during and after antibiotic treatment to help reestablish a normal bacterial flora. All four of these bacteria have an antibiotic effect in whatever area they're working. *Lactobacillus acidophilus* is found primarily in the small intestine. It produces *acidophilin* and *acidolin*, two naturally occuring antibiotics, and is also an antiviral organism that inhibits growth of *Candida albicans* yeast. *Lactobacillus bulgaricus* is active in the circulatory system, which provides the oxygen and other nutrients required by every cell to function. This bacteria also produces the antioxidant bulgarican, which prevents or delays cell deterioration by the oxygen in air. *Bifidobacterium bifidum* effectively retards everything from bacterial and viral invasions to potentially toxic food additives. It is found in high levels in breast milk, and in over 95 percent of all the bacterial flora an infant processes is in this bifidus strain.

You can begin to restore your colon to its natural state by actually reimplanting these four beneficial bacteria. *Lactobacillus acidophilus* is found in cultured products like yogurt, sweet acidophilus milk, and buttermilk. It's the beneficial bacteria in these products that convert lactose to lactic acid that make it easy for your body to digest.

Because these beneficial bacteria are sensitive to the harsh acids of your digestive tract, absorption may be difficult. Therefore, in addition to eating cultured products, you should also use a straight powder formula or a powder in a capsule that contains billions of live beneficial bacteria per dosage. By using the straight powder you can get a greater number of beneficial bacteria and achieve better absorption. There is a powdered formula produced by Natren, Inc., called Mega-dophilus, and it contains all four of these bacteria. You can sprinkle 1 teaspoon of powder on cereal or mix it in yogurt, or take it on an empty stomach in the morning and one hour before each meal—it has a pleasant sweet taste. The nondairy formulas are best for people who are allergic to dairy. If you do not want to use a straight powder, use the capsule formula by Nature's Way called Primadophilus. Both these products are safe to use when breast-feeding and should be taken daily. There are a number of other supplements that can help treat candida vaginitis, such as digestive aids, which are discussed next.

Digestive Aids for Better Nutrient Absorption

You should consider taking supplemental hydrochloric acid (HCL) with meals, followed by digestive enzymes after eating. These supplements will help you to break down and utilize proteins, fats, and carbohydrates from the foods you eat—and help you better absorb other nutrients that are important to the treatment of candida vaginitis. Specific cells in the stomach produce HCL, which is secreted primarily in response to ingested protein or fat. Decreased HCL levels can lead to poor digestion and cause symptoms such as gas and bloating after eating. It also can lead to poor iron absorption and is often associated with iron deficiency anemia.

In addition to taking an HCL supplement with meals, also take a digestive aid after meals that contains bromelain, which is found naturally in pineapple, and papain, which is derived from papaya. Fresh pineapple and papaya do contain these enzymes, but in very low concentrations. Supplemental hydrochloric acid and digestive enzymes are highly concentrated and have a greater effect on the health of the intestinal wall by enhancing the absorption of vitamins and minerals. A healthy intestinal tract is important to fighting yeast infections and preventing them from occurring. Most health food stores carry bromelain, papaya, and HCL supplements in a combination capsule. Look for a supplement that contains animal-based pancreatin; amylase; proteases (trypsin and chymotrypsin); and lipase to break down carbohydrates, proteins, and fats; betaine HCL (betaine hydrochloride); pepsin; bromelaine (from pineapple); and papain (from papaya). These supplements are safe to take when breast-feeding, and it's best to follow the directions on the bottle.

On the next several pages we'll discuss the importance of taking supplemental nutrients such as B_6, biotin, vitamin A (beta carotene), vitamin C, magnesium, fatty acids, caprylic acid, and garlic oil. These health-promoting nutrients provide support by replacing some of these nutrients that are lost because of the diminished intestinal bacteria that produce them. They are all necessary nutrients for combating yeast infections, for weight loss, and for breast-feeding.

Biotin: *Candida Albicans* Fighter

A candida infection can affect the way your body absorbs and excretes biotin. For instance, the production of the B vitamin biotin is dependent for its existence on the beneficial bacteria (lactobacillin) in the intestinal tract, which are often destroyed by antibiotics used to treat candida vaginitis. Biotin can effectively reduce *Candida albicans* to their inactive forms if adequate levels of the vitamin are present in the bloodstream. Biotin is also essential for the release of energy from carbohydrates, the synthesis and oxidation of fatty acids, and the breakdown of amino acids that must take place for energy to be released from protein.

Biotin is important to the metabolism and utilization of the branched-chain amino acids leucine, isoleucine, and valine, known as branched-chain amino acids because of their molecular structure. These amino acids are dependent upon biotin's ability to open pathways so that they can reach their receptor sites without being damaged through oxidation. Thirty-five percent of your muscles are made up of these three amino acids. All three of these amino acids must be present for muscular growth, and are important to preventing candida yeast from destroying healthy cells. A deficiency in any one of them will cause muscle loss and reduce your ability to burn fat. Deficiency symptoms of biotin include persistent yeast infections, fatigue, skin dryness, and depression.

I recommend you eat more foods that contain biotin, such as meat, milk, eggs, cereal, legumes, nuts, and seeds. You should also take a combination B vitamin supplement that contains biotin. If your supplement is too low in biotin, you can purchase it separately as well. Avoid taking a B-vitamin supplement that is yeast-based or contains sugar, artificial colors, dyes, or flavors. A daily allowance of approximately 100 to 300 micrograms of biotin per day is considered safe and will meet your body's needs, even when breast-feeding.

Pyridoxine (B_6) for Effective Candida Treatment

The other B vitamin that may help prevent or eliminate candida vaginitis is B_6, or pyridoxine. B_6 levels are very low after pregnancy, and B_6 deficiencies often occur during periods when you have a yeast infection. This essential vitamin is involved in amino acid and protein metabolism, and a B_6 deficiency may result in impairment of both metabolism and cellular immunity. B_6 is important to the structure of the thymus gland, which contains the T-lymphocytes (T-cells) that are involved in cellular immunity. These T-cells protect your body from viral and bacterial invasions. Vitamin B_6 is also necessary for fatty acid synthesis, which slows down the progress of yeast and maintains the insulating myelin sheath around nerves.

Plants are the main food source of B_6 (pyridoxine), and animals provide vitamin B_6 in the form of pyridoxal and pyridoxamine. B_6 is absorbed in your upper small intestine. Once absorbed all three dietary forms of B_6 are converted to pyridoxal phosphate (PLP) and delivered to all your body tissues.

The RDA for B_6 is very low, only 1.6 milligrams per day. Most mothers need to eat more foods rich in vitamin B_6 and take a B_6 supplement daily. I suggest you take a B-complex supplement that contains 25 milligrams of B_6 (pyridoxine) even when breast-feeding. Make sure it is in a capsule form that is free of yeast and sugar.

Magnesium: Cell, Tissue, and Organ Protector

Magnesium levels are usually low after pregnancy, and magnesium deficiencies occur as a result of a yeast infection. Magnesium is indispensable to your body. Magnesium is involved in every major biological process and a vital component of the water that flows in and out of your cells. Its primary role in the cells is to catalyze virtually hundreds of metabolic reactions that are necessary for removing yeast from your body. Magnesium protects all cells, tissues, and organs from pathogenic invaders like *Candida albicans*. If you keep your magnesium levels up, you'll lessen your chances of contracting yeast infections. Magnesium is also necessary for the transformation of essential fatty acids into prostaglandins, which are important to fighting candida infections.

The RDA for magnesium is 280 milligrams. I recommend you eat food that is rich in magnesium and take a daily vitamin and mineral complex that contains 280 to 600 milligrams of magnesium. Magnesium supplements are safe to take if you're breast-feeding. It's best to take a mineral complex in capsule form because they seldom contain unnecessary additives and are very well assimilated.

Some rich food sources of magnesium include: beef, lamb, pork, turkey, veal, flounder, salmon, shrimp, crab, almonds, peanuts, pistachio nuts, walnuts, almonds, spinach, broccoli, oranges, prunes, bananas, potatoes, and beans.

A Few More Yeast-Fighting Nutritional Guidelines

There are a few more nutritional guidelines that you need to follow if you want to prevent or eliminate candida vaginitis. It is thought that candida thrives in a sugary environment and therefore your diet should contain no carbohydrates (sugars). However, carbohydrates are necessary because they create metabolic activity, which is needed to get yeast out of your system. It's okay to eat carbohydrates (sugars) and complex carbohydrates, just not in excessive amounts. The bulk of your diet, however, should consist of the following foods: eggs, fish, poultry, vegetables, whole grains, nuts, and seeds.

A low-calorie starvation diet or fasting will only make yeast infections worse. They slow down metabolic activity and prevent yeast from moving out of your system. Fasting also depletes your body of essential nutrients that help to reduce yeast by destroying it or by interfering with its growth. Don't forget that fasting is an ineffective way to try to lose weight and can impair liver and kidney functions. Although fasting may cause a rather rapid initial decrease in body weight, it is primarily due to water depletion and decreases in lean muscle mass—not body fat.

A low-fat diet can also cause problems because it deprives the body of adequate stores of essential fatty acids. Essential fatty acids (EFA) include linoleic, linolenic, and arachidonic acids. These are all polyunsaturated fatty acids that cannot be produced in the body. Essential fatty acids strengthen cell membranes, which are your body's first defense against yeast infections. They are part of the structure of cell membranes and prevent yeast from spreading into the bloodstream from the intestinal tract or vagina. Therefore, your diet should incorporate these three essential fatty acids as well as oleic acid, a nonessential fatty acid. Oleic acid is a polyunsaturated fatty acid that also interferes with the yeast conversion to fungus. Food sources of these fatty acids include: high-oleic sunflower oil, sunflower oil, canola oil, sesame oil, and peanut oil. You can supplement your diet with essential fatty acids by using 1 tablespoon of any of these oils on a salad or in hot cereal.

Another fatty acid recently shown to be useful in fighting yeast infections is eicosapentoenoic acid (EPA). It is a polyunsaturated, omega-3 fatty acid found in high concentrations in cold-water fish such as salmon, mackerel, trout (lake), tuna, swordfish, halibut, and red snapper. If you want the benefits of this omega-3 fatty acid, one way to get it is by eating fish at least twice a week. Another way is by taking fish-oil supplements such as MaxEPA, which contains EPA and the omega-3 fatty acid decosahexaenoic acid (DHA). DHA slows down the progress of yeast organisms in the body and is abundant in the brain and eyes. The omega-6 fatty acid called gama-linolenic acid (GLA) that is found in evening primrose oil capsules is helpful in treating yeast problems. If you take fish-oil supplements make sure they do not contain vitamins A or D, and follow the directions on the bottle. If you're breast-feeding, the safest way to get these fatty acids is from eating fish, not taking fish-oil capsules.

Other nutrient oils that help to reduce yeast by killing it or by interfering with its duplication include caprylic acid and fresh garlic. Caprylic acid is fatty acid extracted from coconut oil. Most health food stores carry a caprylic acid supplement called Caprain, from Synergy Plus. Use as directed on the label. If you don't like to eat fresh garlic, you can take a garlic oil supplement called Kyolic. Take two garlic oil capsules three times a day for about three months. If you are breast-feeding and suspect the garlic is causing a problem for your baby, eliminate the garlic from your diet for a couple of weeks. Some babies enjoy the taste of garlicky foods and will actually breast-feed longer.

Two other nutrients that should be included in your anti-yeast nutrient plan are vitamin C and beta carotene, which help regulate yeast and support the immune system. Take a vitamin C supplement of 500 to 2,000 milligrams daily and a beta carotene supplement of 5,000 to 10,000 I.U. (International Units). Both these vitamins are water soluble and safe to take when breast-feeding.

Avoid Foods That Contain Yeast

Listed below are foods you should avoid eating during an active yeast infection or if you have recurring yeast infections. You'll also find below an Anti-Yeast Nutrient Plan that encapsulates the main points discussed in this chapter.

Foods to Avoid

Brewer's yeast	gin	sauerkraut
peanut butter	rum	horseradish
yeast bread	vodka	soy sauce
rolls and pastries	cider	some teas
pretzels	vinegar	pickled and smoked meat
wine	pickles	mushrooms
beer	mayonnaise	cantaloupe
diet soda	mustard	strawberries
whiskey	olives	cottage cheese
brandy	catsup	cheese

packaged processed foods that contain yeast in the list of ingredients

Anti-Yeast Nutrient Plan for Mothers

1. Avoid foods that contain yeast, molds, and products that have been fermented.

2. It's okay to eat simple carbohydrates (sugars) and complex carbohydrates, just not in excessive amounts. Carbohydrates are necessary because they create metabolic activity, which is needed to get yeast out of your system. The bulk of your diet should consist of the following foods: eggs, fish, beef, poultry, vegetables, nuts, and seeds. A low-calorie starvation diet or fasting will only make a yeast infection worse.

3. In addition to eating yogurt, you should take a straight powder formula or a powder in a capsule that contains billions of live beneficial bacteria per dosage. You can sprinkle 1 teaspoon of powder on cereal or mix it in yogurt. Remember that a healthy intestinal tract is important to fighting yeast infections and preventing them from reoccurring.

4. Take hydrochloric acid (HCL) supplement with meals, followed by digestive enzymes after eating. Most health food stores carry digestive enzymes and HCL supplements in a combination capsule. They should be taken before, during, or after meals, and are safe to take when breast-feeding.

5. Eat fish twice a week, and supplement your diet with essential fatty acids by using 1 tablespoon of oil (canola, sunflower, safflower, etc.) on a salad or in hot cereal each day. Take evening primrose oil capsules, and a fish oil supplement called Maxepa, which contains the omega-3 and omega-6 fatty acids. These fatty acids are useful in fighting yeast infections in the vagina and intestinal tract.

6. Eat more foods that are rich in magnesium and take a daily mineral complex that contains 280 to 600 milligrams of magnesium. Magnesium's primary role in the cells is to create hundreds of metabolic reactions that are necessary to removing the yeast from your body.

7. Take a vitamin-C supplement of 500 to 2,000 milligrams and a beta carotene supplement of 5,000 to 10,000 I.U. each day. Both vitamin C and beta carotene are useful in the regulation of yeast and in the support of the immune system.

8. Eat more foods that contain biotin, and take a biotin supplement of 100 to 300 micrograms daily. Biotin can effectively reduce *Candida albicans* to their inactive forms if adequate levels of the vitamin are present in the bloodstream.

9. Take a vitamin B–complex supplement that contains between 1.6 and 25 milligrams of B_6 (pyridoxine), even when breast-feeding. Vitamin B_6 is necessary for fatty-acid synthesis, which slows down the progress of yeast.

10. Take a caprylic acid supplement called Caprain, from Synergy Plus. Also take two garlic oil capsules three times a day for about three months. These nutrient oils help to reduce yeast by killing it or interfering with its duplication.

11

"My Body Feels So Bloated and Fat"
Avoiding Certain Food Additives and Regulating Sodium

When you bake an apple pie at home, do you think of adding a preservative to it? Probably not. Preservatives aren't necessary for the apple pie. Yet when you buy an apple pie at the supermarket you'll get enough emulsifiers, artificial flavorings, thickeners, and synthetic colorings to stock a small chemistry lab. Over 3,500 synthetic chemical additives are approved by the U.S. Food and Drug Administration just for the packaged-food industry.

Each year the average American eats approximately 150 pounds of additives, which come primarily from the processed-foods industry and fast foods. These chemicals are the ones you see listed on food packages, but sadly, there are many hidden additives that never appear on the "truth-in-packaging" labels, and these are classified as "contaminants." Chemicals used during processing may contaminate foods without being direct additives. Chemicals used in packaging can also infiltrate foods.

Synthetic Food Additives: Beware

Chemical processes that modify food not only tamper with the basic structure of a food, but tamper with your health and the health of your baby. Everyone has a certain propensity for having adverse reactions to an additive or chemical in food. Your body's adaptive mechanism must cope with large amounts of synthetic chemicals in foods. Retaining fluid and bloating easily is just one adverse reaction that many people experience.

For many mothers being bloated makes them feel fat, which in turn triggers feelings of frustration and hopelessness about losing weight. These feelings of frustration often lead to overeating. This is a very common reaction, especially after pregnancy, when a mother is still focused on how her body is changing. Another reaction some mothers have to being bloated is to stop eating to counteract their physical and psychological discomfort. This only worsens the problem, because the body doesn't receive the nutrients it needs to get rid of the bloating.

Food manufacturers want you to believe that synthetic additives such as the preservatives BHA and BHT (possible carcinogens) are necessary to keep food prices down because they make food cheaper to produce and distribute, and reduce waste by extending shelf life. This, however, doesn't appear to be the case. The cost of processed packaged foods keeps rising. The bottom line is that synthetic food additives are here to stay because it's easier and more profitable for the food manufacturer to use synthetic additives instead of natural additives derived from food.

Too Many Unanswered Questions

There are still too many unanswered questions about the safety of chemically processed and preserved foods. How is it processed? How is it prepared? Are additives like artificial colors, flavors, and preservatives being used to cover up bad odors and tastes that come from spoiled, unhealthy food? The sad truth is that most food manufacturers fall short of telling you the whole truth by omitting ingredients and using misleading words like *natural flavorings* and *organic*.

Colorings, for example, are used to make food look better than it really is. Flavorings are used to make food more appealing to your nose and taste buds than it would otherwise be, and synthetic preservatives often mask the deterioration of food. Even a food labeled "unsalted" may still contain salt, and a product marked "sugar free" may contain added artificial sweeteners.

For many hundreds or even thousands of years both salt and sugar, as well as spices such as cloves, cinnamon, and vanilla, have been used safely to preserve and improve the taste of food. The herb turmeric, for instance, imparts a yellow coloring and can be used instead of the Yellow Dye #5, which causes allergic reactions in many people. Dehydrated beets can also be used safely in food instead of Red Dye # 3, which has been proven to be unsafe. However, Red Dye # 3 and Yellow Dye # 5 are used because they impart a more vibrant color and are less expensive than turmeric or beets. Another example is Blue Dye #1, a coal-tar derivative used in soda, candy, ice cream, cereal, and pudding, which is on the safe list, but is an allergen and causes cancerous tumors in animals.

Most coloring agents are synthetic and potentially toxic. They are unsafe substitutes for the natural fresh color of foods. The FDA doesn't require food manufacturers to list the specific coloring agent used in their foods. They need only be designated as artificial colors, so you can't differentiate those that are safe and those that are not. What would you rather eat—a safe, natural food that looks a little imperfect or an unsafe food that looks perfect?

Processed Food: Have You Ever Eaten More Than a Moderate Amount?

The U.S. Food and Drug Administration is responsible for monitoring the safety of additives and allows what they consider to be safe levels in food, assuming that you eat these foods in moderation. But how often have you eaten more than a moderate amount of a processed food? The FDA is not concerned with whether additives will improve your health, but only if they prove to be reasonably harmless. Just because certain food additives are used presently in foods and deemed "safe" doesn't mean that they are, in fact, "safe."

It's up to you to take the time to read food labels so you can avoid unsafe food additives and keep your sodium intake to about 1,500 milligrams (¾ teaspoon of salt) per day. Start asking yourself how food can sit on the shelf for three years and not spoil? What is artificial chocolate flavor or imitation flavor? What it means is that the real food is left out. So if the real chocolate is left out what was it replaced with? Will it make you feel bloated or possibly make your child hyperactive? The synthetic versions of natural flavors are made from a mixture of many chemicals. There are over 500 natural flavors and more than 1,500 synthetic flavors. It's usually not the natural sugar in a candy bar that causes harmful side effects, but all the artificial stuff it contains.

Let's take, for example, the flavor enhancer monosodium glutamate, or MSG, which causes you to experience a "flavor rush." This "rush" is an electrical discharge of nerve impulses that are responsible for the sensation of flavor. So if you "can't eat just one," don't blame it on willpower. Instead, check the label. MSG was removed from baby food in 1976 because it produced excitotoxic injury (dangerously high levels of stimulation) in the developing brains of children. Yet MSG is still added to almost all canned soups and processed foods that both children and adults eat. Hydrolyzed vegetable protein (HVP), a seasoning found in everything from canned soups and crackers to fish sticks, and is laden with MSG.

Under FDA regulation, manufacturers need only declare MSG when it is added to products, not when it's part of other ingredients. Additives such as HVP, autolyzed yeast or yeast extract, natural flavors, sodium caseinate, and calcium caseinate all contain harmful amounts of MSG. It can comprise 8 to 40 percent of HVP. It can cause fluid retention, increased thirst, migraines, headaches, and cardiac arrhythmia. Worse still, many foods containing HVP and the others have been labeled "MSG free."

Another example of a harmful food additive is aspartame, the active ingredient in Equal or NutraSweet, which are artificial sweeteners that contain 4 calories per gram, just like table sugar. Aspartame is 180 times sweeter, so you're supposed to eat less. Right? Wrong. You're eating a lot more than you realize. Aspartame is found in a wide variety of products, from diet soda to cereal. There is still controversy and question over the safety of these artificial sweeteners. Adverse reactions to aspartame include increased thirst, bloating, dizziness, ear buzzing, severe muscle aches, and inflammation of the pancreas. This is just one artificial sweetener that you and your children should avoid.

Another sour note to this sweet story is that aspartame can also increase hunger and interfere with sleep. Aspartame affects sleep and hunger by inducing the release of the neurotransmitter serotonin within the brain. Even the methanol added during the manufacturing of aspartame becomes a poisonous substance when your intake exceeds 250 milligrams per day. The aspartame content of a liter of diet soda is about 549 milligrams, of which 55 milligrams is methanol. Drinking diet soda may only be making weight loss more difficult.

Saccharin, a synthetic sweetener with a long history, has been banned in several countries, including Canada. Saccharin and the artificial sweetener cyclamate, which is marketed under the name Sucaryl, contain no calories. They are nonfoods and have no nutritional value. Sucaryl is a combination of ten parts cyclamate (a salt of cyclamic acid) and one part aspartame, and saccharin is made from petroleum products. Sounds appetizing, doesn't it? Both these artificial sweeteners are so much sweeter than natural sugars that they worsen your sweet tooth. When you eat natural sugars you need more in order to satisfy the sweetener level you've become accustomed to through using artificial sweeteners.

Recently, the U.S. Food and Drug Administration approved the use of Olestra (a fat substitute) in snack foods, and soon it will be in almost all processed food. Olestra supposedly enhances the flavor of foods and matches the "feel" of fat in the mouth. This fake fat contains no calories and has no nutritional value. It passes through the digestive tract unabsorbed and can cause cramping, flatulence, diarrhea, and rectal leakage. Olestra also impedes the absorption of certain important nutrients, such as the fat-soluble vitamins A, D, E, and K. It's possible that the next bag of fat-free potato chips you buy will not only contain MSG, but Olestra as well.

When faced with the dizzying array of sugar, aspartame, saccharin, and synthetic fat additives in so-called diet foods, you're better off eating natural sugars and fats in moderation. At least natural sugar and fats have some nutritional benefits. Artificial sweeteners and synthetic fats have *no* nutritional benefits—just harmful side effects. Saving a few extra calories is simply not worth the harmful side effects.

Food Processing: Yet Another Problem

Food processing creates another problem in terms of meeting your body's nutritional needs. When you consume too many salt-laden, processed foods, your potassium requirements increase dramatically. As a rule, processed foods throw off the crucial balance of sodium and potassium in your body. These two minerals work together. If you consume too much of one, you'll need more of the other to balance it.

Sodium and potassium are vital to the regulation of various body processes, including maintenance of normal water balance, conduction and transmission of nerve impulses, muscle contractions and heart action, and functioning of enzymes. Too much or too little sodium can stimulate hunger and cause sleep difficulties, fluid retention (bloating), and fatigue.

Potassium is also vital to maintaining normal water balance. A potassium deficiency can cause fluid retention (bloating) and fatigue, stimulate hunger, and cause sleep difficulties. There is no RDA for potassium, though most doctors and nutritionists will recommend a daily intake of around 2 to 2.5 grams (1,000 milligrams = 1 gram). I recommend you eat several foods each day that contain potassium and take a mineral complex that contains potassium. Some potassium-rich foods include: bananas (440 mg.); oranges, cantaloupe, raisins, 10 prunes (448 mg.); apricots, cabbage, broccoli, cauliflower, squash, tomatoes, mushrooms, asparagus, potatoes (556 mg.); 1 cup milk (335 mg.); 1 egg (65 mg.); 1 cup oatmeal (146 mg.); molasses and apricot.

It is unfortunate that salt has gotten such a bad reputation. There is nothing bad about sodium in and of itself. Sodium is an important element that helps to maintain normal body fluid volume and plays a part in nerve impulse transmission and muscle contractions. The RDA for sodium is 1,000 to 3,000 milligrams daily. The minimum adult requirement is set at 500 milligrams per day. If you're breast-feeding, the safe minimum requirement is approximately 635 milligrams per day.

It's consuming too much sodium that causes physical problems. Try to keep your sodium intake at 1,500 milligrams per day if you bloat easily. Very little of your salt intake comes from the shaker. In fact, the salt you add at the table accounts for only 6 percent of your overall sodium intake.

Most products that are canned, bottled, frozen, processed, packaged, smoked, or pickled are high in sodium. (See chapter 4 for a list of foods high in sodium.) All fish, except breaded fish, crab, lobster, mussels, shrimp, scallops, and clams, are low in sodium. Baking powder and baking soda, which are used to leaven bread and cakes, contain sodium and are sometimes used in processed vegetables to brighten their color.

You can modify your sodium intake by reading labels carefully. The labeling laws listed below specify how terms relating to sodium levels must be used.

Labeling Laws for Sodium

Sodium free—less than 5 milligrams per serving

Very low sodium—35 milligrams or less per serving

Low sodium—140 milligrams or less per serving

Reduced sodium—product is processed to reduce the overall level of sodium by 75 percent

Unsalted—product is processed without the use of salt, but still contains the sodium originally present in the food

Most of your sodium comes from packaged, processed foods that contain additives such as sodium nitrite, disodium phosphate, monosodium glutamate, sodium alginate, sodium benzoate, and sodium sulfite. Sodium compounds are liberally added to commercially processed foods, making it easy to consume too much sodium without even realizing it. Too much sodium will cause the retention of fluids and the swelling of tissues— factors that will leave you feeling bloated.

There are many other food additives that do not contain sodium but will still cause fluid retention and bloating. Next you'll find a list of some of these nonsodium and sodium food additives that should be avoided if you want to stop retaining fluid and feeling bloated.

Common Food Additives to Avoid

Monosodium glutamate (flavor enhancer)

Hydrolyzed Vegetable Protein (HVP) (flavor enhancer)—contains harmful amounts of MSG

Autolyzed yeast or yeast extract—contains harmful amounts of MSG

Sodium and calcium caseinate (preservative)—contains harmful amounts of MSG

Natural flavors or artificial flavors—may contain harmful amounts of MSG or any one of 100 other harmful chemicals

Sodium nitrite or nitrate (preservative)

Brine (table salt and water)

Disodium phosphate (emulsifier and buffer)

Sodium sulfite (preservative and bleaching agent)

Sodium proprionate (preservative)

Sodium hydroxide (preservative)

Sodium benzoate (preservative)

Sodium alginate (thickening and whitening agent)

Sodium carboxymethylcellulose (thickening and stabilizing agent)

Vanillan and ethyl vanillin (flavoring agent and substitute for natural vanilla)

Butylated hydroxyanisole (BHA) (antioxidant)

Butylated hydroxytoluene (BHT) (antioxidant)

Heptyl paraben (preservative in beer)

Phosphoric acid (acidifier)

Propyl gallate (antioxidant)

Sulfur dioxide (preservative)

Sodium bisulfite (preservative)

EDTA (chelating agent)

Brominated vegetable oil (BVO) (emulsifier)

Saccharin (artificial sweetener)

Aspartame (artificial sweetener)

Artificial Colorings
   Yellow #5 and #6

Red #3 and #4

Blue #1 and #2

Green #3

Orange B (hot dogs)

Citrus red #2 (some oranges)

The Truth About Preservatives

There are a few synthetic microbial preservatives that are harmless, and important to maintaining a safe and abundant food supply. Calcium propionate is a safe preservative used to prevent the growth of certain bacteria and molds on bread. Proprionate is found naturally in Swiss cheese, which explains why mold growth on the surface of Swiss cheese is not a problem. Carrageenan, which is made from seaweed, is also harmless, and is used to thicken and whiten ice cream, jelly, chocolate milk, and infant formula.

On the other hand, the microbial preservative sodium nitrite, used to cure processed meat, is harmful, and should be avoided. Research has shown that nitrosamines, the product of nitrites and nitrates, become potent carcinogenic chemicals when combined with the hydrochloric acid of your stomach. You'll find sodium nitrite in hot dogs, bacon, ham, luncheon meat, smoked fish, and corned beef. It is the nitrites that make these meat products red. Otherwise they would be gray, which is not very appetizing, but then neither are nitrites. The nitrite is broken down into nitrous acid, which combines with hemoglobin in the meat to form the red color. This is similar to what happens in your body as nitrites inactivate red blood cells and create a condition called methemoglobinemia (inactivated hemoglobin), which causes extreme fatigue and irritability.

If you or your kids are "hooked" on hot dogs or processed lunch meat, don't buy hot dogs or any processed meats that have been cured with nitrites or nitrates. Purchase lunch meat and hot dogs that use sodium lactates instead of nitrites or nitrates. The New York Style Sausage Co., and Diestel Brand Turkey are safe and flavorful brands.

Also start taking either a vitamin-C supplement or eat more fruits and vegetables that contain vitamin C. Vitamin C is a proven inhibitor of nitrosamine formation. Another commonly recognized role of vitamin C is in the formation of collagen. Throughout all tissue of the body collagen is the main component of the connective tissue that serves to cement the cells and tissue together. After pregnancy the formation of collagen is essential to your recovery and weight loss. Without adequate collagen, wounds do not heal properly and tend to keep breaking open. Vitamin C is important to maintain the elasticity and strength of normal capillary walls. Vitamin C is found in citrus fruits and other fruit sources, cabbage, broccoli, tomatoes, potatoes, green peppers, and other vegetable sources.

Last, try to eat more grains and vegetable oils that contain vitamin E. Vitamin E is extremely important because of its antioxidant properties, which protect your body from the harmful effects of eating synthetic food additives. Vitamin E takes up oxygen very readily and protects other vitamins, like vitamin A, that are oxidized rather easily in the body. With vitamin E available, oxygen is bound by it rather than left free to oxidize vitamin A and C or polyunsaturated fatty acids.

This is not the only function of vitamin E. This vitamin is a factor in maintaining cell membranes, and therefore helps to prevent the destruction of red blood cells. The production of several enzymes involved in oxygen production require vitamin E. If you want to lose weight and stay healthy, vitamin E must be included in your diet. Some good sources of vitamin E are wheat-germ oil, whole-wheat flour, seeds, almonds, walnuts, dried beans, corn oil, safflower oil, peanut oil, hazelnuts, and green leafy vegetables.

Aggravating the Underlying Problem: Diuretics, Coffee, and Chocolate

If you're a heavy coffee drinker or chocolate addict, or are using diuretics, you may be depleting your body of magnesium and potassium, which are vital to the regulation of body fluids. Caffeine, for instance, is a diuretic. It will stimulate the formation of urine and the removal of water from the body. In dosages of 50 to 200 milligrams it may cause increased alertness, but in dosages of 300 to 500 milligrams it can cause nervousness and muscular tremors. Caffeine raises blood sugar levels and increases heart rate. Caffeine also stimulates the secretion of stomach acids, which is why so many people suffer from an upset stomach after drinking several cups of coffee.

Another very popular source of caffeine is chocolate. Chocolate contains caffeine, beta-phenylethylamine, and theobromine, which are all drugs that are habit forming. If you take diuretics, eat too much chocolate, or drink too much coffee you're only going to feel fat and bloated, by depleting your body of magnesium and potassium.

Magnesium, for example, is involved in every major biological process and is a vital component of the water that flows in and out of your cells. It's the magnesium in the extracellular fluid that bathes nerve cells, helping to conduct nerve impulses that relax muscles following contractions. Magnesium activates a number of enzymes and is involved in the regulation of protein synthesis, muscle contraction, and body temperature.

Substantial quantities of magnesium are stored in the skeletal system, which serves as a reserve during short periods when your dietary intake is deficient. It is found in the cells of soft tissue and catalyzes virtually hundreds of metabolic reactions that result in changes in energy states necessary to losing weight. Adequate magnesium intake promotes the retention of calcium in tooth enamel, and even helps regulate your metabolic rate. The RDA for magnesium is 280 milligrams.

Potassium, as we learned earlier in this chapter, is equally vital to the regulation of various body processes, including maintenance of normal water balance, conduction and transmission of nerve impulses, muscle contractions and heart action, and functioning of enzymes. Too little potassium can cause fluid retention (bloating) and fatigue, stimulate hunger, and cause sleep difficulties. There is no RDA for potassium, though it is thought that around 2,000 milligrams per day are needed.

So overeating chocolate or drinking too much coffee may give you temporary psychological relief, but it will worsen your biological distress by robbing your body of vital nutrients. You also need to relax and remember that bloating is water gain, not fat. Eat wisely to combat the problem and stay off the scale because it will only cause you more frustration.

Start Eating "Clean" Food

If you want to stop feeling fat and bloated, your best bet is to get back to basics and start eating what I call "clean" foods—high-quality, wholesome foods that are free of synthetic additives. Start by eating fewer packaged foods that contain synthetic additives. Instead buy organic produce and organically fed poultry and beef, and eat more whole foods such as fresh fruits, vegetables, grains, nuts, and seeds. Eat fruits and vegetables that have been grown organically—without the use of insecticides, herbicides, or growth-stimulating chemicals.

There are several natural sweeteners you may want to use instead of artificial sweeteners, such as barley, malt, bran, and rice syrup. These natural sweeteners, called grain syrups, are produced when natural enzymes convert the starch in the grain to sugar, which your body can metabolize slowly. These sugars are easy to bake with, have more flavor than table sugar, and are more delicate than molasses.

Nature provides an abundance of whole, unrefined foods that are rich in nutrients and flavor. But instead of enjoying these foods close to their natural state, we fill our shopping carts with so-called fast foods that are refined, processed, and packed with sodium and synthetic additives that are harmful. Stripped of most vitamins and minerals, these foods simply can't meet your nutritional needs.

As the health advantages of eating natural whole foods become increasingly evident, more and more natural food stores and natural food products are appearing all across the country. Never fear, there are some good food manufacturers that use organically grown foods as ingredients in their prepared foods. Organically grown foods are processed, packaged, transported, and stored to retain maximum nutritional value, but the products are not drowned in salt and laden with synthetic preservatives, flavorings, and colorings. In other words, the food is "clean." It is high-quality, flavorful, wholesome food that is free of synthetic additives.

Too Busy to Prepare a Meal? Try Amy's Kitchen

If you get too busy to prepare a meal, you don't need to feel guilty. Look for frozen foods made by Amy's Kitchen at your local supermarket. They make over thirty products that are "clean" and made with all organic ingredients, not synthetic additives. All of Amy's frozen foods have a good home-baked taste and are safe for you and your kids to eat. Your kids will like the pepperoni-style pocket pita or the macaroni and cheese. The family-size vegetable lasagna or cheese enchilada taste great. Even the chocolate fudge cake and strawberry cheese cake are delicious and are affordable.

Take a few moments to compare the ingredients in a couple of Amy's frozen foods to those of another *very* popular frozen food that claims to be healthful:

Amy's Kitchen

Lasagna Ingredients:
Organic cooked lasagna pasta (organic whole-wheat durum flour, organic semolina flour), organic tomatoes, filtered water, low-fat cheese, part-skim mozzarella cheese, onions, organic zucchini, organic spinach, carrots, olive oil, spices, Parmesan cheese, AA butter, sea salt, garlic

Another popular brand

Lasagna Ingredients:
Cooked enriched macaroni product (durum semolina, water, egg white solids, niacin, ferrous sulfate, water, thiamine, mononitrate, riboflavin), tomato puree, cottage cheese, water, tomato paste, part-skim ricotta cheese, organic whey, pasteurized part-skim milk, vinegar, water, organic carrageenan, cooked beef, onions, reduced-fat grade low moisture part-skim mozzarella cheese, pasteurized cultured milk, salt enzymes, less than 2% of: spices, concentrated dealcholized burgundy wine, sugar, salt, cheese, pasteurized part-skim cow's milk, cultures, salts, enzymes, food starch, soy protein, yeast, garlic extract, caramel color, hydrolyzed corn and wheat, and more . . .

Amy's Kitchen

Pocket Pizza Ingredients:
Organic tomatoes, organic wheat flour, nonfat milk, part-skim mozzarella cheese, veggie pepperoni (water, soy protein, tofu, wheat, ground mustard, paprika, beet powder, vegetable gum, nutritional yeast, spices, sea salt), olives, organic whole-wheat flour, grade AA butter, red onions, olive oil, sweet dairy whey, nonaluminum baking powder, sea salt, honey, spices, garlic

Another popular brand

Pocket Pita Ingredients:
Unbleached enriched flour (wheat flour, niacin, iron reduced, thiamine mononitrate, riboflavin), cooked white meat turkey (white turkey, turkey broth, isolated soy protein, salt, sodium phosphate, sugar, flavorings), water, ham water, added ground and formed, natural smoked flavor added (cured water, dextrose, salt, sodium phosphate, dextrose, natural smoked flavors, sodium erythorbate, sodium nitrite), reduced-fat cheddar cheese (cultured pasteurized milk, salt, enzymes, annatto blend), granular and blue cheese (milk, cheese cultures, enzymes, yellow #5), turkey flavor (medium-chain triglycerides, artificial flavorings, BHA, TBHQ, and citric acid), matrodextrin, autolyzed yeast extract, disodium phosphate, citric acid, lactic acid, dough conditioners, and more . . .

Below is a list of several other safe and easy-to-prepare food products that you and your kids can feel good about eating. All are available in supermarkets nationwide.

Some Good "Clean" Foods

Lundberg Family Farms (one-step high-fiber soup and cereals—no MSG, HVP, artificial colors, flavors, or preservatives)
StonyField Farms (organic, low-fat yogurt)
Familia (mixed cereal with fruit and nuts and a blend of wholesome grains)

Auburn Farms, Inc. (toaster pastries made with 100% whole-wheat flour for a snack or breakfast—no artificial ingredients like other pop tarts)

WestBrae Natural (noodles made with whole wheat or rice—no MSG, HVP, or artificial flavors). Just add water and simmer.

Arrowmead Mills (soup mixes, organically grown and produced)

New York Style Sausage Co. (uses sodium lactates instead of nitrates or nitrites)

Diestel Brand Turkey (lunch meat made with no synthetic additives)

Aunt Patsy's Pantry (soup mixes that contain no synthetic additives)

Kashi, Kashi Co. (seven whole grain and sesame breakfast pilaf)

There are several ways you can add flavor to the foods you cook at home without using salt. You'll be surprised at how herbs and spices enhance rather than mask the natural flavor of food. The best prepared seasonings on the market that contain no additives are Mrs. Dash and Spike. At the end of this book you'll find the Everyday Herb Chart for an easy reference when cooking.

12

"I'm Constipated All the Time"
How Fiber, Digestive Enzymes, Beneficial Bacteria, and Fewer Processed Foods Can Help

You made it through pregnancy, childbirth, and night after night of interrupted sleep, but constipation still remains a problem. Constipation can certainly be an annoyance, and it can make you feel frustrated and emotionally fatigued. Being constipated after childbirth is painful, and is caused by hormonal and emotional factors as well as by inadequate fiber and nutrients in the diet. Being constipated after pregnancy can make you feel fat and hopeless about losing weight, which often leads to overeating. Most mothers experience these feelings more intensely after pregnancy because they are extremely sensitive to how their bodies are changing.

Another way that many mothers react to being constipated is to stop eating in hopes of getting rid of their physical and psychological discomfort. This will only worsen the problem by depriving your body of the nutrients and fiber needed to get rid of the bloating. Not eating may give you temporary psychological relief, but it will worsen your biological distress. To begin, relax and remember that the bloating that is making you uncomfortable is not fat, but an accumulation of food and gas that has not passed through your digestive tract.

Laxatives: The Wrong Way to Correct Constipation

If you're doctoring yourself for this condition with commercial laxatives while eating a poor diet you'll find that constipation will be a recurring problem. The regular use of laxatives and enemas is the wrong way to correct constipation. Long-term use of laxatives may cause a problem in the ability of your colon to contract normally and will result in dependence if they are used regularly.

After childbirth the abdominal muscles necessary for elimination have been stretched, making them flaccid and ineffective. So if you're straining your sphincter and abdominal muscles to overcome constipation, you'll only become sore and develop hemorrhoids. You need to get to the root of what is wrong by making changes in the way you eat and operate emotionally. Follow these nine steps and you'll solve your constipation problem:

Step One:

Start taking time to eat slowly, rather than rushing through meals. Eating slowly and chewing food will encourage normal digestion and help eliminate or avoid constipation. By doing this, you'll eat less and have a chance to taste what you're eating. Also, when you chew thoroughly, digestion and nutrient absorption are more efficient.

Eat slowly and ask yourself, "Do I feel comfortable?" Stop eating before you have to loosen your clothing or lie down because you're too full. Your brain is always sending you signals about hunger and satiety—listen to it. Listening to your body means eating smaller, more frequent meals and snacks. When you eat too much too quickly you lose touch with your body's needs. Your stomach is only about the size of your fist. It is like an expandable elastic bag that collapses when it is not inflated. There's no need to stuff it!

Step Two:

Eat smaller, more frequent meals and controlled snacks. To overcome constipation you must eat small portion sizes—no large meals. Controlled snacking means eating something nourishing every few hours. This acts as a bridge of energy between meals, while maintaining an even blood sugar level and digestive functioning. You can find snack suggestions and menu plans in the last chapter of this book.

Step Three:

Drink a good amount of water or other liquids with your meals to soften stools. Drinking less than eight glasses of water or liquid daily often leads to or prolongs constipation. Skimping on water can even cause fiber to be constipating. You must drink enough liquid so the fiber can create a soft bulk. If stools become too hard, you may develop painful hemorrhoids.

Hemorrhoids, the abnormal enlargement of veins in the anal area, are often the result of increased pressure at the time of elimination. Warm baths and the use of a pain-relieving spray called Dermoplast will soothe inflammation and itching when flare-ups occur. Cortisone-containing creams and suppositories may be used, but only under the supervision of a physician.

Rutin, a bioflavonoid, is useful in helping to get rid of hemorrhoids. Bioflavonoids are water soluble and are members of the group of compounds called flavonoids. Bioflavonoids, which are present in the rind and pulp of citrus fruits, are found naturally in oranges, grapefruits, and lemons. Keep in mind that the pulpy portion of the fruits contains ten times as many bioflavonoids as the strained juice. Other good food sources of bioflavonoids are apricots, cherries, plums, black currants, grapes, green peppers, tomatoes, broccoli, cantaloupe, and papaya. The buckwheat plant, both the leaf and grain, is also a good source of the bioflavonoid rutin. You can get rutin from these food sources, or you can purchase a rutin supplement at most health food stores. It is sold separately or often combined with a vitamin C supplement.

Vitamin C (ascorbic acid), found in fruits and vegetables, is also a gentle, safe digestive aid. Or you can add 2 grams of pure vitamin C powder or crystals to a glass of water and drink it slowly. Most people can tolerate vitamin C powder or crystals, but not tablets or capsules, even when they are taken with a meal. If you've had a bad reaction to a vitamin C supplement, most likely you were reacting to the coloring agent, binders, and fillers used in the processing of the tablet. A vitamin-C supplement made from pH-neutral mineral ascorbates, like calcium ascorbate, will not irritate the digestive system. Fat-soluble vitamin C, also called ascorbyl palmitate, can be used instead of the usual ascorbic acid vitamin C, which can sometimes irritate the stomach.

Step Four:
Start a moderate exercise program. Physical activities increase bowel functioning. You need to move around. Prolonged sitting will only worsen constipation. Walking is the answer. It fits into the hectic schedule of family life better than any other type of exercise and is available at any time and anywhere. It doesn't require expensive equipment or the need for a baby-sitter. Remember, if you've been sedentary for a while, start out slowly. Your body will appreciate and respond positively to even a short walk.

Step Five:
Set aside time to relax, and try whenever possible to go to the bathroom alone. This might be the most difficult step of all. New mothers often avoid or rush going to the bathroom because they fear splitting open their stitches and the discomfort of hemorrhoids. Allow yourself plenty of private and quiet time. You need to relax. Stress and the emotional upheaval of motherhood can profoundly effect digestion. Digestion is connected to your feelings. This is because both digestion and emotions are controlled by your nervous system. Changes in hormone levels, sleep cycles, and your emotional state after pregnancy can disrupt the production of digestive enzymes and cause digestive problems.

Step Six:
Supplement your diet with digestive aids. By promoting the proper digestion of foods with digestive enzymes, betaine hydrochloride (HCL), and several strains of beneficial bacteria, you can help prevent and eliminate constipation. An HCL supplement will improve digestion of meals containing protein and fat. Hydrochloric acid is available in tablet form and can be taken before, during, or after meals, and is safe to take when breast-feeding. Betaine hydrochloride can be taken alone, or along with

digestive-enzyme capsules, which contain amylase, proteases (trypsin and chymotrypsin), pepsin, bromelaine, and papain.

There are several other digestive aids, such as acidophilus milk, yogurt, and cultured buttermilk. These products have been cultured with the beneficial *lactobacillus acidophilus*, which aids in digestion. There are several other strains of beneficial bacteria, such as *lactobacillus bulgaricus, streptococcus thermophilus*, and *bifidobacterium bifidum*, that combat constipation by aiding in digestion and returning the intestinal flora to a healthier balance. All four of these beneficial bacteria aid in the production of B vitamins by creating a healthy intestinal flora. When you take antibiotics, birth control pills, or corticosteroids, the beneficial bacteria in your digestive tract are destroyed and need to be replaced. Because these beneficial bacteria are also sensitive to the harsh acids of your digestive tract, absorption is usually difficult. Therefore, I recommend you take these beneficial bacteria in powder form. By using a powder supplement you get a greater number of beneficial bacteria and better absorption. There is a powdered formula produced by Natren, Inc., called Mega-dophillus, that contains all four of these bacteria. The nondairy formulas are best for people who are allergic to dairy products. You can sprinkle 1 teaspoon of powder on cereal or mix it into yogurt in the morning, and then take it one hour before lunch and dinner.

Step Seven:
Avoid eating refined or simple carbohydrates (white-flour and sugar products, etc.) that do not contain fiber. Refined carbohydrates and processed foods (synthetic fats and artificial sweeteners) no longer resemble what is found in nature. If refined and fried foods are a large part of your diet, you're lacking not only valuable nutrients, but also fiber and bulk. When there's no fiber to make bulk, the feces become hard and don't move quickly through the colon. The more refined or processed a food is, the less work your digestive system has to do and the more quickly absorption takes place. The more nutrients and fiber a food has, the slower the process of absorption.

For instance, an uncooked apple is an unrefined complex carbohydrate that contains fiber, and you must chew it. It is then broken down further by digestive enzymes before it can be absorbed through the intestinal wall. However, when that apple is refined or processed and made into commercially prepared apple sauce, it becomes a simple carbohydrate that lacks fiber and is broken down into glucose much faster during digestion. So it's much better for you to eat the raw apple.

White flour is another refined food that is low in fiber. It is made from refined wheat grain. During the refining process, most of the fiber, vitamins, and minerals are destroyed when the germ of the wheat is removed. If you regularly purchase white bread, gradually change to 100 percent whole-wheat bread. When baking, substitute ½ cup of 100 percent whole-wheat flour for each cup of white flour. Each time you make a recipe, increase the amount of wheat flour while decreasing the amount of white flour until eventually you use all 100 percent whole-wheat flour.

Fiber is not found in meat, cheese, or refined or processed foods. And you won't find fiber in processed snack foods or fried foods. What you will find is the new synthetic fat substitute called Olestra. You should avoid any foods that contain Olestra because it passes through the digestive tract unabsorbed, and can cause cramping and painful gas, and can worsen constipation.

It is best to avoid drinking soda if you're constipated. Guzzling diet soda is an unhealthy diet behavior. Most diet sodas are laden with artificial flavors, artificial colors, artificial sweeteners, preservatives, and caffeine. They are 99 percent carbonated water and contain saccharin, aspartame (NutraSweet or Equal) or a blend of the two. The artificial sweeteners and the caffeine will cause you to urinate more frequently and lose valuable water, which can aggravate or cause constipation. The carbonation in the soda warms up in the body and produces carbon dioxide, which fills you up with gas. Drinking too much soda can cause carbon dioxide fixation, a condition that occurs when the phosphoric acid in soda that holds the sugar in suspension so it will not crystallize combines with the carbon dioxide and creates an extraction of osteoblast. Because there is too much carbon dioxide in the system, calcium and other minerals in the bones are easily extracted.

Munching on potato chips containing Olestra and guzzling soda will give you more gas pain than you had labor pain. Water with a slice of lemon is a much better choice than diet soda.

Step Eight:

Eat more fiber-rich, unrefined, complex carbohydrates—grains, nuts, fruits, and vegetables. These foods are good sources of B vitamins, iron, and vitamins A and C. Complex carbohydrates are made up of long-chain sugar molecules that are slowly broken down into smaller molecules of glucose during digestion. In other words, fiber slows the rate of absorption of sugar over a longer period of time, and can reduce your craving for more sugar. A fiber-rich diet is the best way to eliminate constipation and lower serum cholesterol.

Fiber also helps control weight in several other ways. It adds bulk to the diet and provides a feeling of fullness. And since the digestive tract does not break the fiber down into forms that can be used for energy, it doesn't contain calories. That's right, fiber contains no calories. Many of the so-called diet drinks, such as Slim Fast, are simply a mixture of various kinds of fiber. However, this is an expensive way to get your fiber.

Fiber is an internal regulator that accelerates the transit of food through the digestive tract while absorbing liquid and producing bulk. An adequate fiber intake means less strain to move your bowels and less risk of hemorrhoid and diverticular disease. Consuming enough fiber also decreases the risk of colon cancer, because food passes through the intestine quickly so that it does not interact with unfriendly intestinal bacteria. And here's one last reason to make fiber an important part of your diet: Fat binds with fiber as it moves through the intestinal tract, resulting in the absorption of fewer calories.

There Are Several Kinds of Dietary Fiber

Fiber is the indigestible part of plant food. There are several kinds of dietary fiber: pectins, gums, cellulose, mucilages, hemicellulose, and lignin.

All fiber sources except lignin (a woody substance found in asparagus and rhubarb) are classified as complex carbohydrates. Gums, pectins, mucilages, and certain hemicelluloses are *soluble* fibers that dissolve in water, and will lower absorption of cholesterol and overall fat, and regulates blood sugar, by slowing the absorption of sugar into the bloodstream. Cellulose, lignin, and hemicellulose are *insoluble* fibers and do not dissolve in water; instead, they absorb water, accelerating the transit time of food and softening stools. Insoluble fibers are those that pass through the digestive tract almost unchanged, except that they have been broken down by chewing. They absorb up to fifteen times their weight in water. Insoluble fibers have little or no effect on blood cholesterol. Instead their role is to prevent constipation.

The calcium pectate present in the soluble fiber of a carrot helps to lower cholesterol. The soluble fiber in other vegetables such as onions and cabbage have similar cholesterol-fighting effects. The soluble fiber in barley has been found to help with the regulation of cholesterol made in the liver. Oat bran and rice bran contain more of the insoluble fibers, which seem to have no effect on cholesterol levels. Other grains, such as buckwheat, amaranth, and quinoa are not true grains. They belong to a botanical family different from that of wheat, rice, oats, rye, corn, barley, millet, and triticale, but their kernels all have a similar composition. They all have an edible seed composed of three parts—the bran, endosperm, and germ.

For bowel regularity, bran (insoluble fiber) is the best option. Two tablespoons of unprocessed bran a day followed by 8 ounces of water can help eliminate constipation. Don't forget you need to increase your intake of liquid considerably. Too little liquid can cause fiber to be constipating. You need liquid to create a soft bulk. The bulky stool stimulates peristalsis, the rhythmic contractions of the bowel that allow easy and rapid movement through the digestive tract. This prevents constipation and related problems, such as hemorrhoids.

Complex carbohydrates have a mixture of soluble and insoluble fibers, but certain foods may have a little more of one than another. Try to eat

FIBER

Soluble	Insoluble
(Lowers absorption of cholesterol and overall fat; regulates blood sugar)	(Accelerates transit time of food; softens stools)
Fruits and vegetables (carrots, cabbage, onions, apples, and citrus fruits)	Some fruits and vegetables (pears, peaches, prunes, plums, asparagus)
Oats (oatmeal, oat bran)	Whole grains (wheat bread or muffins, wheat bran, rice bran, hulled barley, rye, millet, buckwheat, quinoa, amaranth, oat bran)
Barley (pearl)	
Legumes (beans, peas, lentils)	
Psyllium seeds (found in most commercial laxatives)	
Flaxseeds	Nuts and seeds (sunflower, pumpkin)
Sea vegetables (kombu, kelp, agar, carrageenan)	

a wide variety of fruits, vegetables, and grains so you get a total of 20 to 35 grams from both soluble and insoluble fibers per day.

The Side-Effects of Eating Too Much Fiber

There is no RDA for fiber. The Center for Food Safety and Applied Nutrition recommends a range of 20 to 35 grams of dietary fiber per day. Consuming large amounts of bran and other high-fiber supplements can produce intestinal obstruction. Although fiber supplements are available in tablets and powder mixes, it's best to start eating foods high in fiber. Both prunes and figs are natural laxatives that are high in fiber. Any increase in fiber intake should be gradual, in order to give your digestive system time to adjust. But if you become constipated in spite of all your best efforts, here's what to do: If you feel that you need a laxative, use a natural one. Take a fiber supplement, such as psyllium seed or pectin, and use only the powder mixes. Avoid fiber supplements in capsule or pill form. If you use fiber supplements, be sure to take them with an 8-ounce glass of water. Anytime you add fiber to your diet you must drink at least eight 8-ounce glasses of water every day, whether you're thirsty or not.

There is another side effect that comes from consuming too much fiber. That's right—intestinal gas and bloating. Beans contain soluble fiber and two nonabsorbable sugars (raffinose and stachyose) that are fermented by intestinal bacteria. This fermentation creates large quantities of intestinal gas. Soybeans, cabbage, spinach, broccoli, brussels sprouts, cauliflower, and eggplant are all gas-producing. You don't want to avoid eating these nutritious and high-fiber foods. So your best approach for eating these foods is to eat small amounts at a time. Another suggestion is to remove the cover for one minute when you're steaming these vegetables.

Salads are excellent sources of fiber. Skip the iceberg lettuce and experiment with lettuces and leafy greens from other botanical families. They are terrific sources of dietary fiber as well as vitamin C, beta carotene, iron, calcium, and folic acid. As a general rule, the darker green the leaves, the more nutritious the salad green. Romaine and loose-leaf lettuce, for example, have up to eight times as much vitamin C and almost ten times as much beta carotene as iceberg lettuce.

By varying the greens in your salad, you can enhance the nutritional content as well as the taste and texture. You can create endless combinations, from a simple mix of lettuce and greens to main-course salads that incorporate a selection of other vegetables, cheeses, and even turkey or chicken. Try a few new leafy combinations from the following list.

Lettuce	Nonlettuce Greens
Butter (Boston & Bibb)	Arugula
Loose-leaf (green leaf, red leaf, red oak leaf, limestone)	Belgian endive
	Chicory
Romaine	Escarole
	Radicchio
	Watercress
	Spinach
	Baby bok choy

The following chart lists the amount of soluble and insoluble fiber contained in a selection of nutritious foods.

FIBER CONTENT OF FOODS

Foods	Serving Size	Total Fiber (grams)	Soluble Fiber (grams)	Insoluble Fiber (grams)
Apple	1 small	3.9	2.3	1.6
Pear	1 small	2.5	0.6	1.9
Prunes	3 medium	2.3	1.3	1.0
Strawberries	3/4 cup	2.4	0.9	1.5
Apricots	2 medium	1.3	0.9	0.4
Banana	1 small	1.3	0.6	0.7
Peach	1 small	1.0	0.5	0.5
Grapefruit	1 medium	1.3	0.9	0.4
Pinto beans	1/2 cup	3.0	0.3	2.7
Peanuts	10	1.0	0	1.0
Almonds	10	1.0	0	1.0
Sweet potato	1 small	3.8	2.2	1.6
Broccoli	1/2 cup	2.6	1.6	1.0
Zucchini	1/2 cup	2.5	1.1	1.4
Lettuce	1 cup	0.5	0.2	0.3
Pasta (whole wheat)	1/2 cup	1.1	0.3	0.8
Popcorn	3 cups	2.8	0.8	2.0
Bread (whole-wheat)	1 slice	2.8	.08	2.7
Oatmeal	1/2 cup	1.6	0.5	1.1
Brown rice	1/2 cup	1.3	0	1.3

Step Nine:

Make sure that your vitamin and mineral supplement contains a nonconstipating form of iron. Try an iron supplement that contains ferrous gluconate or ferrous fumarate. When these iron supplements are taken, they do not cause constipation and intestinal upset. Try your best to make these changes—you'll feel the result immediately! On the following page are the nine steps we just discussed.

Nine Steps to Avoiding and Overcoming Constipation

Step One: Start taking time to eat slowly—don't rush through meals.

Step Two: Eat smaller, more frequent meals. Try to eat a snack every few hours to maintain an even blood sugar level and digestive function.

Step Three: Drink eight glasses of water or liquid daily to soften stools.

Step Four: Move around or take a walk to increase bowel function. Prolonged sitting can worsen constipation.

Step Five: Set aside time to relax and try whenever possible to go to the bathroom alone.

Step Six: Use digestive aids such as betaine hydrochloride (HCL) and digestive enzyme capsules before, during, or after meals to prevent or eliminate constipation.

Step Seven: Eat fewer refined simple carbohydrates (white flour, sugar products, etc.) that do not contain fiber.

Step Eight: Eat more fiber-rich unrefined complex carbohydrates like grains, nuts, fruits, and vegetables.

Step Nine: Take a vitamin and mineral supplement that contains a form of iron that is nonconstipating.

13

"I Really Need Some Help Getting Started"

So, you say you're a procrastinator and just can't seem to get going. Getting started is the most difficult part about changing your eating habits. What makes it so difficult is that you have to be totally self-motivated until you experience some success and positive reinforcement. You must also take the time to make these changes specifically for yourself. Not only will you be happier, but your children will hopefully grow up with the understanding that Mom has needs and desires as well.

Doing Nothing

Your first step is to stop thinking about all the changes you have to make, and start doing something—anything. Doing nothing but thinking produces anxiety. Doing nothing requires more energy because you're always worrying about what you are supposed to do. Eventually, all the worrying tires you out, and no change has occurred. Any change, no matter how small, will give you a feeling of accomplishment.

Do you sometimes feel you'd prefer to eat nothing rather than just a teensy bit of food? It's this type of rigid and inflexible behavior that will keep you struggling with your body weight forever. If you want to lose weight you must engage in self-fulfilling behavior that is kind and compassionate, not self-depriving behavior that leaves you frustrated and angry.

Do you think it's easier to lose weight when you don't have to make any choices? Not wanting to make choices will once again lead you to stagnation. It is by making choices that you develop the motivation that comes from deep within. You need to make choices and decisions about what you eat. It is the only way to become healthy, happy, and in control of eating.

This chapter has Forty Helpful Review Tips, which will get you off to a good start, along with an Everyday Herb Chart and Food Substitute Chart, which will help you regulate the sodium, sugar, and fat in your diet. The four week-long menu plans are easy to prepare, wholesome, and taste good. The food is different each day, so you can freeze leftovers and repeat a menu that you like.

In the following pages, you'll find over fifty recipes, including snack suggestions, that look, smell, and taste terrific. All recipes are quick and easy to prepare and are rich in the nutrients you need after pregnancy. At the end of each recipe you'll find a list of the nutrients contained in the dish. By knowing what nutrients a recipe contains, you can select one that best meets your nutritional needs.

You'll be pleased to know that fat, sugar, salt, and eggs have not been eliminated from the recipes. Instead, all ingredients have been carefully used so that each recipe reaches its desired flavor point, which is when food tastes its best and is still healthful. When you're cooking foods at home, keep in mind that once you've reached the flavor point, adding more sugar or fat will only add calories. Also, when you eat at a restaurant you must always ask how each dish is cooked. Then tell the waiter that you want your food either steamed, boiled, or broiled without a mountain of butter and salt. And when you go to a party, eat beforehand so you won't nibble on high-calorie foods.

As we have learned, you need not become a health nut, nor do you have to give up everything you love to eat to lose weight. You can have your cake and eat it, too, as long as it's not too much cake too often. Whether or not you are aware of it, nutrition can help you enormously. Incredible though it may seem, every vitamin, mineral, and protein found in the food you eat has a distinct and specific effect on both your mind and body.

You can start by reading through the "Forty Helpful Review Tips" below. Don't forget: If you take care of your body, it will take care of you. Give your body a chance to work for you. It will all be well worth your patience.

Forty Helpful Review Tips

1. Give yourself credit for any progress you make. Being a mother is a difficult job; don't make it more difficult by trying to do too much. You'll get your body back. It just takes time and patience.

2. Taking care of yourself emotionally and physically is truly the greastest contribution you can make to your family.

3. You need to adjust to the new you. Once you have a baby, you change significantly as your body chemistry undergoes specific bio-chemical, biological, and psychological changes. You are no longer the same person.

4. Express how you feel. Emotions were meant to be expressed. If they are not expressed, fear, frustration, love, and anger can all be displaced onto food.

5. Asking for help from others doesn't make you morally weaker than another mother. You may need help at the moment, but this doesn't suggest a lifelong weakness of character.

6. Your thoughts and emotions are the result of chemical processes going on within your brain. Proper nutrition can help stabilize your brain chemistry and your mood.

7. When you're depressed, you overeat because of an emotional hunger rather than a physical hunger.

8. Knowledge is power: The more you know about your own body, the more patient you'll be and the greater your chances of losing weight without a struggle.

9. Don't try to force your body to lose weight by restricting food or overexercising. Give your body all the time it needs to make the necessary metabolic changes.

10. Learn how to identify and adjust to your own metabolic type. Read chapter 2.

11. After pregnancy you need a greater supply of certain nutrients, not only for milk production, but for regulating hunger and balancing your brain's chemistry. Remember, it's food that supplies your brain with nutrients.

12. After pregnancy hunger and satiety signals change significantly. So it's important that you pay attention and work with these new signals if you want to control your hunger and lose weight.

13. Try not to skip meals or leave yourself hungry. Instead, eat smaller, more frequent meals and controlled snacks.

14. Eat slowly, rather than rushing through meals. Eating slowly and chewing food will encourage normal digestion and help eliminate or avoid constipation.

15. Don't get hung up on calorie counting. Instead, evaluate the amount you eat. Stick with the foods you've been eating; just cut down on portion sizes.

16. Always drink water before, during, and after exercise, and when you're losing weight. When you breast-feed you must not only eat well, but most important drink plenty of fluids.

17. Hunger is a function of brain and mind. The nutrients found in the food you eat are brain- and mind-altering substances. So you must learn how to satisfy your hunger, and stop trying to ignore it.

18. Your brain's ability to regulate hunger and satiety is remarkable, but it can't do it alone. Without proper carbohydrates, protein, fats, vitamins, and minerals, neurotransmitters are unable to function effectively. Just as your digestive tract absorbs nutrients, so does your brain.

19. Compare the vitamin and mineral content of a food to its caloric content. This way you can easily determine why a bag of potato chips with little nutritional value will never satisfy your hunger.

20. If you don't eat enough protein while breast-feeding, the protein your baby needs will be drawn from your muscles. You must con-

serve muscle mass; it's muscle that burns fat, and the more muscle you have, the more fat you'll burn.

21. After you have a baby it's important that you maintain your lean body mass. To do this it's essential you have sufficient carbohydrates and fat calories in your diet to create a protein-sparing effect.

22. Although breast-feeding does utilize more calories, it will also increase hunger.

23. Most mothers experience more salt cravings than they do sugar cravings. Part of your hunger after pregnancy is due to an increase in thirst and the retention of body fluids.

24. Too much or too little sodium can stimulate hunger and cause sleep difficulties and a potassium deficiency, which, in turn, can cause fluid retention and bloating.

25. Getting a restful sleep is not only refreshing but biologically necessary if you are to lose weight.

26. When you eat hot foods you reach a sense of satiety or fullness sooner than if you eat cold foods.

27. The metabolism of fat is a complex process and cannot be rushed. No diet pill has ever been able to change the way fat functions or burns in the body.

28. Fats are important nutrients. In fact, you need fat to burn fat. Fats are essential for the utilization of other nutrients and for the production of hormones. Eating the right types of fats in moderation can actually help you lose weight.

29. The essential fatty acids strengthen cell membranes, which are your body's first defense against yeast infections.

30. *Candida albicans* infection can affect the way your body absorbs and excretes biotin, B_6, and magnesium. Most mothers don't eat enough foods rich in these nutrients.

31. When you have a yeast infection, avoid foods that contain yeast as well as molds and products that have been fermented.

32. Chemical processes that modify foods tamper not only with the basic structure of a food, but with your health and the health of your baby.

33. If refined foods are a large part of your diet, then you're lacking valuable nutrients, fiber, and bulk. Eat more fiber-rich, unrefined, complex carbohydrates, which include grains, nuts, fruits, and vegetables.

34. It's up to you to take the time to read food labels so you can avoid unsafe food additives and keep your sodium intake to about 1,500 milligrams per day.

35. If you're constipated, try taking a digestive aid, which is available at health food stores.

36. Take a daily vitamin and mineral supplement (capsule or straight powder) that is free of yeast, corn, wheat, lactose (milk sugar), sugar, salt, artificial sweeteners, fillers, binders, coatings, colorings, preservatives, or salicylates. Salicylates decrease the effectiveness of vitamin C and increase the need for vitamin K when used over a long period of time. Your supplement should contain a form of iron that is nonconstipating, like a combination of ferrous sulfate and sodium fumarate or an elemental iron from carbonyl.

37. Start exercising faithfully.

38. Try eating foods that are close to their natural state. Nature provides an abundance of whole, unrefined foods that are rich in nutrients and flavor.

39. When you eat at any restaurant, you must always ask how each dish is cooked. When you go to a party, eat beforehand, so you won't nibble on high-calorie foods.

40. If you take care of your body, it will take care of you. Give your body a chance to work for you. It will be well worth your patience.

Four Week-Long Menu Plans

Just because you're cooking on a tight schedule doesn't mean you have to live on processed prepared foods. With a little planning and know-how you can easily prepare flavorful, high-quality, wholesome foods. In fact, your family can be fed more healthfully and economically with fresh whole foods than with any processed prepared foods. As a mother, you have the greatest influence on the health of your family. Whenever you prepare fresh whole foods, you have invested in your family's mental and physical health, and the value of that cannot be measured in dollars and cents. You and your family also need to take a daily multivitamin and mineral supplement. Supplements should always be taken with meals to facilitate absorption and to prevent the nausea that often occurs when supplements are simply swallowed with water or juice.

The following four week-long menu plans will help you get off to a good start. The menus are simple and well balanced. Food items marked with an asterisk (*) appear in the recipe section that follows. The ingredients in the recipes are designed to provide a better variety and amount of important nutrients than that normally found in an average diet. You may want to repeat menus so that you don't end up with too many leftover ingredients. Remember that leftover foods easily lend themselves to casseroles, and sometimes taste better than when they were first served.

WEEK ONE

	Breakfast	Snack	Lunch	Snack	Dinner
Day One	1 cup oatmeal with 2 Tbsp. 100% bran cereal 1 Tbsp. raisins 1 cup skim milk	3 Tbsp. cottage cheese on whole-wheat bagel with cucumber slices Water with lemon	Grilled cheese sandwich (2 oz. cheese) 1 bunch grapes Water with lemon	1 Tbsp. peanut butter on 1/2 apple, sliced 1/2 cup skim milk	4 oz. salmon, broiled 1/2 cup carrots 1 small baked potato 1 cup skim milk
Day Two	1 cup yogurt 1 Tbsp. wheat germ 1 cup strawberries	1 bran muffin 1 cup skim milk	*Tomato and Ricotta on rye bread 1 cup skim milk	*Cauliflower Salad Water with lemon	*Creamy Almond Chicken 1 cup skim milk

	Breakfast	Snack	Lunch	Snack	Dinner
Day Three	Cinnamon French toast (use 2 eggs) 1/4 cup milk 1/2 cup blueberries Water with lemon	1/2 grapefruit 4 whole-grain crackers	*2 Vegetarian Tostadas 1 cup skim milk	1/2 whole-wheat bagel with 1 Tbsp. cottage cheese and 1 Tbsp. orange marmalade Water with lemon	3/4 cup spaghetti sauce over 1 cup pasta 1/2 cup zucchini 1 cup skim milk
Day Four	1 (7-grain) waffle 1/2 grapefruit 1 cup skim milk	*Fresh Peanut Butter and Pear Spread on 2 graham crackers 1/2 cup skim milk	1 sandwich (2 oz. Diestel brand turkey) 1/2 apple 1 cup skim milk	*Cauliflower Salad Water with lemon	4 oz. shrimp 1 cup brown rice 1/2 cup broccoli Water with lemon
Day Five	2-egg omelet with tomatoes and onions 1 slice whole-wheat toast 1 cup cranberry juice	1 bran muffin 1 cup skim milk	*1 bowl Barley Mushroom Soup 2 whole-wheat crackers Small salad 1/2 cup skim milk	1 apple 1 oz. cheese Water with lemon	1 Amy's Kitchen Bean Burrito 1 cup brown rice bunch of grapes 1 cup skim milk
Day Six	1 cup Raisin Bran cereal 1 cup milk 1/2 orange	*Fresh Peanut Butter and Pear Spread on 2 graham crackers 1 cup skim milk	*Cheese-Stuffed Potato 1/2 cup strawberries Water with lemon	*1 cup Barley Mushroom Soup 1 peach Water with lemon	*Beef with Pea Pods 1 cup skim milk
Day Seven	1 cup yogurt 2 Tbsp. 100% bran cereal Water with lemon	1/2 grapefruit 4 whole-wheat crackers 1 cup skim milk	*2 Vegetarian Tostadas 1 cup skim milk	*Fresh Peanut Butter and Pear Spread on 2 graham crackers Water with lemon	3/4 cup spaghetti sauce over 1 cup pasta 1 cup skim milk

WEEK TWO

	Breakfast	Snack	Lunch	Snack	Dinner
Day One	1/2 cantaloupe 1 Tbsp. peanut butter on 1 slice whole-wheat toast 1 cup skim milk	1/2 cup low-fat cottage cheese with 1 peach, sliced Water with lemon	*Zucchini Sandwich 1 cup skim milk	1 apple, chopped, added to 1 cup coleslaw (use yogurt for the dressing) Water with lemon	4 oz. chicken, sliced, added to frozen stir-fried vegetables and noodles 1 cup skim milk
Day Two	*Kashi with Honey 1 cup skim milk	1 cup acorn squash, baked raisins Water with lemon	1 pita sandwich with zucchini, bean 2 Tbsp. shredded cheese 2 Tbsp. yogurt with mustard	1/2 cup low-fat cottage cheese with peaches Water with lemon	*Fillet of Sole 1 cup brown rice 6 asparagus spears 1 cup skim milk
Day Three	1 (7-grain) waffle 1/2 grapefruit 1 cup skim milk	*1 Orange-Yogurt Muffin 1 cup skim milk	*Zesty Lentil Salad 1/2 apple Water with lemon	*Peanut Butter and Pear Spread on 2 graham crackers 1 cup skim milk	Amy's Organic Vegetable and Pot Pie 1/2 cup pears Water with lemon
Day Four	Couscous (cook like rice) 1 Tbsp. honey 3 pitted prunes 1 cup skim milk	*Sesame Carrots Water with lemon	*Spiced beans 1/2 whole-wheat bagel 1 cup skim milk	1/2 grapefruit Water with lemon	*Braised Veal Chops with Fennel 1/2 cup corn 1 cup skim milk
Day Five	*2 Apple Cheese pancakes (freeze remaining pancakes) Water with lemon	*1 Orange-Yogurt Muffin 1 cup skim milk	*1 bowl Corn Chowder 1/2 orange Water with lemon	1 apple 4 crackers 1 cup skim milk	*Cajun-Style Red Snapper 1 cup cauliflower 1 cup skim milk

	Breakfast	Snack	Lunch	Snack	Dinner
Day Six	1 cup oatmeal 2 Tbsp. 100% bran cereal 1 Tbsp. raisins 1 cup skim milk	*Gingered Sweet Potatoes 1 cup skim milk	*Amy's Organic Macaroni and Cheese Water with lemon	*1 Apple-Cheese Pancake Water with lemon	*Sweet and Sour Pork 1 small baked potato 1/2 cup green beans 1 cup skim milk
Day Seven	2-egg omelet with tomatoes and onions 1 slice whole-wheat toast 1 cup cranberry juice	1 bran muffin 1 cup skim milk	*1 bowl Corn Chowder 1/2 whole-wheat bagel	1 apple 4 crackers 1 cup skim milk	Amy's Organic Ravioli and Cheese 1/2 cantaloupe 1 cup skim milk

WEEK THREE

	Breakfast	Snack	Lunch	Snack	Dinner
Day One	2 whole-wheat pancakes with blueberries 1 cup skim milk	1 string cheese stick 1/2 apple Water with lemon	Spinach salad with tomatoes, mushrooms, sesame seeds & 2 Tbsp. olive oil & vinegar 1 cup skim milk	1 pear 1 oz. cheese Water with lemon	Amy's Organic Pasta and Vegetable Lasagna 1 cup skim milk
Day Two	1 cup yogurt 2 Tbsp. wheat germ 1 cup strawberries Water with lemon	*1 Pumpkin Square 1 cup skim milk	Pita Sandwich with 2 oz. Diestel brand turkey, 1 oz. feta cheese, tomatoes, radishes Water with lemon	1 banana dipped in honey and peanuts 1 cup skim milk	4 oz. beef sirloin steak, sliced thinly Stir-fried pea pods 1 cup pasta 1 cup skim milk

	Breakfast	Snack	Lunch	Snack	Dinner
Day Three	1 cup Raisin Bran cereal 1 cup skim milk 1/2 banana	1 rice cake with sliced tomatoes, avocado, onions, and cucumbers 1 cup skim milk	*1 bowl Cream of Broccoli Soup 3 crackers Water with lemon	*Low-Fat French Fries 1 cup skim milk	1 cup red cabbage 1/2 cup diced carrots and onions stir-fried with 1 Tbsp. olive oil & 6 shrimp Water with lemon
Day Four	2-egg omelet with tomatoes and onions 1 slice whole-wheat toast 1 orange Water with lemon	1/2 apple 4 crackers Water with lemon	*1 bowl Vegetable & Beef Stew 1 corn muffin 1 cup skim milk	*1 Pumpkin Square 1 cup skim milk	Amy's Organic Pocket Pizza 1 cup skim milk
Day Five	1 (7-grain) waffle 1/2 grapefruit 1 cup skim milk	*1 Strawberry-Oatmeal Bar 1 cup skim milk	1 bowl *Cream of Broccoli Soup 3 crackers Water and lemon	1/2 apple 1 oz. cheese Water with lemon	4 oz. halibut steak 1 baked potato 1/2 cup brussels sprouts 1 cup skim milk
Day Six	1 cup oatmeal 1 Tbsp. raisins 1 cup skim milk	1 apple 1 oz. cheese Water with lemon	*Tomato and Riccota Sandwich on rye bread Water with lemon	*Low-Fat French Fries 1 cup skim milk	*1 bowl Vegetable Beef Stew 1 corn muffin 1 cup skim milk
Day Seven	1 bran muffin 1/2 banana 1 cup skim milk	*1 Strawberry-Oatmeal Bar 1 cup skim milk	1 cup yogurt with blueberries 1 Tbsp. wheat germ Water with lemon	1/2 bagel 1 string cheese stick 1/2 grapefruit Water with lemon	Amy's Organic Black Bean Vegetable Tortillas 1 cup skim milk

WEEK FOUR

	Breakfast	Snack	Lunch	Snack	Dinner
Day One	1/2 grapefruit 1 slice whole-wheat toast Water with lemon	*Spicy Carrot Muffin 1 cup skim milk	Pita sandwich (Diestel brand turkey) 1 oz. feta cheese, tomatoes, radishes Water with lemon	1 rice cake with avocado, tomato, and cucumber 1 cup skim milk	Amy's Country Dinner with Gravy, mashed potatoes, green beans, apple crisp 1 cup skim milk
Day Two	1 cup cream of wheat with cinnamon & honey 1/2 banana 1 cup cranberry juice	Bunch of grapes Water with lemon	*Mixed Vegetable Marinade 1 cup skim milk	*1 Spicy Carrot Muffin 1 cup skim milk	1 small baked potato 6 asparagus spears 1 cup skim milk
Day Three	1 (7-grain) waffle 1 orange 1 cup skim milk	*Spicy Carrot Muffin 1 cup skim milk	*Zucchini Sandwich 1 cup cranberry juice	1/2 cup low-fat cottage cheese with peaches Water with lemon	4 oz. broiled fillet of sole 1 cup cole slaw with chopped apples (use plain yogurt as dressing) 1 cup skim milk
Day Four	*Kashi with Honey 3 pitted prunes 1 cup skim milk	1/2 acorn squash, baked, with cinnamon	*Mixed Vegetable Marinade 1 cup skim milk	1 cup yogurt with 2 Tbsp. wheat germ 1/2 cup blueberries Water with lemon	4 oz. hamburger (extra-lean) 1/2 cup corn 1 sweet potato 1 cup skim milk
Day Five	*Rice Pilaf 1/2 grapefruit 1/2 cup skim milk	*Fresh Peanut Butter and Pear Spread on 2 graham crackers	*Cheese-Stuffed Potato 1 cup strawberries Water with lemon	*1 Spicy Carrot Muffin 1 cup skim milk	Amy's Organic Veggie Loaf with Mashed Potatoes and Vegetables 1 cup skim milk

	Breakfast	**Snack**	**Lunch**	**Snack**	**Dinner**
Day Six	2-egg omelet with tomatoes and onions 1 slice whole-wheat toast 1/2 cantaloupe Water with lemon	1 bran muffin 1 cup skim milk	*1 bowl Minestrone Soup 1/2 bagel 1 cup skim milk	1 pear 1 oz. cheese Water with lemon	*Scallops with Fresh Ginger 1 cup brown rice 1 cup skim milk
Day Seven	1 cup cream of rice creal 1 cup skim milk	*1 cup Minestrone Soup 1/2 bagel Water with lemon	1 grilled cheese sandwich (2 oz. cheese) 1 small apple	*Fresh Peanut Butter and Pear Spread on 2 graham crackers 1 cup skim milk	*Salmon Steak with Rosemary and Mustard 1 cup brown rice 1 cup skim milk

Recipes: Meat and Poultry

Meat (beef, veal, pork, and lamb) and poultry are excellent sources of protein, vitamins, and minerals. It's not necessary to eat large portions of meat to get enough protein. Meat can be part of a low-fat diet as long as you choose lean cuts, eat small portions (3 to 4 ounces, cooked), and trim all visible fat before cooking. It is the quality of the meat and poultry and how it's prepared that give it flavor. Try organically fed meat and poultry from your local natural food store; they are flavorful and free of growth-stimulating hormones, pesticides, and antibiotics.

Good-quality lean beef is bright to deep red in color and should feel firm and dry, not soft and moist. An extra-lean piece of beef can have more flavor than one marbled with fat. Beef is an excellent source of iron, zinc, and vitamin B_{12}, which are difficult to obtain, especially if you're a strict vegetarian. Veal is usually lower in fat than beef. For example, 4 ounces of trimmed, roasted veal sirloin contains 6 grams of fat and a similar-sized portion of choice beef sirloin has 11 grams of fat. When buying veal, it should be light pink in color.

Most of the leanest cuts of lamb contain the same amount of fat, protein, iron, zinc, and vitamin B_{12} as the leanest cuts of beef. You can use ground lamb just like you would use ground beef or turkey. The leanest cuts of pork are comparable in fat to the leanest cut of beef. However, the fat in pork is slightly less saturated than that in beef. Pork is not as lean as skinless chicken or turkey breast. The healthiest methods of cooking pork are roasting and broiling. The leanest part of the chicken is the breast. It has less than half the fat of meat and is less saturated than the fat in beef. Always choose lean meat and poultry for grinding. Ask the butcher to trim off any fat and grind it for you. When preparing stew, soup, or gravy made from meat, chill them first, then skim off the fat that rises to the top.

Beef with Pea Pods

SERVES 4 to 6

1 pound beef flank or sirloin steak
   (can also use chicken or turkey
   breast)
1 green onion, sliced
1 tablespoon soy sauce

1 tablespoon vermouth
2 tablespoons cornstarch
2 tablespoons vegetable oil
1 (10-oz.) package frozen pea
   pods, thawed, or ¼ lb. fresh

Slice meat into 2-inch strips. Combine meat and onion in a medium bowl. In a separate bowl, mix together soy sauce, vermouth, and cornstarch; add mixture to meat and onion. Marinate 30 minutes or longer in the refrigerator.

Heat 1 tablespoon of the vegetable oil in a large skillet over medium-high heat. Stir-fry ingredients until brown. In a separate skillet, stir-fry pea pods for about 2 minutes in 1 tablespoon of vegetable oil. Add cooked pea pods to meat mixture and serve immediately.

Nutrients: Protein, saturated fats, cholesterol, iron, phosphorus, zinc, B_{12}, B_6, B_2, niacin, vitamin E

Vegetable and Beef Stew

SERVES 6

3 pounds beef chuck (stew beef)
4 tablespoons vegetable oil
1 cup chopped green bell pepper
1 cup chopped onion
¾ cup chopped celery
½ cup beef broth
½ cup water
2 cups chopped tomatoes
1 clove garlic, finely chopped

¼ teaspoon pepper
1 bay leaf
⅛ teaspoon dried thyme
6 small red potatoes, chopped
8 medium carrots, diced
½ cup pearl onions
2 tablespoons all-purpose flour
¼ cup water

Cut meat into bite-size pieces. Heat oil in a large skillet over medium heat. Add meat, green pepper, and onion and sauté until meat is brown and vegetables are softened. Set aside.

In a large stockpot combine celery, beef broth, water, tomatoes, garlic, pepper, bay leaf, thyme, red potatoes, carrots, and pearl onions and simmer 1 hour. Then add sautéed meat mixture.

Whisk together flour and water in a small bowl and slowly stir into stew. Simmer, stirring, 10 more minutes or until stew thickens.

Nutrients: Protein, saturated fats, cholesterol, iron, vitamin C, vitamin E, calcium, potassium, phosphorus, zinc, B_{12}, B_6, niacin, fiber

Braised Veal Chops with Fennel Seeds

SERVES 4

2 tablespoons vegetable oil	½ teaspoon salt
4 (1½-inch-thick) veal chops	¼ cup chopped onion
2 tablespoons dry white wine	¾ cup chopped carrots
¼ teaspoon fennel seeds, crushed	2 cups chopped tomatoes
¼ teaspoon sugar	⅓ cup chopped green peppers

Heat vegetable oil in a large skillet over medium-high heat and brown veal chops. Add remaining ingredients, cover, and cook over medium heat for 35 minutes or until chops are tender.

Nutrients: Protein, saturated fats, cholesterol, iron, phosphorus, zinc, vitamin C, B_{12}, B_6, B_2, niacin, fiber

Lamb Chops with Orange Marmalade

SERVES 4

4 (1½-inch-thick) lamb rib chops	½ cup orange marmalade
½ teaspoon garlic powder	4 (¼-inch-thick) orange slices

Preheat oven to 350°F (175°C). Sprinkle both sides of lamb chops with garlic powder. Place in a medium baking dish. Spoon one-fourth of the marmalade on each lamb chop. Top each with 1 orange slice. Cover. Bake for 30 minutes.

Nutrients: Protein, saturated fats, cholesterol, iron, phosphorus, zinc, vitamin C, B_{12}, B_6, B_2, niacin, fiber

Creamy Almond Chicken

SERVES 4

4 boneless and skinless chicken
  breast halves
Dash of salt
Dash of pepper
4 tablespoons vegetable oil
⅔ cup sliced almonds

1 cup low-fat milk
3 tablespoons apricot nectar
⅛ teaspoon ground red pepper
2 tablespoons all-purpose flour
¼ cup cold water

Preheat oven to 325°F (115°C). Season chicken breasts with salt and pepper. Place in a baking dish: set aside. Toast almonds in small dry skillet over medium heat until golden brown; set aside. Combine oil, salt, pepper, milk, apricot nectar, and red pepper in a medium saucepan and cook, stirring, over medium heat 6 minutes.

Whisk together flour and water, and slowly stir into apricot mixture to create a creamy low-fat sauce. Baste each piece of chicken with sauce. Bake for 30 minutes.

Warm remaining sauce and pour over baked chicken. Sprinkle with sliced almonds.

Nutrients: Protein, saturated fats (less than beef), cholesterol, iron, vitamin E, calcium, zinc, B_2, B_6, B_{12}, niacin

Chicken Cacciatore

SERVES 4

2 teaspoons olive oil
4 boneless, skinless chicken breast
   halves
1 onion, chopped
1 garlic clove, minced
1 teaspoon salt
1 bay leaf

¼ teaspoon dried basil
¼ teaspoon dried oregano
½ cup white wine
1 cup tomato sauce
1 cup stewed tomatoes
1 cup sliced mushrooms

Heat olive oil in a large skillet over medium-high heat and brown chicken, onion, and garlic. Add remaining ingredients, except mushrooms, and bring to a boil. Cover and simmer about 20 minutes. Add mushrooms, and cook 10 minutes more.

To serve, spoon sauce from the pan over each piece of chicken.

Nutrients: Protein, saturated fats (less than beef), iron, phosphorus, calcium, cholesterol, zinc, vitamin D, niacin, B_6

Turkey Turnovers

SERVES 4 to 5

1 tablespoon vegetable oil
1 pound ground turkey
2 medium onions, chopped
4 medium tomatoes, cut up
1 medium green bell pepper,
   chopped
½ cup shredded carrots

¼ cup raisins
1 teaspoon curry powder
½ teaspoon salt
½ teaspoon cumin
¼ teaspoon pepper
2 ready-made pie crusts

Preheat oven to 400°F (205°C). Heat oil in a skillet over medium heat. Add turkey and onions and cook 3 minutes. Add remaining ingredients and bring to a boil, then reduce heat and simmer 10 minutes.

Roll out pie crust, and spoon filling on half of crust. Fold crust over filling, making a half round, and pinch edges together to seal. Place turnover on a baking sheet. Prick top of crust to let out steam. Bake for 30 minutes.

Nutrients: Protein, saturated fats (less than beef), cholesterol, iron, phosphorus, vitamin C, vitamin A, B_{12}, B_2, B_6, niacin, fiber

Sweet and Sour Pork

SERVES 4 to 6

1 teaspoon ground ginger	6 medium lean pork cutlets
1 teaspoon salt	1 tablespoon sesame seed oil
½ teaspoon pepper	1 cup pineapple juice
1 teaspoon paprika	2 tablespoons balsamic vinegar
¼ cup all-purpose flour	3 tablespoons honey

Combine ginger, salt, pepper, paprika, and flour in a plastic bag. Toss each cutlet in bag, shake, and coat. Heat sesame oil in a skillet over medium-high heat and brown pork cutlets.

Mix together pineapple juice, vinegar, and honey, and add to cutlets. Cover and cook over low heat 30 minutes.

Nutrients: Protein, saturated fats (less than beef) cholesterol, iron, B_{12}, B_2, B_6, niacin, vitamin C, phosphorus, zinc, vitamin E

Recipes: Fish and Seafood

The flavor of fish is outstanding. Like meat and poultry, fish and shellfish are also excellent sources of protein. Fish and other seafoods are rich in iodine, phosphorus, zinc, selenium, and vitamin B_{12}. They're low in saturated fat, and low in cholesterol and calories.

Most fish will cook in the oven at 350°F (175°C) in only twelve minutes because it has little connective tissue. When done, the fish will flake and the translucent texture of fish will be opaque. When buying frozen fish, the best rule of thumb is to make sure it is solidly frozen, with no soft spots. The package should be tightly wrapped, with no ice-crystal deposits on the inside of the package. The ice crystals destroy the cells in the flesh of the fish and dry it out.

Although it's always best to buy fresh fish, you can also find high-quality frozen fish. Quick freezing is the key to preserving fish and seafood. By using temperatures of 20 to 40 degrees below zero, this method does not destroy flavor or the health-promoting polyunsaturated fatty acids— known as the omega-3s. Fish can also be cooked in its frozen state, which keeps it tender. If you want to thaw fish, do so in the refrigerator or place the sealed package under cold, not warm, running water. When freezing fish at home, freeze the fish in its original wrapper, which is made of special coated paper designed to retain moisture. Don't eat breaded or battered frozen fish. Try grilling fish instead; it gives fish a unique flavor and aroma.

Cajun-Style Red Snapper

SERVES 4

1 tablespoon paprika

1 teaspoon salt

1 teaspoon onion powder

1 teaspoon garlic powder

½ teaspoon ground red pepper

½ teaspoon black pepper

½ teaspoon dried thyme

½ teaspoon dried oregano

4 (½- to ¾-inch-thick) red snapper fillets (other firm fillets can be used)

2 tablespoons vegetable oil

In a small bowl, mix together paprika, salt, onion powder, garlic powder, red pepper, black pepper, thyme, and oregano. Sprinkle both sides of red snapper fillets with seasoning mixture. Heat oil in a skillet over medium heat and cook fillets 3 minutes on each side or until red snapper flakes when pierced with a fork.

Nutrients: Protein, polyunsaturated fats, B_{12}, iodine, phosphorus, calcium, selenium, zinc, vitamin D, vitamin E, B_2, niacin

Shrimp with Broccoli

SERVES 4

4 tablespoons olive oil
Dash of dried basil
3 tablespoons fresh lemon juice
3 tablespoons freshly grated
   Parmesan cheese

4 small heads of broccoli
1 pound shrimp, cleaned
1 pound pasta (optional), cooked

Heat oil in a skillet over medium heat. Add basil, lemon juice, Parmesan cheese, and broccoli. Cover and cook for 5 minutes. Add shrimp and cook 2 to 3 minutes or until shrimp turns pink.

Serve with pasta, if desired.

Nutrients: Protein, polyunsaturated fats, B_{12}, B_2, niacin, folic acid, iodine, phosphorus, selenium, zinc, calcium, vitamin D, vitamin C, fiber

Broiled Swordfish with Toasted Almonds

SERVES 4

4 medium swordfish steaks
¼ cup almonds, finely
   chopped

2 tablespoons fresh lemon juice
2 tablespoons sesame oil
1 teaspoon dried oregano

Preheat broiler. Toast almonds in a small dry skillet over medium heat until golden brown; set aside. In a small bowl, mix together lemon juice, sesame oil, oregano, and almonds. Brush marinade generously over swordfish. Broil swordfish 6 minutes for each ½ inch of thickness or until swordfish flakes when pierced with a fork.

Nutrients: Protein, polyunsaturated fats, B_{12}, B_2, niacin, iodine, phosphorus, selenium, zinc, vitamin D, calcium

Breaded Pike Parmesan

SERVES 4

1 cup herb-seasoned stuffing
  croutons, crushed
⅓ cup freshly grated Parmesan
  cheese
2 tablespoons chopped green
  onion

Dash of paprika
Dash of dill weed
4 medium pike fillets or halibut

Preheat oven to 400°F (205°C). In a plastic bag, mix together croutons, Parmesan cheese, onion, paprika, and dill. Place each fillet in bag, shake, and coat. Place breaded fillets in baking dish. Bake 6 minutes for each ½ inch of thickness or until fish flakes when pierced with a fork.

Nutrients: Protein, polyunsaturated fats, B_{12}, B_2, niacin, iodine, selenium, phosphorus, zinc, vitamin D, calcium

Scallops with Ginger

SERVES 4

3 tablespoons vegetable oil
1 teaspoon ginger root, grated
¾ cup shredded carrots

½ cup chopped green onions
2 tablespoons fresh lemon juice
1 pound scallops, cleaned

Combine all ingredients except scallops in a skillet over medium heat. Sauté 5 minutes until carrots are crispy and bright. Add scallops and cook 3 more minutes or until scallops are opaque.

Nutrients: Protein, polyunsaturated fats, B_{12}, B_2, niacin, iodine, selenium, phosphorus, zinc, vitamin D, vitamin A, fiber

Fillet of Sole with Mint

SERVES 4

2 tablespoons chopped onion
1 tablespoon finely chopped fresh
  mint
2 tablespoons fresh lime juice

1 clove garlic, minced
Dash of pepper
Dash of salt
1 pound fresh or frozen sole fillets

Preheat oven to 400°F (205°C). In a small bowl mix together all ingredients except fillets. Brush mixture generously over sole fillets and place in a baking pan. Bake for 6 minutes or until sole flakes when pierced with a fork.

Nutrients: Protein, polyunsaturated fats, B_{12}, B_2, niacin, iodine, selenium, phosphorus, zinc, vitamin D

Salmon Steaks with Rosemary Mustard

SERVES 4

1 tablespoon finely crushed dried
  rosemary
1 small clove garlic, crushed
¼ cup Dijon mustard

2 tablespoons vegetable oil
1 pound fresh or frozen salmon
  steaks

Preheat broiler. In a small bowl mix together all ingredients except salmon. Brush marinade generously over salmon steaks. Place salmon in a baking dish. Broil 4 to 6 minutes for each ½ inch of thickness. Baste occasionally with remaining mixture, until salmon flakes when pierced with a fork.

Nutrients: Protein, polyunsaturated fats, B_{12}, B_2, niacin, iodine, selenium, phosphorus, zinc, vitamin D, vitamin E

Mackerel Parmesan

SERVES 4

¼ cup sesame oil
¼ cup fresh lemon juice
1 tablespoon dried basil
1 pound fresh or frozen mackerel

½ cup freshly grated Parmesan
cheese
¼ teaspoon garlic powder

Preheat oven to 400°F (205°C). In a small bowl mix together sesame oil, lemon juice, and basil. Pour over mackerel and marinate 1 hour. Drain mackerel and place in a baking dish. Sprinkle with Parmesan cheese and garlic powder, and bake 10 minutes or until mackerel flakes when pierced with a fork.

Nutrients: Protein, polyunsaturated fats, B_{12}, B_2, niacin, iodine, selenium, phosphorus, zinc, vitamin D, vitamin E

Swordfish and Apples

SERVES 4

2 tablespoons vegetable oil
4 tablespoons brown sugar or rice
syrup
3 large apples, sliced or diced

½ teaspoon grated nutmeg
1½ pounds fresh or frozen
swordfish steaks

Heat vegetable oil in a skillet over medium heat. Add rice syrup or brown sugar, apples, and nutmeg and sauté 2 minutes. Add swordfish, cover, and simmer 15 minutes or until swordfish flakes when pierced with a fork.

Nutrients: Protein, polyunsaturated fats, B_{12}, B_2, niacin, iodine, selenium, phosphorus, zinc, vitamin D, vitamin C, fiber, vitamin A

Snack Suggestions for Busy Moms

The recipes in this section can be used for snacks, desserts, or side dishes. Snacking has gotten a bad reputation and is often associated with junk food and poor nutrition. I recommend controlled snacking, not random snacking. Controlled snacking means having something nourishing every few hours. It acts as an energy bridge between meals. Controlled snacking can prevent overeating.

The main purpose of snacking is to provide a constant and even supply of energy to your body. The snack prevents a dip in blood sugar between meals, so you can feel alert all day long. Snacking can give you a nutritional boost. Some quick and simple snack suggestions include: cinnamon toast on whole-wheat bread, carrots and zucchini dipped in seasoned yogurt, fresh fruit, popcorn with a splash of honey, or whole-wheat crackers and tuna.

You can always use leftovers from previous meals as a quick snack—just eat less. Soups can be either a meal-in-a-bowl or, in a smaller portion, a quick snack. This is why I included soup recipes in this section. They are high in nutrition, flavor, and texture, and will help you reach satiety or fullness sooner than cold foods will.

Cauliflower Salad

SERVES 8 to 10

1 head lettuce
1 head cauliflower
1 red onion, sliced
¼ cup pine nuts

Dressing:
1 cup plain yogurt
½ cup freshly grated Parmesan
   cheese
1 tablespoon honey
1 teaspoon ground coriander

Tear lettuce into pieces, break cauliflower into florets. Layer all ingredients in a large salad bowl.

In a small bowl thoroughly whisk together yogurt, Parmesan cheese, honey, and coriander. Pour over salad. Cover the bowl and place in the refrigerator for a few hours or overnight. Toss before serving.

Nutrients: Vitamin A, vitamin C, folic acid, calcium, fiber, protein

Gingered Sweet Potatoes

SERVES 4 to 5

5 medium sweet potatoes,
   scrubbed
1 tablespoon margarine
2 tablespoons honey

1 tablespoon peeled and finely
   chopped fresh ginger root
¼ teaspoon salt
¼ cup finely chopped walnuts and
   pecans

Preheat oven to 375°F (190°C). Grease a medium baking dish. Cut potatoes into thin slices. Place potato slices in baking dish. Mix together remaining ingredients, then pour evenly over potatoes. Bake for 35 minutes.

Nutrients: Vitamin A, vitamin C, folic acid, calcium, fiber, protein

Cheese-Stuffed Potatoes

SERVES 2

2 medium potatoes
4 tablespoons low-fat cottage
   cheese
4 tablespoons plain low-fat yogurt

1 teaspoon dill weed
4 tablespoons chopped green
   onion
Paprika

Preheat oven to 375°F (190°C). Microwave potatoes on high until tender, about 8 minutes. Cut in half and place in a baking dish. In a small bowl, mix remaining ingredients together except for paprika. Spoon cheese mixture into center of potatoes. Sprinkle paprika over potatoes. Bake in preheated oven for 12 minutes.

Nutrients: Vitamin A, vitamin C, folic acid, calcium, protein, fiber

Mixed Vegetable Marinade

SERVES 6 to 8

1 pound broccoli, cut into florets

2 yellow summer squash, cut into thin strips

1 large head cauliflower, cut into florets

2 cups sliced carrots

1 medium red onion, diced

Dressing

½ cup vegetable oil

¼ cup red wine vinegar

2 teaspoons sugar

1 teaspoon salt

1 teaspoon dried basil

1 teaspoon Dijon mustard

½ teaspoon pepper

Dash of nutmeg

2 cloves garlic, crushed

Toss all vegetables in a large bowl. Combine all salad dressing ingredients and whisk together thoroughly. Pour dressing over vegetables. Cover and marinate 1 hour in the refrigerator. May be kept refrigerated in a covered container up to 3 to 4 days.

Nutrients: Vitamin A, vitamin C, folic acid, calcium, fiber, vitamin E

Low-Fat French Fries

SERVES 4

5 large potatoes with skin
Vegetable-oil cooking spray
Mrs. Dash seasoning

Preheat oven to 475°F (265°C). Scrub potatoes, but don't peel them. Slice each potato lengthwise into ¼-inch-thick ovals, then slice each oval lengthwise into long thin strips.

Arrange potato strips in a single layer on a large baking sheet. Spray potato strips with cooking spray. Sprinkle generously with Mrs. Dash. Bake potatoes 30 minutes or until crisp and golden brown.

Nutrients: Vitamin A, vitamin C, folic acid, calcium, fiber, vitamin E

Sesame Carrots

SERVES 4 to 5

2 cups diced carrots
2 teaspoons sesame oil
1 teaspoon salt
2 teaspoons soy sauce

½ cup orange juice
2 teaspoons barley malt
2 teaspoons sesame seeds

In a medium saucepan, combine all ingredients except sesame seeds. Bring to a boil, reduce heat, and simmer 15 minutes. Place in a serving dish and sprinkle with sesame seeds.

Nutrients: Vitamin A, vitamin C, folic acid, calcium, fiber, vitamin E

Swiss-Style Green Beans

SERVES 4 to 5

1½ pounds fresh whole green
  beans
1 cup sliced green and red bell
  peppers
⅓ cup fresh lemon juice
2 cloves garlic, crushed
½ cup olive oil
1 teaspoon dried tarragon

1 teaspoon dried dill weed
¼ teaspoon salt
2 teaspoons Dijon mustard
2 tablespoons chopped fresh
  parsley
4 ounces low-fat Swiss cheese,
  shredded
⅓ cup chopped walnuts

In a medium saucepan, steam green beans and bell peppers until tender, about 15 minutes. In a small bowl, mix together remaining ingredients except walnuts. Add to steamed vegetables and stir. Place on a serving dish and top with walnuts.

Nutrients: Vitamin A, vitamin C, folic acid, calcium, fiber, vitamin E, protein

Italian Broccoli

SERVES 6 to 8

6 heads of broccoli
¼ cup olive oil
1 clove garlic, minced

¼ cup fresh lemon juice
2 teaspoons Mrs. Dash
  seasoning

In a large stockpot steam broccoli until tender, then place in serving bowl. In a small bowl, mix together olive oil, garlic, lemon juice, and seasoning. Pour mixture over broccoli and toss.

Nutrients: Vitamin A, vitamin C, folic acid, calcium, fiber, vitamin E

Zesty Lentil Salad

SERVES 2

3 cups water
1 cup dried lentils
1 bay leaf
¼ teaspoon pepper
1 teaspoon dried thyme
1 teaspoon dried basil

2 tablespoons olive oil
¼ cup red wine vinegar
1 garlic clove, minced
1 small mint leaf
1 cup chopped onion
½ cup shredded carrot

In a medium saucepan, combine water and lentils. Cook over medium heat 30 minutes. Drain and discard any liquid from lentils. Add remaining ingredients to cooked lentils. Stir and cook 10 more minutes. Place in a serving bowl.

Nutrients: Vitamin A, vitamin C, folic acid, calcium, fiber, vitamin E, protein

Mixed Vegetable Bake

SERVES 6 to 8

6 cups fresh cut-up vegetables
(such as cauliflower, broccoli,
carrots, onions, turnips,
rutabaga, etc.)
¾ cup cold milk
1 tablespoon cornstarch
½ teaspoon salt
⅛ teaspoon pepper

2 tablespoons vegetable oil
3 tablespoons fresh dill or 1
tablespoon dried
2 tablespoons lemon juice
1 tablespoon chopped parsley
½ cup bread crumbs
¼ cup grated Parmesan cheese
1 tablespoon chopped parsley

Preheat oven to 350°F (175°C).

In a large stockpot, steam vegetables until tender, then add milk, cornstarch, salt, pepper, oil, dill, lemon juice, and parsley to steamed vegetables. Mix well.

Grease a medium baking dish and pour in vegetable mixture. Sprinkle top with bread crumbs, Parmesan, and parsley. Bake for 15 minutes.

Nutrients: Vitamin A, vitamin C, folic acid, calcium, fiber, vitamin E, protein

Vegetarian Tostadas

SERVES 4 to 6

6 corn tortillas

1 (16-oz.) can refried beans

2 medium avocados, peeled,
  pitted, and coarsely mashed

½ cup salsa

Dash of pepper

1 teaspoon fresh lemon juice

8 ounces shredded zucchini

2 tomatoes, chopped

1 cup chopped green leaf lettuce

1 red pepper, diced

Preheat oven to 375°F (190°C). Grease a baking sheet. Place tortillas on prepared baking sheet. Spread each tortilla with refried beans. In a bowl, combine avocados, salsa, pepper, and lemon juice and blend well. Spoon avocado mixture on each tortilla. Mix together zucchini, tomatoes, green leaf lettuce, and red pepper. Top each tortilla with some vegetable mixture. Bake 3 minutes.

Nutrients: Vitamin A, vitamin C, folic acid, calcium, fiber, vitamin E, protein, iron

Spicy Beans

SERVES 4 to 5

1 cup dry navy beans, sorted and rinsed

1 cup dry pinto beans, sorted and rinsed

¼ teaspoon oregano

¼ teaspoon pepper

¼ teaspoon thyme

1 small bay leaf

3 tablespoons chopped onion

½ cup diced green and red peppers

1½ teaspoons Dijon mustard

4-oz. jar pimientos, diced and drained

¼ cup cider vinegar

1 tablespoon olive oil

In a medium saucepan, bring 6 quarts of water to a boil. Pour beans into boiling water, cover, and reduce heat to medium. Cook 60 minutes or until beans are tender. Drain and discard any liquid from beans. Add all remaining ingredients to beans, cover, and cook over medium heat 15 minutes. Remove bay leaf and serve.

Nutrients: Vitamin A, vitamin C, folic acid, calcium, fiber, vitamin E, protein, iron

Kashi and Lavender Honey

SERVES 4

2 cups water
1 cup kashi (seven grains and
  sesame)
2 tablespoons lavender honey

1 teaspoon ground cinnamon
1 tablespoon safflower oil
2 medium apples, diced

In a medium saucepan, bring water to a boil. Pour kashi into boiling water, cover, and cook over medium heat 25 minutes, or until liquid is absorbed and the Kashi is tender. Stir in honey, oil, and cinnamon. Top with apples.

Nutrients: Complex carbohydrates, fiber, B_6, B_2, B_1, niacin, iron, zinc, calcium, selenium, magnesium, vitamin E, vitamin A, vitamin C

Rice Pilaf with Cinnamon and Raisins

SERVES 4

½ cup diced onion

3 tablespoons vegetable oil

1 cup white rice

1 cup brown rice

3 cups chicken broth

Pinch each of thyme, basil,
   parsley, and ground cinnamon

2 medium eggs

2 tablespoons raisins

In a large skillet, sauté onions in oil, then add the uncooked rice, stirring 2 to 3 minutes or until rice is slightly browned. Add 3 cups boiling chicken broth, thyme, basil, parsley, and cinnamon. Cover and cook over low heat until liquid is absorbed and the rice is tender.

In a small bowl whisk together eggs until blended and add to rice pilaf. Cook, stirring, over low heat 1 minute or until eggs are cooked. Top rice pilaf with raisins.

Nutrients: Complex carbohydrates, protein, fiber, B_6, B_2, B_1, niacin, iron, zinc, calcium, selenium, magnesium, vitamin E, vitamin A, protein

Acorn Squash with Apple and Onion Stuffing

SERVES 4

4 acorn squash halves, with seeds removed

3 cups chopped tart apples

1 cup chopped onion

½ teaspoon salt

½ teaspoon thyme

¼ teaspoon pepper

1 cup plain bread crumbs

¼ cup water

2 eggs

¼ cup chopped walnuts

Bake squash in a 375°F (190°C) oven until just tender; set aside. In a large skillet, sauté apples, onion, salt, thyme, and pepper over medium heat. Add bread crumbs, water, egg, and walnuts and mix well. Spoon stuffing into cavity of squash. Return stuffed squash to 375°F oven and bake 20 minutes more.

Nutrients: Complex carbohydrates, fiber, B_6, B_2, B_1, niacin, iron, zinc, calcium, selenium, magnesium, vitamin E, vitamin A, vitamin C, protein

Tomato and Ricotta Sandwiches

SERVES 2

4 ounces low-fat ricotta cheese
1 large tomato, chopped
1 tablespoon chopped onion

¼ teaspoon basil
1 tablespoon sunflower seeds
4 slices rye bread

In a bowl, mix together cheese, tomato, onion, basil, and sunflower seeds. Toast rye bread and spread ricotta mixture on toast.

Nutrients: Complex carbohydrates, fiber, B_6, B_2, B_1, niacin, iron, zinc, calcium, selenium, magnesium, vitamin E, vitamin A, vitamin C, protein, potassium

Zucchini Sandwich

SERVES 2

4 slices 100 percent whole-wheat
  bread
1 medium zucchini, thinly sliced
1 tomato, sliced

1 small onion, thinly sliced
⅓ cup grated low-fat Cheddar
  cheese

Toast whole-wheat bread. Place zucchini, tomato, onions, and cheese on toasted bread. Microwave sandwiches until cheese is melted.

Nutrients: Complex carbohydrates, fiber, B_6, B_2, B_1, niacin, iron, zinc, calcium, selenium, magnesium, vitamin E, vitamin A, vitamin C, protein

Minestrone Soup

SERVES 4 to 6

1 clove garlic, minced
¾ cup chopped onion
3 tablespoons olive oil
¾ cup diced carrots
¾ cup finely chopped celery
½ cup baby peas
½ cup corn
Dash of pepper
1 teaspoon dried oregano

1 teaspoon dried basil
3½ cups water
2 cups tomato sauce
¾ cup chopped green bell peppers
1 cup garbanzo beans in can
   already cooked
¼ cup chopped parsley
½ cup whole-grain macaroni

In a large stockpot, combine all ingredients except macaroni and bring to a boil. Cover and cook over medium heat 50 minutes. Then add macaroni noodles and cook for 15 more minutes. Serve hot in soup bowls.

Nutrients: Complex carbohydrates, fiber, B_6, B_2, B_1, niacin, iron, zinc, calcium, selenium, magnesium, vitamin E, vitamin A, vitamin C, protein, potassium

Corn Chowder

SERVES 4

2 tablespoons vegetable oil
1 cup chopped onion
½ cup finely chopped celery
1 finely chopped sweet red pepper
5 cups corn

½ teaspoon salt
1 teaspoon Italian seasoning
1 cup chicken broth
1 cup low-fat milk
2 (12-oz.) cans evaporated milk

Combine all ingredients in a blender and puree. Pour puree into a medium saucepan. Cover and cook over medium heat 30 minutes. Serve hot in soup bowls.

Nutrients: Complex carbohydrates, fiber, B_6, B_2, B_1, niacin, iron, zinc, calcium, selenium, magnesium, vitamin E, vitamin A, vitamin C, protein

Creamy Broccoli Soup

SERVES 6

1 tablespoon safflower oil
¾ cup chopped onion
1 cup water
6 vegetable bouillon cubes
1 pound broccoli, chopped
2 cups diced potatoes
¾ cup sliced carrots
1 teaspoon dried thyme

1 teaspoon celery seeds
¼ teaspoon dried marjoram
¼ teaspoon pepper
4 cups low-fat milk
1 (12-oz.) can evaporated milk
2 tablespoons all-purpose flour
¼ cup water

In a large stockpot, combine all ingredients except flour and ¼ cup water. Bring to a boil, cover, and cook over medium heat 1 hour until potatoes are tender.

Whisk together flour and water and slowly stir into soup. Simmer, stirring frequently, 10 more minutes or until soup is thick and creamy. Serve hot in soup bowls.

Nutrients: Complex carbohydrates, fiber, B_6, B_2, B_1, niacin, iron, zinc, calcium, selenium, magnesium, vitamin E, vitamin A, vitamin C, protein

Mushroom-Barley Soup

SERVES 6

½ cup raw pearl barley

6½ cups stock or water

1 teaspoon salt

4 tablespoons tamari

¼ cup dry sherry

¼ vegetable oil

2 cloves garlic, minced

1 cup chopped onions

1 pound mushrooms, sliced

Dash of pepper

In a medium stockpot, combine all ingredients and bring to a boil. Cover and cook over medium heat 1 hour or until barley is tender. Serve hot in soup bowls.

Nutrients: Complex carbohydrates, fiber, B_6, B_2, B_1, niacin, iron, potassium, zinc, calcium, selenium, magnesium, potassium, vitamin E, vitamin C, protein

Cream of Celery Soup

SERVES 6

5 cups low-fat milk	¼ teaspoon celery seeds
4 cups chopped celery	Dash of pepper
2 cups 1-inch potato chunks	3 tablespoons vegetable oil
½ teaspoon salt	1 cup low-fat milk
1 clove garlic, chopped	1 (12-oz.) can evaporated milk
1 cup minced onion	2 tablespoons all-purpose flour
1 cup celery, minced	¼ cup water

In a large stockpot, combine milk, celery, potatoes, and ¼ teaspoon salt. Cover and cook over medium heat until potatoes are tender. Then place potato mixture in blender and puree. Pour puree back into stockpot.

Heat oil in a large skillet over medium heat and, sauté garlic, onion, chopped celery, celery seeds, remaining salt, and pepper. Add to puree.

Pour low-fat milk and evaporated milk into stockpot and stir. Whisk together flour and water and slowly stir into soup. Cover and cook, stirring occasionally, over medium heat 40 minutes or until soup is thick and creamy.

Nutrients: Complex carbohydrates, fiber, B_6, B_2, B_1, niacin, iron, zinc, calcium, selenium, magnesium, vitamin E, vitamin A, vitamin C, protein

Oatmeal Bread

(NO RISING REQUIRED)
1 LOAF

1 cup whole-wheat flour

1 cup unbleached white flour

1½ teaspoons baking soda

½ teaspoon baking powder

½ teaspoon salt

1¾ cups rolled oats

2 medium eggs, beaten

¼ cup molasses

1¼ cups low-fat milk

½ teaspoon vanilla extract

3 tablespoons vegetable oil

2 tablespoons fresh lemon juice

1 tablespoon water

Vegetable-oil cooking spray

Preheat oven to 350°F (175°C). In a large bowl, stir together flours, baking soda, baking powder, and salt. Then add oats to dry ingredients. In a medium bowl, combine eggs, molasses, milk, vanilla, oil, lemon juice, and water. Add to dry ingredients and stir well.

Spray 9 × 5-inch loaf pan with vegetable-oil cooking spray and pour in bread batter. Bake for 55 minutes or until a wooden pick inserted in center comes out clean.

Cool in pan 10 minutes, then turn bread out on a wire rack to finish cooling.

Nutrients: Complex carbohydrates, fiber, protein, B_1, B_2, niacin, vitamin E, vitamin A, iron, zinc, calcium, selenium, magnesium, potassium

Apricot-Walnut Bread

1 LOAF

1 cup whole-wheat flour
1 cup unbleached white flour
1 teaspoon baking soda
¼ teaspoon salt
1 egg, beaten
2 teaspoons vegetable oil

1 teaspoon vanilla extract
1 teaspoon almond extract
½ cup chopped walnuts
1 cup chopped dried apricots
    (without sulfites)
Vegetable-oil cooking spray

Preheat oven to 375°F (190°C). In a large bowl, mix together flours, baking powder, baking soda, and salt; set aside. In a small bowl, combine egg, oil, vanilla, almond extract, walnuts, and apricots and stir. Then add the apricot mixture to the dry ingredients and mix well.

Spray 9 × 5-inch loaf pan with vegetable-oil cooking spray and pour in bread batter. Bake for 45 minutes or until a wooden pick inserted in center comes out clean.

Cool in pan 10 minutes, then turn bread out on a wire rack to finish cooling.

Nutrients: Complex carbohydrates, fiber, B_6, B_2, B_1, niacin, iron, zinc, calcium, selenium, magnesium, vitamin E, vitamin A, vitamin C, protein, potassium

Cranberry Bread

1 LOAF

1¾ cups cranberries

⅓ cup vegetable oil

½ teaspoon ground cinnamon

⅓ cup minced walnuts

1 cup whole-wheat flour

1½ cups unbleached white flour

2 teaspoons baking powder

½ teaspoon baking soda

½ teaspoon vanilla extract

Dash of nutmeg

2 medium eggs, beaten

⅓ cup honey

Vegetable-oil cooking spray

Preheat oven to 350°F (175°C). In a medium skillet combine cranberries, oil, cinnamon, and walnuts and cook over medium heat 3 minutes. Remove from heat and pour into a large bowl.

In a medium bowl, mix together flour, baking powder, and baking soda; add to warm cranberry mixture. Whisk together vanilla, nutmeg, eggs, and honey until blended, then add to cranberry mixture and stir well.

Spray 9 × 5-inch loaf pan with vegetable-oil cooking spray and pour in bread batter. Bake for 55 minutes or until a wooden pick inserted in center comes out clean.

Cool in pan for 10 minutes, then turn bread out on a wire rack to finish cooling.

Nutrients: Complex carbohydrates, fiber, B_6, B_2, B_1, niacin, iron, zinc, calcium, selenium, magnesium, vitamin E, vitamin A, vitamin C, protein

Banana Bread

1 LOAF

2 cups whole-wheat flour
1 teaspoon baking soda
1 teaspoon baking powder
1 teaspoon salt
¼ cup vegetable oil
1 tablespoon sugar

3 large bananas, mashed
2 eggs, beaten
½ cup low-fat milk
⅓ cup chopped walnuts
Vegetable-oil cooking spray

Preheat oven to 325°F (165°C). In a large bowl, mix together flour, baking soda, baking powder, and salt. In a medium bowl, combine vegetable oil, sugar, bananas, eggs, and milk and stir until blended. Add banana mixture to dry ingredients and mix thoroughly. Gently stir in walnuts.

Spray 9 × 5-inch loaf pan with vegetable-oil cooking spray and pour in bread batter. Bake for 55 to 65 minutes, or until a wooden pick inserted in center comes out clean.

Cool in pan 10 minutes, then turn out bread on a wire rack to finish cooling.

Nutrients: Complex carbohydrates, fiber, B_6, B_2, B_1, niacin, iron, zinc, calcium, selenium, magnesium, vitamin E, vitamin A, vitamin C, protein, potassium

Orange Yogurt Muffins

12 MUFFINS

¼ cup honey

¼ cup vegetable oil

1 cup plain yogurt

1 medium egg, beaten

¼ cup freshly squeezed orange
 juice

½ teaspoon orange peel, grated

1 cup unbleached all-purpose flour

1 cup whole-wheat flour

⅛ teaspoon grated nutmeg

1½ teaspoons baking soda

¼ teaspoon salt

⅓ cup finely chopped walnuts

Vegetable-oil cooking spray

Preheat oven to 375°F (190°C). In a small saucepan, melt together honey and oil. Remove from heat and pour into a large bowl. In a medium bowl, blend together yogurt, egg, orange juice, and orange peel. Pour into honey mixture and stir.

In a large bowl, mix together flour, nutmeg, baking soda, salt, and walnuts. Add to liquid ingredients and mix well.

Coat a 12-cup muffin pan with cooking spray and pour in muffin batter. Bake for 30 minutes.

Nutrients: Complex carbohydrates, fiber, B_6, B_2, B_1, niacin, iron, zinc, calcium, selenium, magnesium, vitamin E, vitamin A, vitamin C, protein, potassium

Spicy Carrot Muffins

12 MUFFINS

1 cup unbleached flour
1 cup whole-wheat flour
1 tablespoon baking powder
1 teaspoon ground cinnamon
½ teaspoon salt
½ cup honey

¾ cup low-fat milk
⅓ cup vegetable oil
2 medium eggs, beaten
1 cup shredded carrots
Vegetable-oil cooking spray

Preheat oven to 375°F (190°C). In a large bowl, mix together flours, baking powder, cinnamon, and salt. In a medium bowl, combine honey, milk, oil, eggs, and carrots and stir.

Coat a 12-cup muffin pan with cooking spray and pour in muffin batter. Bake for 15 to 20 minutes.

Nutrients: Complex carbohydrates, fiber, B_6, B_2, B_1, niacin, iron, zinc, calcium, selenium, magnesium, vitamin E, vitamin A, vitamin C, protein

Bran Muffins with Honey

12 MUFFINS

1 cup unprocessed wheat bran
1 cup unbleached all-purpose flour
1 teaspoon baking soda
½ teaspoon ground cinnamon
¼ teaspoon salt
1 cup low-fat milk

1 medium egg, beaten
⅓ cup orange blossom honey
2 tablespoons vegetable oil
⅓ cup raisins
Vegetable-oil cooking spray

Preheat oven to 350°F (175°C). In a large bowl, mix together bran, flour, baking soda, cinnamon, and salt. In a medium bowl, whisk together milk, egg, honey, and oil. Add to dry ingredients and mix thoroughly. Add raisins and stir.

Coat a 12-cup muffin pan with cooking spray and pour in batter. Bake for 25 minutes.

Nutrients: Complex carbohydrates, fiber, B_6, B_2, B_1, niacin, iron, zinc, calcium, selenium, magnesium, vitamin E, vitamin A, vitamin C, protein, potassium

Raisin Oat Muffins

12 MUFFINS

1 cup unbleached all-purpose flour
¾ cup whole-wheat flour
½ cup rolled oats
1 teaspoon baking soda
¼ teaspoon salt
3 tablespoons vegetable oil

2 tablespoons honey
1½ cups low-fat milk
1 medium egg, beaten
½ cup raisins
Vegetable-oil cooking spray

Preheat oven to 375°F (190°C). In a large bowl, mix together flours, oats, baking soda, and salt. In a medium bowl, whisk together oil, honey, milk, and egg. Add to dry ingredients and mix thoroughly. Add raisins and stir.

Coat a 12-cup muffin pan with cooking spray and pour in batter. Bake for 25 minutes.

Nutrients: Complex carbohydrates, fiber, B_6, B_2, B_1, niacin, iron, zinc, calcium, selenium, magnesium, vitamin E, vitamin A, vitamin C, protein, potassium

Apple-Cheese Pancakes

MAKES 12

1 cup low-fat cottage cheese
1½ cups grated apples
½ cup unbleached all-purpose
   flour
1 cup whole-wheat flour
¼ cup low-fat milk
1 tablespoon honey

1 tablespoon sunflower seeds
1 teaspoon ground cinnamon
Dash of allspice
Dash of nutmeg
Dash of salt
4 eggs
Vegetable-oil cooking spray

In a large bowl, mix together all ingredients except eggs and cooking spray. Whisk eggs until firm and pour into cottage cheese mixture; stir.

Preheat a large griddle at medium heat for about 1 minute. Spray with vegetable oil. Spoon about 4 tablespoons batter into the griddle to form a medium-size pancake. Cook for 1 minute and then flip the pancake with a spatula and cook for 1 minute more on other side, until golden brown. Continue with remaining batter. Serve with yogurt or fresh fruit.

Nutrients: Complex carbohydrates, fiber, B_6, B_2, B_1, niacin, iron, zinc, calcium, selenium, magnesium, vitamin E, vitamin A, vitamin C, protein, potassium

Pumpkin Squares

8 SQUARES

2 medium eggs
½ cup honey
¾ cup plain canned pumpkin
1 teaspoon vanilla extract
½ cup unbleached all-purpose flour

¼ cup whole-wheat flour
1 teaspoon baking powder
1 teaspoon ground cinnamon
½ teaspoon ground ginger
¼ teaspoon salt
¼ teaspoon ground nutmeg

Preheat oven to 350°F (175°C). Spray an 8-inch-square baking dish with cooking spray.

In a large bowl, whisk eggs until firm. Add honey, pumpkin, and vanilla to eggs. Combine flours, baking powder, cinnamon, ginger, salt, and nutmeg in a large bowl and mix. Add to pumpkin mixture and stir well.

Pour pumpkin batter into baking dish. Bake for 40 minutes. Let cool and refrigerate 1 hour before serving. Top with yogurt if desired.

Nutrients: Complex carbohydrates, fiber, B_6, B_2, B_1, niacin, iron, zinc, calcium, selenium, magnesium, vitamin E, vitamin A, vitamin C, protein, potassium

Apricot Cookies

1 DOZEN

¾ cup apricot preserves

1 egg, beaten

¼ cup honey

½ teaspoon vanilla extract

¼ cup vegetable oil

1 cup unbleached all-purpose flour

1 cup whole-wheat flour

¼ teaspoon baking powder

½ teaspoon salt

Vegetable-oil cooking spray

Preheat oven to 375°F (190°C). In a large bowl, mix together preserves, egg, honey, vanilla, and oil. Add flours, baking soda, and salt; stir well.

Spray baking sheet with vegetable oil. Roll small pieces of dough into ¾-inch-diameter balls and flatten on baking sheet. Bake for 10 to 12 minutes or until the bottom edges begin to brown. Let cool on the sheet for 1 minute, then transfer to a wire rack. Sprinkle with powdered sugar, if desired.

Nutrients: Complex carbohydrates, fiber, B_6, B_2, B_1, niacin, iron, zinc, calcium, selenium, magnesium, vitamin E, vitamin A, vitamin C, protein, potassium

Fudge Cookies

1 DOZEN

2 squares (2 ounces) unsweetened chocolate *or* 6 tablespoons unsweetened cocoa *or* powdered carob + 3 tablespoons milk

1½ cups unbleached all-purpose flour

¼ cup honey

¼ cup vegetable oil

2 tablespoons low-fat milk

2 teaspoons vanilla extract

2 medium eggs, beaten

½ cup whole-wheat flour

2 teaspoons baking powder

½ teaspoon salt

Vegetable-oil cooking spray

Preheat oven to 375°F (175°C). In a small saucepan, melt chocolate or 6 tablespoons cocoa or carob and 3 tablespoons milk over very low heat. Remove from heat and place in large mixing bowl. Add honey, oil, milk, vanilla, and eggs to melted chocolate and stir thoroughly. Slowly stir in flour, baking powder, and salt.

Spray baking sheet with vegetable oil. Roll small pieces of dough into ¾-inch-diameter balls and flatten on baking sheet. Bake for 10 to 12 minutes or until the bottom edges begin to brown. Let cool on the sheet for 1 minute, then transfer to a wire rack.

Nutrients: Simple carbohydrates, B_6, B_2, B_1, niacin, iron, zinc, selenium, magnesium, vitamin E, vitamin A, vitamin C, protein

Carob and Peanut Butter Brownies

1 DOZEN

½ cup peanut butter
1 cup carob powder
¼ cup vegetable oil
½ cup honey
¼ cup water
3 medium eggs, beaten

2 teaspoons vanilla extract
½ cup unbleached all-purpose
  flour
¼ cup whole-wheat flour
Vegetable-oil cooking spray

Preheat oven to 325°F (165°C). In a large bowl, blend together peanut butter, carob, oil, honey, water, eggs, and vanilla. Then add in flours and stir well.

Spray 9-inch-square baking dish with vegetable-oil cooking spray and pour in brownie batter. Bake for 45 minutes.

Nutrients: Simple carbohydrates, B_6, B_2, B_1, niacin, iron, zinc, selenium, magnesium, vitamin E, vitamin A, vitamin C, protein

Strawberry Oatmeal Bars

MAKES 12

½ cup honey
⅓ cup vegetable oil
1 teaspoon vanilla extract
1 cup quick-cooking oats,
   uncooked
¾ cup unbleached all-purpose
   flour
¼ cup 100% whole-wheat flour

½ teaspoon baking soda
Dash of salt
10 ounces unsweetened fresh or
   frozen strawberries
1 tablespoon honey
2 tablespoons cornstarch
¼ teaspoon almond extract
Vegetable-oil cooking spray

Preheat oven to 375°F (190°C). In a large bowl, blend together honey, oil, and vanilla. Add oats, flours, baking soda, and salt and mix well.

Spray a 9-inch-square baking dish with vegetable-oil cooking oil. Then press 2 cups of oatmeal mixture into bottom and up sides of dish. Bake crust for 8 minutes. Let cool.

In a small bowl, combine strawberries, honey, cornstarch, and almond extract. Pour evenly into baked crust, and spoon remaining oat mixture over strawberries. Return to oven and bake for 30 minutes.

Nutrients: Complex carbohydrates, fiber, B_6, B_2, B_1, niacin, iron, zinc, selenium, magnesium, vitamin E, vitamin A, vitamin C, potassium

Baked Apples

SERVES 4

4 large apples
1⅓ cups granola
½ teaspoon ground cinnamon
½ teaspoon ground coriander
½ cup honey

1 tablespoon vegetable oil
¼ cup apple juice
1 tablespoon orange juice
Vegetable-oil cooking spray

Preheat oven to 325°F (165°C). Core apples and set aside. In a large bowl, mix together granola, cinnamon, coriander, honey, oil, apple juice, and orange juice. Pack apples with filling.

Spray baking dish with vegetable oil, and place apples upright in dish. Cover and bake for 25 minutes or until apples are tender.

Nutrients: Complex carbohydrates, fiber, B_6, B_2, B_1, niacin, iron, zinc, selenium, magnesium, vitamin E, vitamin A, vitamin C

Fresh Peanut Butter and Pear Spread

ABOUT 2½ CUPS

Your kids will love to spread this on bagels or graham crackers. You can make large quantities of this and keep it on hand in the refrigerator for about 2 months.

2 cups peanut butter
4 ounces canned pears, drained

Place peanut butter and pears in a mixer and blend until creamy.

Nutrients: Simple carbohydrates, B_6, B_2, B_1, niacin, iron, zinc, selenium, magnesium, vitamin E, vitamin A, vitamin C, protein

Everyday Herb Chart

Herbs and spices can add a variety of taste sensations to foods that otherwise might strike you as bland. Seasoning with herbs and spices enhances the flavor and nutritional value of foods. You don't need to use chemical additives and sodium-laden seasoning when cooking. Herbs and spices can make an ordinary dish simply fantastic! Try a little basil on your carrots, or sprinkle a touch of ginger or curry on your chicken. Zucchini tastes wonderful sprinkled with basil, tarragon, and thyme. Dill and caraway are delicious in breads.

Herbs, Spices, Seeds	How It Tastes	How It Is Used
Allspice	A blend of cinnamon, nutmeg, and cloves	Fish, soups, fruitcakes, cookies, red and yellow vegetables
Basil	Sweet and pungent flavor that is sometimes peppery	Pesto, fish, eggs, tomatoes, salads, sauces, pasta, stews, meat
Bay Leaf	Distinctly aromatic, woody	Lentils, poultry, eggs, soups, salads, chowders, marinades, artichokes, eggplant
Chervil	Tasty parsley flavor	Vegetables, cottage cheese, meat, figs, stews, salads, sauces, eggs
Cinnamon	Spicy, pleasantly aromatic	Pastries, desserts, fruits, puddings, sweet potatoes, carrots, squash, beans
Cloves	Spicy, hot	Sweet pork, soups, desserts, potatoes, sauces, fruits, beans, carrots, squash
Coriander	Subtle lemon-orange flavor	Cookies, soups, cheese, meat, pastries, casseroles, cheese, meat, Mexican dishes
Cumin	Sweet and salty taste	Chili, fish, meat loaf, eggs, beans, cabbage, pies, cheese

Herbs, Spices, Seeds	How It Tastes	How It Is Used
Curry	A combination of many spices; pleasant fragrance	Soups, shellfish, poultry, meat, fruits, potatoes, creamed and scalloped potatoes, vegetables
Ginger	Sweet, spicy, and aromatic	Cakes, pies, carrots, fruits, meat, yellow vegetables, beets, salad dressings
Marjoram	Slight mint flavor, delicate	Omelets, pork, lamb, beef, fish, vegetables, soups, chowders, stews
Mint	Fruity, aromatic	Lamb, veal, fish, fruits, sauces, carrots, cabbage, beans, potatoes
Nutmeg	Spicy, sweet	All kinds of desserts, vegetables, sauces, fruits, meat
Oregano	Similar to thyme; stronger than marjoram	Pizza, Italian food, meat, fish, vegetables, mushrooms, dips
Rosemary	Refreshing, pungent, savory flavor	Poultry, omelets, breads, sauces, marinades, vegetables, soups, fruits, stuffing, eggs
Saffron	Pleasantly bittersweet	Rice dishes, potatoes, fish, stews, sauces, soups, veal, chicken
Sage	Pungent, long-lasting flavor	Pork, lamb, veal, poultry, fish, squash, stuffings, salads, pumpkin, dips, cream soups
Savory	Aromatic, sagey flavor	Lentils, soups, salads, tomatoes, beets, peas
Tarragon	Pleasant, licorice-anise flavor	Eggs, fish, shellfish, poultry, vinegar, broccoli, cauliflower, soups, sauces

Herbs, Spices, Seeds	How It Tastes	How It Is Used
Thyme	Pleasant clovelike flavor	Fish, gumbo, tomatoes, soups, sauces, onions, carrots, potatoes, poultry, cheese

Food-Substitute Chart

This chart will give you some useful substitutes for sugar, fat, eggs, and other foods. I included this section not to make you feel that these foods are bad, but to help you cook without adding *unnecessary* fat, cholesterol, sugar, and salt. Keep in mind that fat, sugar, salt, and eggs are naturally healthful foods when eaten in moderation.

Main Ingredient	Substitute
Whole milk	Evaporated milk, non-fat or skim milk, buttermilk, soy milk, acidophilus milk
One egg	1/4 cup egg substitute, or 1 egg white plus 2 tablespoons baking powder and 1 teaspoon vegetable oil
Two eggs	1 egg plus 1 egg white, 2 egg whites plus 1 tablespoon vegetable oil, 1/4 cup mashed tofu
Butter (saturated)	Unsaturated, more healthful: Mazola Extra-Light Corn Oil Spread or Kraft Touch of Butter Spread, canola oil, olive oil, safflower oil, peanut oil, corn oil, vegetable oil, sesame oil, or broth for sautéing or frying
Sour cream	Plain yogurt, sour half and half, sour milk, plain kefir (cultured milk)
Cream sauce	Use cornstarch, white flour, arrowroot flour, or kuzu and mix with low-fat milk. Use 2 teaspoons arrowroot in place of 1 tablespoon cornstarch. Use 1 1/2 teaspoons arrowroot in place of 1 tablespoon flour.
Chocolate	Use 3 tablespoons carob or cocoa powder plus 1 tablespoon milk for 1 square baking chocolate

Main Ingredient	Substitute
Unbleached all-purpose flour	Whole wheat, cake flour, pastry flour, whole-wheat pastry flour. (Rye flour, rice flour, soy flour, barley flour, corn flour, and buckwheat flour all need an addition of approximately 1/4 cup gluten flour per cup to rise.)
Regular cheese	Low-cholesterol cheese, low-fat cheese, soy cheese
Cream cheese	Tofu
Table sugar	Honey, barley malt, rice syrup, fruit juices. Reduce liquid by 1/8 cup in recipe, and sweetener like honey 1/4 cup and heavier sweetener by 1/2 cup.
Peanut butter	Almond butter, sesame seed tahini. Use same amount as peanut butter.
Jelly or jam	Apple or pear butter
Whipping cream	Low-fat milk (9 ounces mixed with 1/2 teaspoon cream of tartar)
Yeast	Gluten flour (gives bread its structure and texture), egg, baking powder
Non-yeast breads	Essence bread, flat bread, quick bread
Ground beef	Ground skinless turkey or chicken and tofu—all good for lasagna, spaghetti, chili, casseroles
Rice or potatoes	Buckwheat, wild rice, quinoa, bulgur, kashi
Hot dogs and sausage	Turkey or chicken sausages, soy sausage
Pan-frying	Pan-broiling, baking, or roasting
Beef stock	Vegetable stocks from carrots, onions, leeks, or celery
Iceberg lettuce	Spinach, chard, chicory, collards, romaine, mustard, curly endive, kale, escarole
Salt	Kelp powder

Bibliography

American Heart Association. *The American Heart Association Cookbook*. New York: Ballantine Books, 1984.

Bass, Marianne; Kathy N. Kolasa; and L. Wakefield. *Community Nutrition and Individual Food Behavior*. Minneapolis, MN: Burgess Publishing Co., 1979.

Bloomfield, Molly M. *Chemistry and the Living Organism*. New York: John Wiley and Sons, Inc., 1980.

Brazelton, T. Berry, M.D. *Touchpoints: Your Child's Emotional and Behavioral Development*. New York: Addison Wesley, 1994.

Butler, Charles M. *Neuropsychology: The Study of the Brain and Behavior*. Belmont, CA: Brook/Cole Publishing Company, 1968.

Crapo, Lawrence. *Hormones: The Messengers of Life*. Stanford, CA: Alumni Association, 1985.

Gates, June C. *Basic Foods*. New York: Holt, Rinehart & Winston, 1981.

Griffth, H. Winter, Ph.D. *Complete Guide to Vitamins and Mineral Supplements*. Tucson, AZ: Fisher Book Publishing, 1985.

Hatfield, Fredrick C., Ph.D. *Ultimate Sports Nutrition: A Scientific Approach to Peak Athletic Performance*. New York: Contemporary Books, Inc., 1987.

Leach, Penelope, M.D. *Your Baby and Child*. New York: Knopf, 1978.

Lesser, Michael, M.D. *Nutrition and Vitamin Therapy*. New York: Bantam Books, 1981.

McClintic, Robert. *Physiology of the Human Body*. New York: John Wiley and Sons, Inc., 1975.

Mennler, Ruth L. *The Human Body in Health and Disease*. Philadelphia, PA: J. B. Lippincott Company, 1970.

Picatella, Joseph C. *Choices for a Healthy Heart*. New York: Workman Publishing Company, 1987.

Tapley, Donald, M.D. *The Columbia University College of Physicians and Surgeons: Complete Home Medical Guide*. New York: Crown Publishing, Inc., 1989.

Worthington-Roberts, Bonnie S. *Contemporary Developments in Nutrition*. St. Louis, MO: The C. V. Mosby Company, 1989.

Index